FRIENDS
OF ACPL

JUN 1 7 2010

OFFICE 2010

Simplified®

W9-BZM-265

Visual

by Kate Shoup

WILEY

Wiley Publishing, Inc.

OFFICE 2010 SIMPLIFIED®

Published by
Wiley Publishing, Inc.
10475 Crosspoint Boulevard
Indianapolis, IN 46256

www.wiley.com

Published simultaneously in Canada

Copyright © 2010 by Wiley Publishing, Inc., Indianapolis, Indiana

No part of this publication may be reproduced, stored in a retrieval system or transmitted in any form or by any means, electronic, mechanical, photocopying, recording, scanning or otherwise, except as permitted under Sections 107 or 108 of the 1976 United States Copyright Act, without either the prior written permission of the Publisher, or authorization through payment of the appropriate per-copy fee to the Copyright Clearance Center, 222 Rosewood Drive, Danvers, MA 01923, 978-750-8400, fax 978-646-8600. Requests to the Publisher for permission should be addressed to the Permissions Department, John Wiley & Sons, Inc., 111 River Street, Hoboken, NJ 07030, 201-748-6011, fax 201-748-6008, or online at www.wiley.com/go/permissions.

Library of Congress Control Number: 2010925238

ISBN: 978-0-470-57194-1

Manufactured in the United States of America

10 9 8 7 6 5 4 3 2 1

Trademark Acknowledgments

Wiley, the Wiley Publishing logo, Visual, the Visual logo, Simplified, Read Less - Learn More and related trade dress are trademarks or registered trademarks of John Wiley & Sons, Inc. and/or its affiliates. Microsoft is a registered trademark of Microsoft Corporation in the U.S. and/or other countries. All other trademarks are the property of their respective owners. Wiley Publishing, Inc. is not associated with any product or vendor mentioned in this book.

Disclaimer

In order to get this information to you in a timely manner, this book was based on a pre-release version of Microsoft Office 2010. There may be some minor changes between the screenshots in this book and what you see on your desktop. As always, Microsoft has the final word on how programs look and function; if you have any questions or see any discrepancies, consult the online help for further information about the software.

LIMIT OF LIABILITY/DISCLAIMER OF WARRANTY: THE PUBLISHER AND THE AUTHOR MAKE NO REPRESENTATIONS OR WARRANTIES WITH RESPECT TO THE ACCURACY OR COMPLETENESS OF THE CONTENTS OF THIS WORK AND SPECIFICALLY DISCLAIM ALL WARRANTIES, INCLUDING WITHOUT LIMITATION WARRANTIES OF FITNESS FOR A PARTICULAR PURPOSE. NO WARRANTY MAY BE CREATED OR EXTENDED BY SALES OR PROMOTIONAL MATERIALS. THE ADVICE AND STRATEGIES CONTAINED HEREIN MAY NOT BE SUITABLE FOR EVERY SITUATION. THIS WORK IS SOLD WITH THE UNDERSTANDING THAT THE PUBLISHER IS NOT ENGAGED IN RENDERING LEGAL, ACCOUNTING, OR OTHER PROFESSIONAL SERVICES. IF PROFESSIONAL ASSISTANCE IS REQUIRED, THE SERVICES OF A COMPETENT PROFESSIONAL PERSON SHOULD BE SOUGHT. NEITHER THE PUBLISHER NOR THE AUTHOR SHALL BE LIABLE FOR DAMAGES ARISING HEREFROM. THE FACT THAT AN ORGANIZATION OR WEBSITE IS REFERRED TO IN THIS WORK AS A CITATION AND/OR A POTENTIAL SOURCE OF FURTHER INFORMATION DOES NOT MEAN THAT THE AUTHOR OR THE PUBLISHER ENDORSES THE INFORMATION THE ORGANIZATION OR WEBSITE MAY PROVIDE OR RECOMMENDATIONS IT MAY MAKE. FURTHER, READERS SHOULD BE AWARE THAT INTERNET WEBSITES LISTED IN THIS WORK MAY HAVE CHANGED OR DISAPPEARED BETWEEN WHEN THIS WORK WAS WRITTEN AND WHEN IT IS READ.

FOR PURPOSES OF ILLUSTRATING THE CONCEPTS AND TECHNIQUES DESCRIBED IN THIS BOOK, THE AUTHOR HAS CREATED VARIOUS NAMES, COMPANY NAMES, MAILING, E-MAIL AND INTERNET ADDRESSES, PHONE AND FAX NUMBERS AND SIMILAR INFORMATION, ALL OF WHICH ARE FICTITIOUS. ANY RESEMBLANCE OF THESE FICTITIOUS NAMES, ADDRESSES, PHONE AND FAX NUMBERS AND SIMILAR INFORMATION TO ANY ACTUAL PERSON, COMPANY AND/OR ORGANIZATION IS UNINTENTIONAL AND PURELY COINCIDENTAL.

Contact Us

FOR GENERAL INFORMATION ON OUR OTHER PRODUCTS AND SERVICES PLEASE CONTACT OUR CUSTOMER CARE DEPARTMENT WITHIN THE U.S. AT 877-762-2974, OUTSIDE THE U.S. AT 317-572-3993 OR FAX 317-572-4002.

For technical support please visit www.wiley.com/techsupport.

WILEY
Wiley Publishing, Inc.

Sales
Contact Wiley at (877) 762-2974 or fax (317) 572-4002.

Credits

Executive Editor
Jody Lefevere

Sr. Project Editor
Sarah Hellert

Technical Editor
Vince Averello

Copy Editor
Scott Tullis

Editorial Director
Robyn Siesky

Business Manager
Amy Knies

Sr. Marketing Manager
Sandy Smith

Vice President and
Executive Group Publisher
Richard Swadley

Vice President and
Executive Publisher
Barry Pruett

Sr. Project Coordinator
Lynsey Stanford

Graphics and Production
Specialists
Andrea Hornberger

Quality Control Technician
Jessica Kramer

Proofreader
Cindy Ballew

Indexer
Potomac Indexing, LLC

Screen Artists
Ana Carrillo
Jill A. Proll

About the Author

Freelance writer/editor **Kate Shoup** has authored 20 books and edited scores more. Recent titles include *Windows 7 Digital Classroom*, *Teach Yourself VISUALLY Outlook 2007*, *Office 2007: Top 100 Simplified Tips & Tricks*, and *Internet Visual Quick Tips*. When not working, Kate loves to ski (she was once nationally ranked), read, and ride her motorcycle — and she plays a mean game of 9-ball. Kate lives in Indianapolis with her daughter and their dog.

Table of Contents

Part I: Office Features

1

Office Basics

2

Working with Files

3

Office Graphics Tools

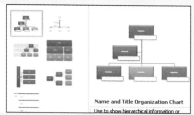

Working with Office Files Online

Part II: Word

Adding Text

KO RACING

3212 Raceway Ln.

Indianapolis, IN

Formatting Text

Table of Contents

7

Adding Extra Touches

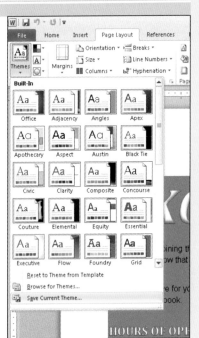

8

Reviewing Documents

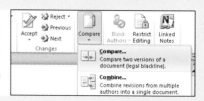

Part III: Excel

9

Building Spreadsheets

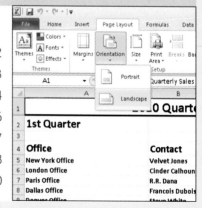

10

Worksheet Basics

Table of Contents

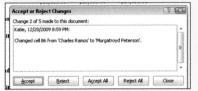

11

Working with Formulas and Functions

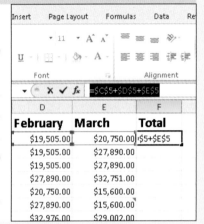

12

Working with Charts

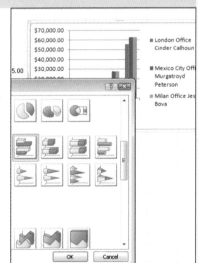

Part IV: PowerPoint

13

Creating a Presentation

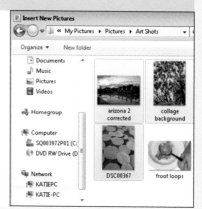

14

Populating Presentation Slides

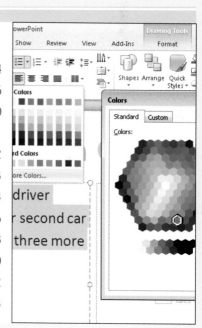

15

Assembling and Presenting a Slide Show

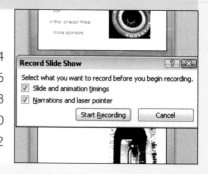

Table of Contents

Part V: Access

16

Database Basics

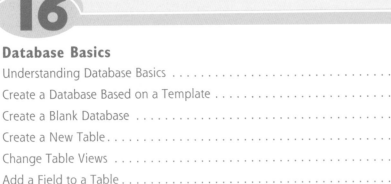

17

Adding, Finding, and Querying Data

Part VI: Outlook

18

Organizing with Outlook

19

E-mailing with Outlook

Table of Contents

Part VII: Publisher

20

Publisher Basics

21

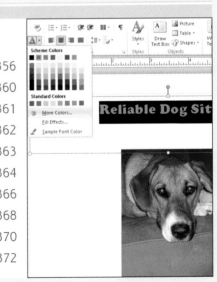

Fine-Tuning a Publication

Part VIII: OneNote

22

Taking Notes with OneNote

23

Organizing and Sharing Notes

Part I

Office Features

In Office 2010, the applications share a common look and feel. You can find many of the same features in each program, such as the Ribbon, the Quick Access toolbar, various program window controls, and the File tab. Many of the tasks you perform in Office, such as creating new files, opening existing files, working with text and data in files, saving files, printing files, and executing commands, involve similar processes and features throughout the Office suite. In this part, you learn how to navigate the common Office features and perform basic Office tasks.

Start and Exit Office Applications

Before you can begin working with a Microsoft Office application, also called a program, you must open the application.

There are a few ways to start an application. One is to launch it from the Start menu, as described in this task. Another is to double-click the program's shortcut icon on the desktop.

(You learn how to create a shortcut icon for a program in the tip at the end of this section.)

When you finish your work, you can close the program. If applicable, you can save your work before exiting a program completely.

Start and Exit Office Applications

Start an Office Application

1. Click **Start**.

2. Click **All Programs**. The All Programs menu option changes to a Back menu option.

3. Click **Microsoft Office**.

4. Click the name of the program that you want to open.

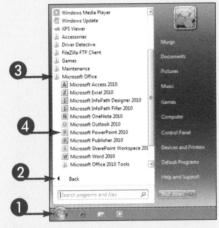

● The program that you selected opens in a new window.

Note: See the next section to learn how to identify different areas of the program window.

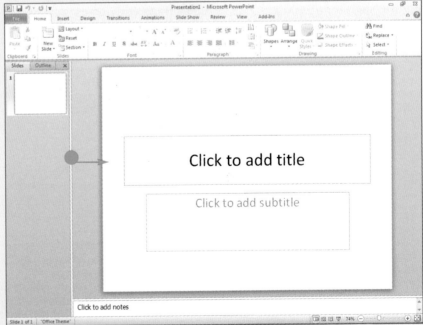

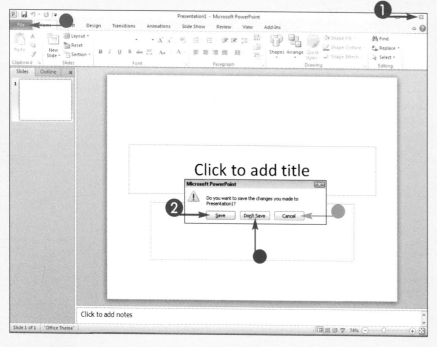

Exit an Office Application

① Click the **Close** button (❌).

● You can also click the **File** tab and then click **Exit**.

If you have not yet saved your work, the program prompts you to do so before exiting.

② Click **Save**.

The program window closes.

● If you click **Don't Save**, the program closes without saving your data.

● If you click **Cancel**, the program window remains open.

How do I create a shortcut icon for an Office application?

To create a shortcut icon that appears on the Windows desktop, follow these steps:

① Right-click a blank area of the desktop and click **New** and then **Shortcut**.

The Create Shortcut dialog box appears.

② Click **Browse**, navigate to the Office program, click the filename, and click **OK**.

③ Click **Next**.

④ Type a name for the shortcut.

⑤ Click **Finish**.

The new shortcut icon appears on the desktop.

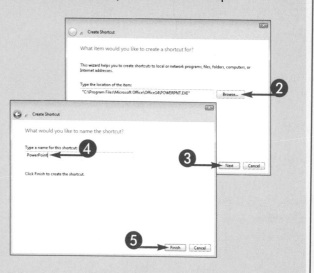

Navigate the Program Windows

All Office programs share a common appearance and many of the same features. These features include a Ribbon, which appears instead of the menus and toolbars found in previous versions of Microsoft Office; a Quick Launch toolbar, which features a customizable set of frequently used commands; and scroll bars, which you can use to navigate an open file in a program window. When you learn how to navigate one Office program, you can use the same skills to navigate the others. If you are new to Office, you should take a moment to familiarize yourself with the suite's various on-screen elements.

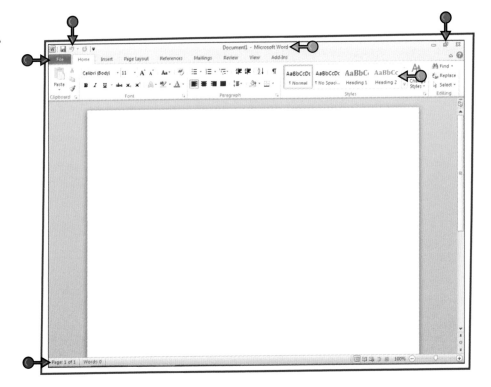

Title Bar
Displays the name of the open file and the Office program.

Quick Access Toolbar
Displays quick access buttons to the Save, Undo, and Redo commands.

File Tab Menu
Click to display a menu of file commands, such as New and Open.

Ribbon
Displays groups of related commands in tabs. Each tab offers buttons for performing common tasks.

Status Bar
Displays information about the current worksheet or file.

Program Window Controls
Use these buttons to minimize the program window, restore the window to full size, or close the window.

Formula Bar

This appears only in Excel. Use this bar to type and edit formulas and perform calculations on your worksheet data.

Work Area

The area where you add and work with data in a program. Depending on the Office program, the work area may be a document, a worksheet, or a slide.

Document Window Controls

Use these buttons to minimize or restore the current document within the program window.

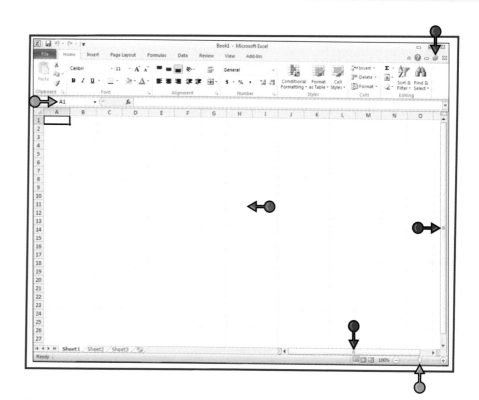

Zoom Controls

Use this feature to zoom your view of a document.

Scroll Bars

Use the vertical and horizontal scroll bars to scroll through the item shown in the work area, such as a document or worksheet.

Work with the Ribbon

Instead of the menus and toolbars found in earlier versions of Office, Office 2010 features the Ribbon, which offers an intuitive way to locate and execute commands.

The Ribbon is grouped into tabs, each containing groups of related commands. For example, the Home tab in Microsoft Word contains commands for changing the font,

setting text alignment, indenting text, and so on. Some tabs appear only when needed, such as when you are working with a table or picture in a document.

The Ribbon is maximized by default, but you can minimize it to view more of your program window.

Work with the Ribbon

Use the Ribbon

1 Click a tab.

The tab organizes related tasks and commands into logical groups.

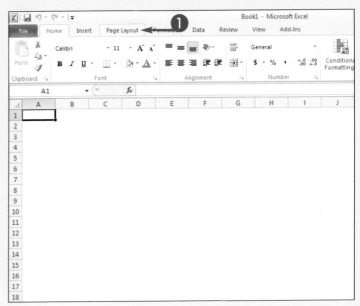

2 Click a button to activate a command or feature.

● Buttons with arrows display additional commands.

● With some groups of commands, you can click the corner group button (⬚) to display a dialog box of additional settings.

When you position the mouse pointer over Live Preview options on the Ribbon, you see the results in the document before applying the command.

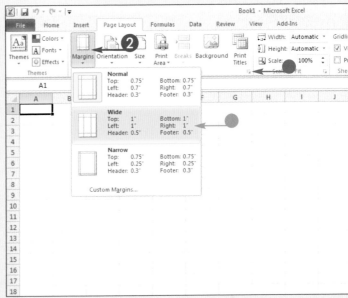

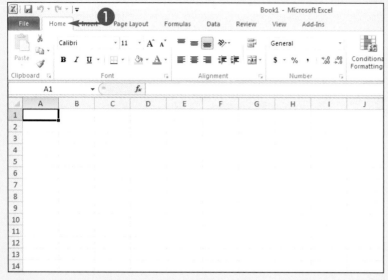

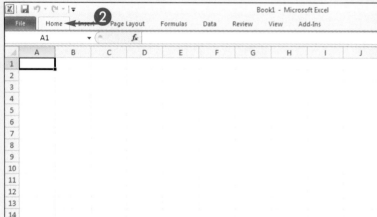

Minimize the Ribbon

1 Double-click a tab name.

The Ribbon is minimized.

2 Double-click the tab name again to maximize the Ribbon.

Can I keep the Ribbon minimized?
Yes. To keep the Ribbon minimized, follow these steps:

1 Right-click a tab on the Ribbon.

2 Click **Minimize the Ribbon**.

The program's Ribbon is minimized at the top of the screen.

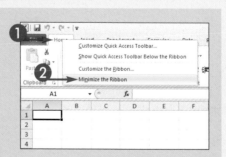

To use a Ribbon while it is minimized, simply click the tab containing the tools that you want to access to reveal it.

Customize the Quick Access Toolbar

The Quick Access toolbar, which appears on-screen regardless of what tab is currently shown in the Ribbon, offers quick access to the Save, Undo, and Redo commands.

You can customize this toolbar to include other commands, such as the Quick Print command or another command you use often. Alternatively,

you might customize the toolbar to omit those commands that appear by default.

By default, the Quick Access toolbar appears in the top left corner of the program window, above the Ribbon. You can choose to display the toolbar below the Ribbon instead.

Customize the Quick Access Toolbar

① Click the **Customize Quick Access Toolbar** button (▾).

② Click **More Commands**.

● You can click any of the common commands to add them to the toolbar.

● You can click **Show Below the Ribbon** if you want to display the toolbar below the Ribbon.

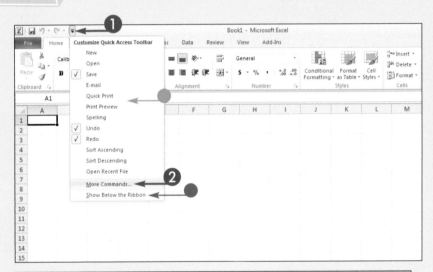

The Options dialog box opens with the Customize options shown.

③ Click the **Choose commands from** ▾.

④ Click a command group.

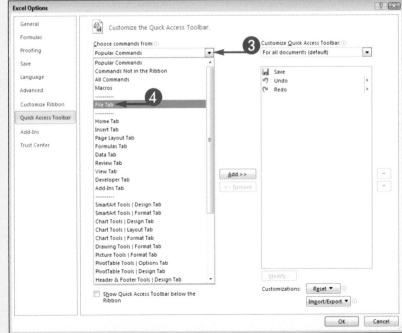

3 1833 05605 1409

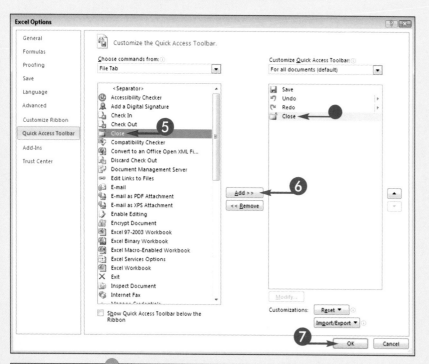

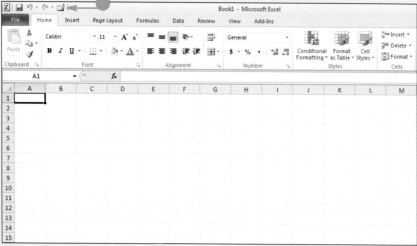

5 Click the command that you want to add to the toolbar.

6 Click the **Add** button.

● Office adds the command.

You can repeat Steps **3** to **6** to move additional buttons to the toolbar.

7 Click **OK**.

● The new command appears on the Quick Access toolbar.

Can I remove a button from the Quick Access toolbar?
Yes. To remove a command, open the Options dialog box, click the command name in the list box on the right, click the **Remove** button, and click **OK**. The button no longer appears on the toolbar.

Are there other ways to customize the Quick Access toolbar?
Yes. You can add commands to the toolbar directly from the Ribbon. Simply click the tab containing the command that you want to add, right-click the command, and then click **Add to Quick Access Toolbar**. The command is immediately added as a button on the toolbar.

Find Help with Office

You can use Office Help to assist you when you run into a problem or need more information about how to complete a particular task.

The Help window offers tools that enable you to search for topics that you want to learn more about. For example, if you want to learn how to print an Office document, you can type

Print in the Help window to locate articles on that topic. Alternatively, you can browse for articles by category.

If you are connected to the Internet, you can access Microsoft's online help files for even more comprehensive information.

Find Help with Office

1 Click the **Help** button (🔞).

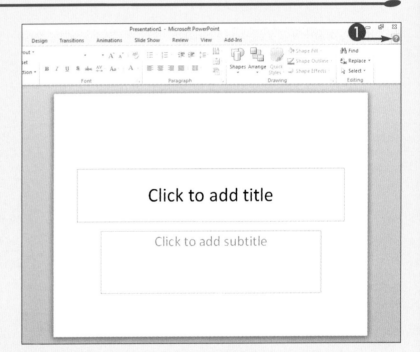

The Help window opens.

2 Type a word or phrase that you want to learn more about.

3 Click the **Search** button.

You can also press Enter to start the search.

Note: *You must be connected to the Internet to access Microsoft's online help files.*

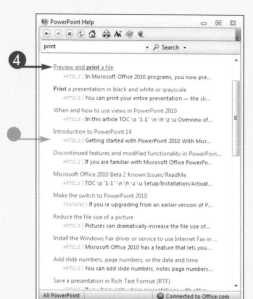

● The results window displays a list of possible matches.

④ Click a link to learn more about a topic.

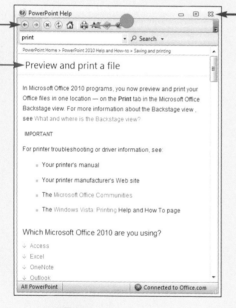

● The Help window displays the article, enabling you to read more about the topic.

● You can use the **Back** and **Forward** buttons (◉ and ◉) to move back and forth between help topics.

● You can click the **Print** button (◉) to print the information.

⑤ Click ◉ to close the window.

Simplify It

Can I use the Help feature if I am offline?
Yes. You can still access the help files that are installed with Office. However, the online resources offer you more help topics, as well as links to demos and other help tools.

How do I browse help files?
Click the **Home** button (◉) on the Help window's toolbar to display a table of contents for the help files for the Office program that you are using. Click a help category to display subtopics of help information. Click an article to view more about a topic. Many articles include links to related articles.

Create a New File

To work with data in Office 2010, you must create a file in which to store it. If the file you want to create is a Word document, an Excel workbook, an Access database, a PowerPoint presentation, or a Publisher publication, you create a new file using the Getting Started screen. When you do, you are given the option of creating a blank file or basing the file on an existing template. To create a new item in Outlook, whether it is an e-mail message, a calendar appointment, a contact, or a task item, you use the Ribbon.

Create a New File

Create a New Word, Excel, PowerPoint, Access, or Publisher File

1 Click the **File** tab.

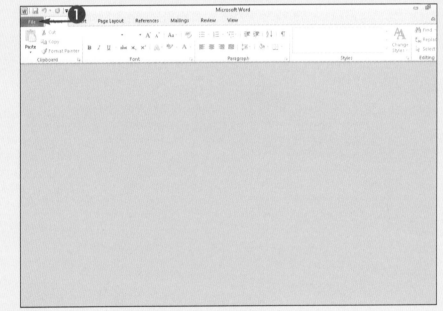

2 Click **New**.

The New screen appears.

3 Click the type of file that you want to create.

4 Click **Create**.

The new file opens.

Note: *Another way to create a new file is to press* `Ctrl` + `N`. *Office creates a new file using the default settings.*

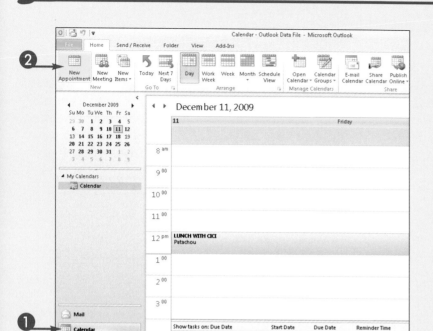

Create a New Outlook Item

1 In the lower left corner of the Outlook window, click the type of item you want to create — Mail, Calendar, Contacts, or Task.

2 Click the **New *Type*** button. For example, if you are creating a Mail item, the button is labeled New E-mail. If you are creating a Calendar item, the button is labeled New Appointment, New Meeting, and so on.

The new item opens.

How do I create a new file based on a template?

In many Office programs, you can create a new file from a template. For example, in Word, you can choose from templates for letters, memos, and more. Simply click the desired template in the New screen.

If you are connected to the Internet, you can access even more Office templates online. Simply click a template category under Office.com Templates in the New screen to display a list of available templates in the selected category; double-click one to download the template and apply it to a new file.

Save
a File

If you want to be able to refer to the data in a file at some later time, you must save the file. You should also frequently save any file you are working on in case of a power failure or computer crash.

When you save a file, you can give it a unique filename and store it in the folder or drive of your choice. You can also change the file type, as described in the tip in this section. You can then open the saved file at a later time. (See the next section for help opening Office files.)

❶ Click the **File** tab.

● For subsequent saves, you can click the **Save** button (⊟) on the Quick Access toolbar to quickly save the file.

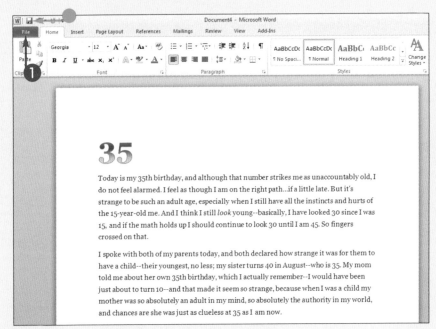

The document's Info screen appears.

❷ Click **Save** or **Save As**.

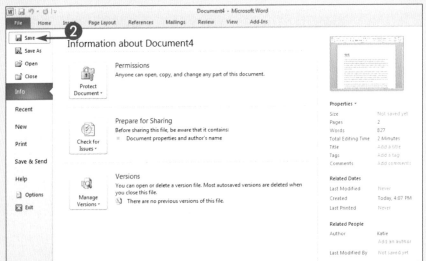

The Save As dialog box appears.

Note: *Another way to save a file is to press* Ctrl *+* S*. If this is the first time the file has been saved, Office launches the Save As dialog box.*

③ In the Navigation pane, click the library in which you want to save the file (here, Documents).

④ In the file list, navigate to the folder in which you want to save the file.

⑤ Type a name for the file in the **File name** field.

⑥ Click **Save**.

● The Office program saves the file and the new filename appears on the program window's title bar.

35

Today is my 35th birthday, and although that number strikes me as unaccountably old, I do not feel alarmed. I feel as though I am on the right path...if a little late. But it's strange to be such an adult age, especially when I still have all the instincts and hurts of the 15-year-old me. And I think I still *look* young--basically, I have looked 30 since I was 15, and if the math holds up I should continue to look 30 until I am 45. So fingers crossed on that.

I spoke with both of my parents today, and both declared how strange it was for them to have a child--their youngest, no less; my sister turns 40 in August--who is 35. My mom told me about her own 35th birthday, which I actually remember--I would have been just about to turn 10--and that made it seem so strange, because when I was a child my mother was so absolutely an adult in my mind, so absolutely the authority in my world, and chances are she was just as clueless at 35 as I am now.

Simplify It

Can I save a file using a different file type?
Yes. Although each Office program saves to a default file type — for example, a Word document uses the DOCX file format — you can save the file in a format compatible with previous versions of Office or with other programs. To save a file in a different format, click the **Save as Type** ⏷ in the Save As dialog box and choose the desired format from the list that appears. Alternatively, with the file open, click the **File** tab, click **Share**, click **Change File Type**, and choose the desired file type from the options that appear.

Open a File

In addition to creating new files, you can open files that you have created and saved previously in order to continue adding data or to edit existing data.

Regardless of whether you store a file in a folder on your computer's hard drive, or on a CD, you can easily access files using the Open dialog box. If you are not sure where you saved a file, you can use the Open dialog box's Search function to locate it.

When you are finished using a file, you should close it. Closing unnecessary files and programs frees up processing power on your computer.

Open a File

① Click the **File** tab.

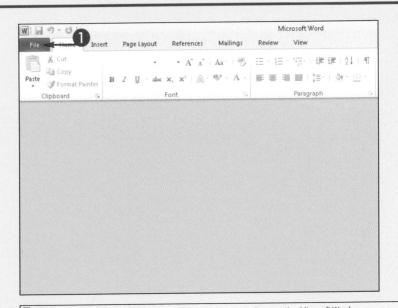

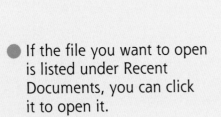

● If the file you want to open is listed under Recent Documents, you can click it to open it.

② Click **Open**.

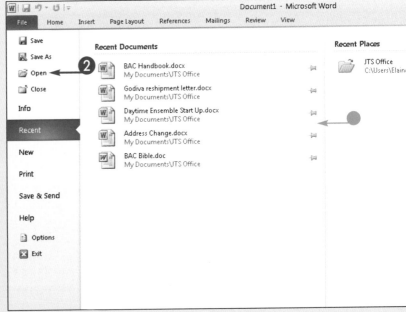

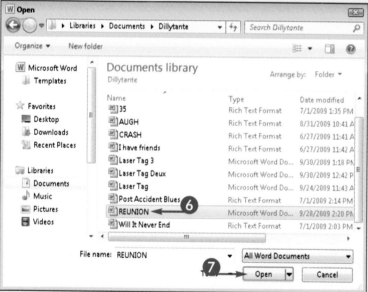

The Open dialog box appears.

Note: *Another way to launch the Open dialog box is to press* Ctrl + O.

③ In the Navigation pane, click the library in which the file you want to open has been saved (here, Documents).

④ In the file list, locate and click the folder in which the file you want to open has been saved.

⑤ Click **Open**.

⑥ Click the name of the file that you want to open.

⑦ Click **Open**.

The file opens in the program window.

Simplify It

How do I close a file?
To close a file, click the **File** tab and click **Close** in the screen that appears. Office closes the file, leaving the program window open. To close the open file and the program window, click the ✕ button in the upper right corner of the program window.

What if I cannot find my file?
You can use the Search box in the upper right corner of the Open dialog box to locate files. Simply locate and open the folder in which you believe the file was saved and type the file's name in the Search box.

Print
a File

If a printer is connected to your computer, you can print your Office files. For example, you might distribute printouts of a file as handouts in a meeting.

When you print a file, you have two options. You can send a file directly to the printer using the default settings or you can open the Office application's Print screen to change these settings. For example, you might opt to print just a portion of the file, print using a different printer, print multiple copies of a file, collate the printouts, and so on. (Printer settings vary slightly among Office programs.)

Print a File

1 Click the **File** tab.

2 Click **Print**.

The Print screen appears.

Note: *Another way to open the Print screen is to press* **Ctrl** + **P**.

● You can specify the number of copies to print using the **Copies** spin box.

● You can choose a printer from the **Printer** drop-down list.

● You can choose to print a selection from the file or specific pages using the available settings in the Settings list.

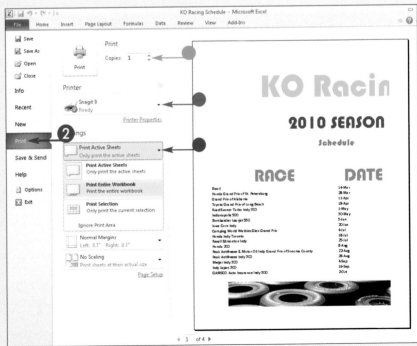

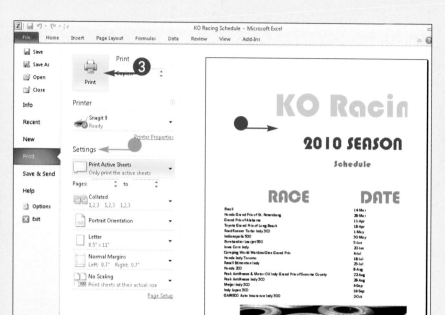

● You can access additional print options under Settings.

● View a preview of the printed file here.

❸ Click **Print**.

The Office program sends the file to the printer for printing.

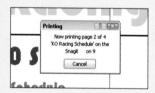

How do I print using default settings?
If you do not need to change any of your default print settings, you can simply click the **Quick Print** button (🖨) on the Quick Access toolbar. If the Quick Print button does not appear on your Quick Access toolbar, you can add it. To do so, click the **Customize Quick Access Toolbar** button (▾) to the right of the Quick Access toolbar and click Quick Print in the list of commands that appears. (You can also add a Print Preview button to the Quick Access toolbar; clicking that button opens the Print screen.)

Select Data

Before you can perform different operations on data, such as deleting it, changing its font or alignment, applying a border around it, formatting it as a list, or copying and pasting it elsewhere in a file or in a different file altogether, you must select the data. Selected data appears highlighted.

Depending on what program you are using, Office offers several different techniques for selecting data. For example, in Word, PowerPoint, and Publisher, you can use your mouse or your keyboard to select a single character, a word, a sentence, a paragraph, or all the data in the file.

Select Data

Click and Drag to Select Data

❶ Click to one side of the word or character that you want to select.

REUNION

Last night I enjoyed a lovely dinner with some very old friends--people I hadn't seen in almost a decade, since before Heidi was born, let alone conceived. It was wonderful to catch up.

They live in Boston, which I am visiting on business. For one ill-fated semester in college, I lived here, attending Boston College and skiing for the ski team there. It was a disaster--everyone hated me (or at least I thought they did). My only refuge was at the home of these friends, Pepper and Stephanie, who took me in far more often than they probably would have liked. The house was plenty full without me. Pepper's mother had been recently divorced, and she had moved in with Pepper and Stephanie and their toddler daughter, Laura, as had two of Pepper's younger brothers, one of whom was about my age. But they never made me feel anything less than completely welcome. They were my family during a time when I desperately needed one.

❷ Drag the cursor across the text that you want to select.

Word selects any characters that you drag across.

You can use this technique to select characters, words, sentences, and paragraphs.

To deselect selected text, simply click anywhere outside the text or press any arrow key on your keyboard.

Note: *This technique also works for selecting images in your Office files. In addition, you can select images by simply clicking them.*

REUNION

Last night I enjoyed a lovely dinner with some very old friends--people I hadn't seen in almost a decade, since before Heidi was born, let alone conceived. It was wonderful to catch up.

They live in Boston, which I am visiting on business. For one ill-fated semester in college, I lived here, attending Boston College and skiing for the ski team there. It was a disaster--everyone hated me (or at least I thought they did). My only refuge was at the home of these friends, Pepper and Stephanie, who took me in far more often than they probably would have liked. The house was plenty full without me. Pepper's mother had been recently divorced, and she had moved in with Pepper and Stephanie and their toddler daughter, Laura, as had two of Pepper's younger brothers, one of whom was about my age. But they never made me feel anything less than completely welcome. They were my family during a time when I desperately needed one.

REUNION

Last night I enjoyed a lovely dinner with some very old friends--people I hadn't seen in almost a decade, since before Heidi was born, let alone conceived. It was wonderful to catch up.

They live in Boston, which I am visiting on business. For one ill-fated semester in college, I lived here, attending Boston College and skiing for the ski team there. It was a disaster--everyone hated me (or at least I thought they did). My only refuge was at the home of these friends, Pepper and Stephanie, who took me in far more often than they probably would have liked. The house was plenty full without me. Pepper's mother had been recently divorced, and she had moved in with Pepper and Stephanie and their toddler daughter, Laura, as had two of Pepper's younger brothers, one of whom was about my age. But they never made me feel anything less than completely welcome. They were my family during a time when I desperately needed one.

REUNION

Last night I enjoyed a lovely dinner with some very old friends--people I hadn't seen in almost a decade, since before Heidi was born, let alone conceived. It was wonderful to catch up.

They live in Boston, which I am visiting on business. For one ill-fated semester in college, I lived here, attending Boston College and skiing for the ski team there. It was a disaster--everyone hated me (or at least I thought they did). My only refuge was at the home of these friends, Pepper and Stephanie, who took me in far more often than they probably would have liked. The house was plenty full without me. Pepper's mother had been recently divorced, and she had moved in with Pepper and Stephanie and their toddler daughter, Laura, as had two of Pepper's younger brothers, one of whom was about my age. But they never made me feel anything less than completely welcome. They were my family during a time when I desperately needed one.

Select Text with a Mouse

1 Double-click the word that you want to select.

Word selects the text.

You can triple-click a paragraph to select it.

Note: *To select data in Excel, click the cell that contains the data. To select a range of cells, click in the upper left corner of the range and drag down and to the right. To select cells that are not part of a continuous series, press* Ctrl *as you click each cell.*

Select Text from the Margin

Note: *This technique works only in Word.*

1 Click in the left margin.

Word selects the entire line of text next to where you clicked.

You can double-click inside the left margin to select a paragraph.

You can triple-click inside the left margin to select all the text in the document.

Simplify It

Can I use my keyboard to select text?
Yes. As mentioned in the introduction for this section, in addition to using your mouse to select text, you can use keyboard shortcuts to select text in a file. To select a single word, press Ctrl + Shift + ← or Ctrl + Shift + →. To select a paragraph from the cursor down or up, press Ctrl + Shift + ↓ or Ctrl + Shift + ↑. To select all of the text from the cursor onward, press Ctrl + Shift + End. To select all of the text above the current cursor location, press Ctrl + Shift + Home. To select all the text in the file, press Ctrl + A.

Cut, Copy, and Paste Data

You can use the Cut, Copy, and Paste commands to move or copy data. For example, you might cut or copy a picture from a Word document and paste it elsewhere in the same Word document, in another Word document, or in a PowerPoint slide or a Publisher file.

When you cut data, it is removed from its original location; when you copy data, Office makes a duplicate of the selected data, leaving it in its original location. In addition to using the Cut, Copy, and Paste commands to move and copy data, you can also use drag-and-drop.

Cut, Copy, and Paste Data

Drag and Drop Data

❶ Select the data that you want to cut or copy.

❷ Click and drag the data to a new location.

The ⌀ changes to ⌀.

To copy the data as you drag it, you can press and hold `Ctrl`.

REUNION

Last night I enjoyed a lovely dinner with some very old friends--people I hadn't seen in almost a decade, since before Heidi was born, let alone conceived. It was wonderful to catch up.

They live in Boston, which I am visiting on business. For one ill-fated semester in college, I lived here, attending Boston College and skiing for the ski team there. It was a disaster--everyone hated me (or at least I thought they did). My only refuge was at the home of these friends, Pepper and Stephanie, who took me in far more often than they probably would have liked. The house was plenty full without me. Pepper's mother had been recently divorced, and she had moved in with Pepper and Stephanie and their toddler daughter, Laura, as had two of Pepper's younger brothers, one of whom was about my age. But they never made me feel anything less than completely welcome. They were my family during a time when I desperately needed one.

❸ Release the mouse to drop the data in place.

The data appears in the new location.

REUNION

Last night I enjoyed a lovely dinner with some very old friends--people I hadn't seen in almost a decade, since before Heidi was born, let alone conceived. It was wonderful to catch up.

They live in Boston, which I am visiting on business. For one ill-fated semester in college, I lived here, attending Boston College and skiing for the ski team there. It was a disaster--everyone hated me (or at least I thought they did). My only refuge was at the home of these friends, Pepper and Stephanie, who took me in far more often than they probably would have liked. Pepper's mother had been recently divorced, and she had moved in with Pepper and Stephanie and their toddler daughter, Laura, as had two of Pepper's younger brothers, one of whom was about my age. The house was plenty full without me. But they never made me feel anything less than completely welcome. They were my fam (Ctrl) ▾ g a time when I desperately needed one.

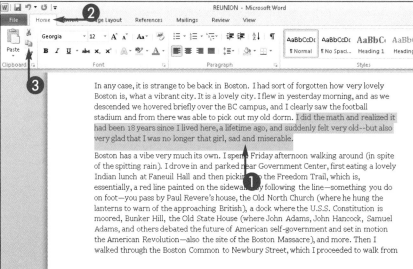

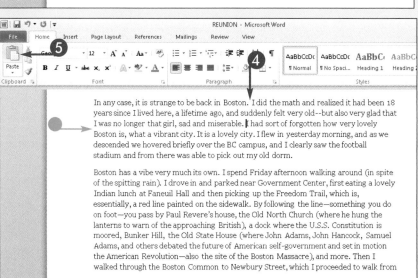

Cut and Copy Data

① Select the data that you want to cut or copy.

② Click the **Home** tab.

③ Click the **Cut** button (✄) to move data or the **Copy** button (📋) to copy data.

> **Note:** You can also press
> Ctrl + X to cut data or
> Ctrl + C to copy data.

The data is stored in the Windows Clipboard.

④ Click the point where you want to insert the cut or copied data.

You can also open another file into which you can paste the data.

⑤ On the Home tab, click the **Paste** button.

> **Note:** You can also press
> Ctrl + V to paste data.

● The data appears in the new location.

> **Note:** You can click the Paste Options smart tag (📋) that appears when you paste, cut, or copy data to view various paste-related options.

Can I cut or copy multiple pieces of data?
Yes. You can cut or copy multiple pieces of data, and open the Office Clipboard task pane to paste the data. The Office Clipboard holds up to 24 items. You can paste them in whatever order you choose, or you can opt to paste them all at the same time. To display the task pane, click the corner group button (▣) in the Clipboard group on the Ribbon's Home tab. The Office Clipboard is just one of many task panes available in the Office programs.

View Multiple Files

You can display different views of a file or view multiple files at once. For example, you might view two versions of a Word document side by side to compare their contents or view two Excel workbooks to compare data. If the files you want to compare are particularly long, you can enable the Synchronous Scrolling option to scroll both files at the same time.

In addition to viewing multiple files at once, you can split a long file into two scrollable panes to view different portions of it. For example, you might split a document to compare how portions of it are formatted.

View Multiple Files

① Open two or more files.

② Click the **View** tab.

③ Click **Arrange All**.

Note: *In Excel, the Arrange Windows dialog box opens, and you can select how you want to display multiple files.*

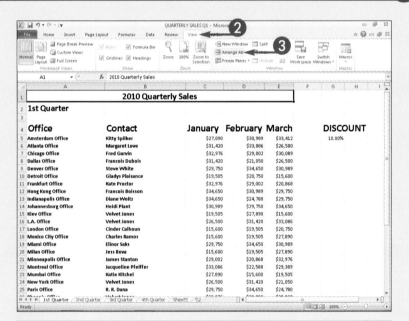

● Both files appear on-screen.

④ Click the **View Side by Side** button (▣) on the View menu to switch between viewing the open files side by side and stacked one on top of the other.

● You can click the **Synchronous Scrolling** button (▣) to scroll both files at the same time.

26

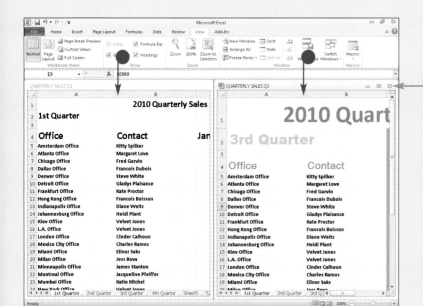

● The files appear side by side.

● You can click the **Close** button () to close a file.

5 To split a single file into scrollable panes, click the **Split** button.

● A horizontal bar appears over the file.

6 Drag the bar up or down to resize the panes, and click to set the bar in place when the panes are the desired size.

Note: To return the page to a full document again, click the Split button again.

What does the Switch Windows button do?
If you have two or more files open, you can click the **Switch Windows** button on the View tab to view a list of every open file in the current Office program. You can then choose a file in the list to view it.

How do I redisplay full windows again?
If you use the Arrange All command to display multiple open files at once, you can click the **Maximize** button (□) in the upper right corner of a file's pane to open the file to its full window size again.

Insert Clip Art

You can add interest to your Office files by inserting clip art images in them. Clip art is simply premade artwork or other types of media. Word, Excel, PowerPoint, Publisher, and Outlook install with the Office clip art collection.

You insert clip art using the Office 2010 Clip Art pane. This pane enables you to search the clip

art that comes preinstalled with Office 2010 to locate images and other media that suit your purposes. In addition, you can use the Clip Art pane to look for more clip art on the Web using the Clip Art task pane.

Insert Clip Art

① Click where you want to add clip art.

You can move the clip art to a different location after you insert the art.

② Click the **Insert** tab.

③ In the Illustrations group, click **Clip Art**.

The Clip Art task pane opens.

④ To search for a particular category of clip art, type a keyword or phrase in the **Search for** field.

● To specify what type of item you need — illustration, photograph, video, or audio — click the **Results should be** ▾ and click the type of item.

● You can also search for clip art on the Office Web site by clicking to select the **Include Office.com content** check box.

⑤ Click **Go**.

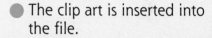

The Clip Art task pane displays any matches for the keyword or phrase that you typed.

● You can use the scroll bar to move through the list of matches.

❻ To add a clip art image, click the image.

● The clip art is inserted into the file.

● The Picture tools appear on the Format tab.

You can resize or move the clip art.

Note: *See the "Resize and Move Objects" section, later in this chapter, to learn more.*

To deselect the clip art, you can click anywhere else in the work area.

● You can click ⊠ to close the pane.

Can I search for a particular type of media?
Yes. To search for, say, a photo or sound file, click the **Results should be** ▾ and select from the list of media types that appears. Alternatively, leave **All media file types** selected to search for a match among all available media formats.

How do I find details about the clip art?
To find out more about a piece of clip art, position the ⌖ over it in the Clip Art task pane, click the ▾, and then click **Preview/Properties**. The Preview/Properties dialog box opens, displaying the file's size, name, type, creation date, and more.

Insert a Picture

In addition to using clip art to add punch to your Office files, you can illustrate your files with images that you store on your computer. For example, if you have a photo or graphic file that relates to your Excel data, you can insert it onto the worksheet. After you insert an image, you can resize, reposition, rotate, and flip it.

You can also perform other types of edits on the image, such as cropping, image correction, color correction, and more. Office 2010 also includes several tools, sometimes called filters, for applying artistic effects to images you insert in files.

Insert a Picture

① Click the area where you want to add a picture.

You can move the image to a different location after inserting it onto the page.

② Click the **Insert** tab.

③ In the Illustrations group, click **Picture**.

The Insert Picture dialog box appears.

④ Navigate to the folder or drive containing the image file that you want to use.

● To browse for a particular file type, you can click the ⊡ and choose a file format.

5 Click the file you want to add.

6 Click **Insert**.

Note: Image files, also called objects, come in a variety of file formats, including GIF, JPEG, and PNG.

● The picture is added to the file.

● The Picture tools appear on the Format tab.

You may need to resize or reposition the picture to fit the space.

Note: See the "Resize and Move Objects" section to learn more.

To remove a picture that you no longer want, you can click the picture and press Delete.

Simplify It

Can I compress images to save space?
Yes. To compress an image that you add to an Office file, click the image, click the **Format** tab on the Ribbon, and click the **Compress Pictures** button (⬚) in the Adjust group. Adjust settings as needed in the Compress Pictures dialog box and click **OK**.

Can I undo changes to my picture?
Yes. Click the **Reset Picture** button (⬚), located in the Adjust group on the Format tab, to restore the selected picture to its original state. (Note that activating this command does not restore the image to its original size.)

Resize and Move Objects

Clip art and other types of images, such as smart art and word art (discussed later in this chapter), are called *objects*. When you insert an object, such as an image, into an Office file, you may find that you need to make it larger or smaller in order to achieve the desired effect. Fortunately, doing so is easy. When you select an object in an Office file, handles appear around that object; you can use these handles to make the object larger or smaller. You can also move objects that you place in a file.

Resize and Move Objects

Resize an Object

1 Click the object that you want to resize.

2 Click a selection handle.

3 Drag inward or outward to resize the object.

> **Note:** To maintain an object's height-to-width ratio when resizing, drag one of the corner handles.

● When you release the mouse button, the object is resized.

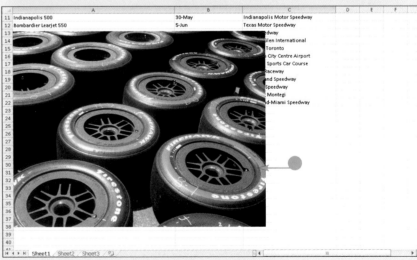

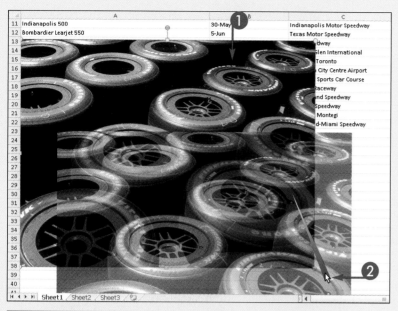

Move an Object

1 Click the object that you want to move.

2 Drag the object to a new location on the worksheet.

● When you release the mouse button, the object moves to the new location.

Note: *You can also move an object by cutting it from its current location and pasting it in the desired spot. For help, refer to the section "Cut, Copy, and Paste Data" in Chapter 2.*

Simplify It

How can I wrap text around an object?
If you insert an object into a Word or Publisher file, you can control how text in the file wraps around the object. For example, you may want the text to wrap tightly around a clip art graphic; alternatively, you might prefer for the text to overlap an image. Regardless of your preferences, you can establish text-wrapping settings by clicking the object, clicking the **Text Wrapping** button in the Format tab, and choosing a wrap style (●).

Rotate and Flip Objects

After you insert an object such as a piece of clip art or a photo from your hard drive into a Word document, an Excel worksheet, a PowerPoint slide, or a Publisher brochure, you may find that the object appears upside down or inverted. To rectify this, you can rotate or flip the object. For example, you might flip a clip art image to face another direction, or rotate an arrow object to point elsewhere on the page. Alternatively, you might rotate or flip an object that you place in an Office 2010 file simply to change the appearance of that object.

Rotate and Flip Objects

Rotate an Object

1 Click the object that you want to rotate.

● A rotation handle appears on the selected object.

2 Click and drag the handle to rotate the object.

● When you release the mouse, the object rotates.

Note: You can also use the **Rotate** button (⬛) on the Format tab on the Ribbon to rotate an object 90 degrees left or right.

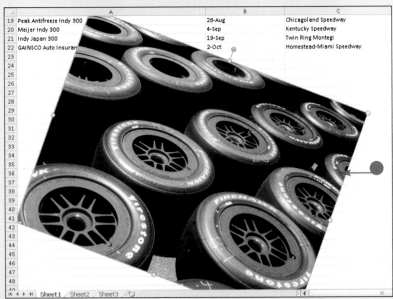

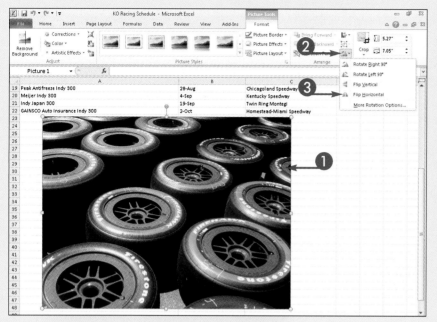

Flip an Object

1 Click the object that you want to flip.

The Format tab opens and displays the Picture tools.

2 Click the **Rotate** button ( ) on the Format tab.

3 Click **Flip Vertical** or **Flip Horizontal**.

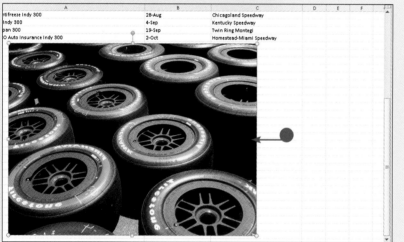

● The object flips.

Simplify It

How do I rotate text?	Can I constrain the rotation?
The easiest way to rotate text is to first insert the text as a WordArt object (see the upcoming section "Create a WordArt Object" for details). After the text has been inserted as a WordArt object, you can rotate it as you would any other object.	Yes. To constrain the rotation to 15-degree increments, press and hold **Shift** while using the rotation handle to rotate the object. Alternatively, rotate the object in 90-degree increments by clicking the **Rotate** button ( ) on the Format tab and choosing **Rotate Right 90°** or **Rotate Left 90°**.

Crop a Picture

In addition to resizing an Office object, such as a clip art image or a photo you have stored on your computer's hard drive, you can use the Crop tool to crop it. When you crop an object, you remove vertical and/or horizontal edges from the object. For example, you might use the Crop tool to create a better fit, to omit a portion of the image, or to focus the viewer on an important area of the image. The Crop tool is located on the Format tab on the Ribbon, which appears when you click the object you want to crop.

Crop a Picture

1 Click the image that you want to edit.

● The Format tab opens and displays the Picture tools.

2 Click the **Crop** button.

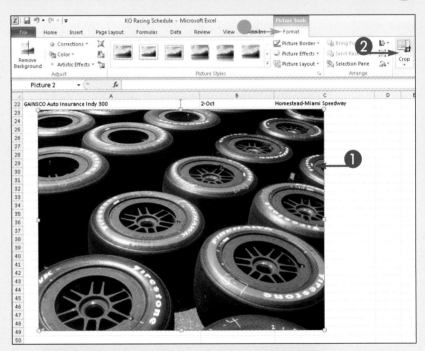

● Crop handles surround the image.

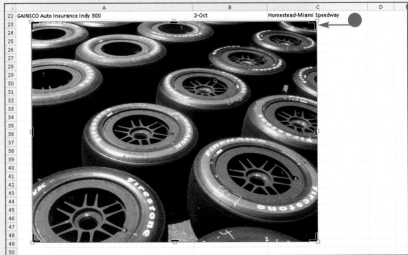

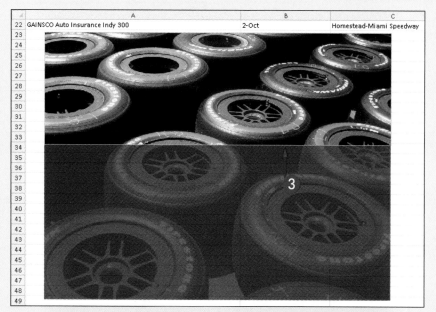

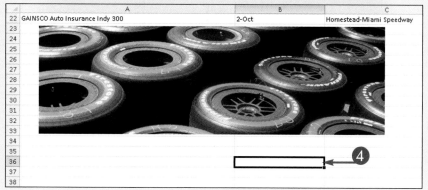

③ Click and drag a crop handle to crop out an area of the image.

When you release the mouse button, the image is cropped.

④ Click outside the image to finalize the crop operation.

Note: *See the "Resize and Move Objects" section, earlier in this chapter, to learn how to resize an image.*

Simplify It

Are there other cropping options?

In addition to cropping your objects into square or rectangular shapes, you can crop your objects using one of any number of predefined shapes. These predefined shapes include ovals, triangles, hearts, moons, arrows, and more. To access these additional cropping options, click the object you want to crop to select it, click the **Format** tab that appears on the Ribbon, click the down arrow under the Crop button, click **Crop to Shape**, and choose the desired shape from the menu that appears.

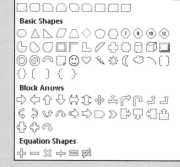

Add a Picture Effect

You can use the Picture Effect tool included with many Office 2010 programs to assign unique and interesting special effects to your objects. For example, you can apply a shadow effect, create a mirrored reflection, apply a glow effect, soften the object's edges, make a bevel effect, or generate a 3D rotation effect. You access the Picture Effects tools from the Format tab on the Ribbon; this tab appears when you click to select the object to which you want to apply the effect. (Note that that the Picture Effects tool is not available in Publisher.)

Add a Picture Effect

① Click the picture that you want to edit.

The Format tab appears on the Ribbon with the Picture tools shown.

② In the Picture Styles group, click the **Picture Effects** button.

③ Click an effect category.

④ Click an effect style.

● As you drag over each effect in the menu, the picture displays what the effect looks like when you apply it.

● The new effect is applied to the picture.

Note: To cancel any picture effect, display the Picture Effects menu again and the style that you applied, and then select the **No** option at the top of the category palette to remove the effect.

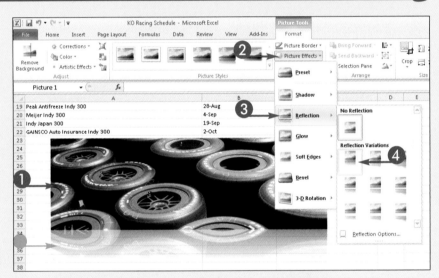

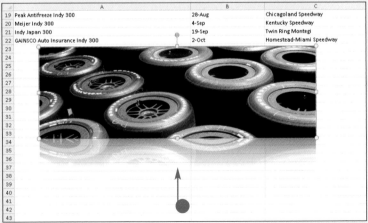

Make Image Corrections

Suppose the image object you have inserted in your Word, Excel, or PowerPoint file is less than perfect. Perhaps it is slightly blurry, or lacks contrast. Fortunately, Office 2010 offers tools that enable you to make corrections to clip art and images even after they have been inserted into your file. For example, you can sharpen and soften images, as well as adjust their brightness and contrast. You access the image-correction tools from the Format tab on the Ribbon; this tab appears when you click to select the object to which you want to apply the effect.

Make Image Corrections

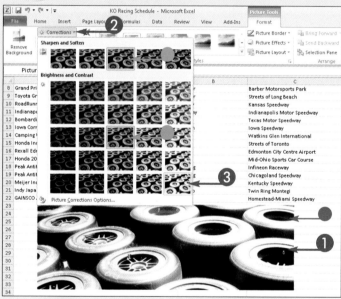

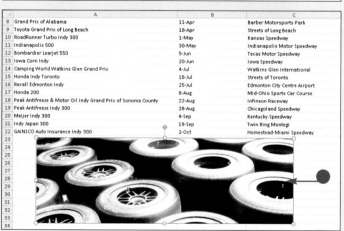

① Click the picture that you want to edit.

The Format tab appears on the Ribbon with the Picture tools shown.

② In the Adjust group, click the **Corrections** button.

● Office highlights the image's current correction settings.

● As you drag over each setting in the menu, the picture displays what the setting looks like when you apply it.

③ Click a correction setting.

● The new setting is applied to the picture.

Make Color Adjustments

If you find that the color in an image you insert in an Office 2010 file seems off, you can adjust it using the Office 2010 Color Saturation, Color Tone, and Recolor tools. The Color Saturation tool enables you to make the color in your image more or less intense; the Color Tone tool enables you to make the colors in your image appear warmer or cooler; and the Recolor tool enables you to apply a color cast to your image. You can also use these tools to apply artistic effects to an image, such as converting a color image to black and white.

Make Color Adjustments

1 Click the picture that you want to edit.

The Format tab appears on the Ribbon with the Picture tools shown.

2 In the Adjust group, click the **Color** button.

● Office highlights the image's current color settings.

● As you drag over each setting in the menu, the picture displays what the setting looks like when you apply it.

3 Click a color setting.

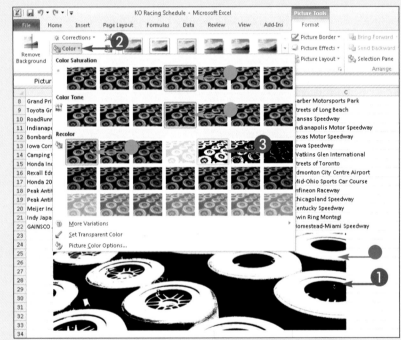

● The new setting is applied to the picture.

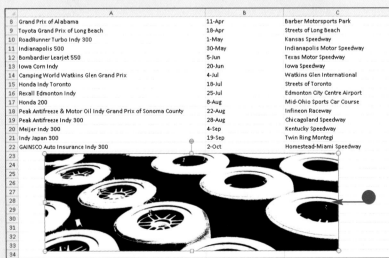

Apply Artistic Effects

Office 2010 includes several tools, sometimes referred to as *filters*, for applying artistic effects to images and clip art in order to liven them up. For example, you can apply an artistic effect to an image to make that image appear as though it was rendered in marker, pencil, chalk, or paint. Applying certain other filters creates an effect reminiscent of mosaics, film grain, or glass. You access these artistic effects from the Format tab on the Ribbon; this tab appears when you click to select the object to which you want to apply the effect.

Apply Artistic Effects

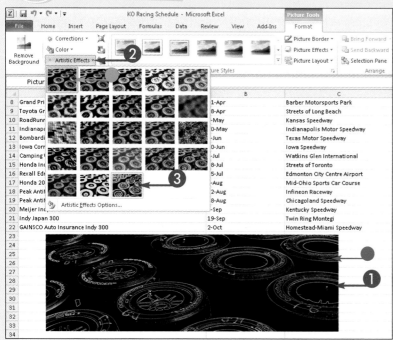

① Click the picture that you want to edit.

The Format tab appears on the Ribbon with the Picture tools shown.

② In the Adjust group, click the **Artistic Effects** button.

● Office highlights the image's current effect.

● As you drag over each effect in the menu, the picture displays what the effect looks like when you apply it.

③ Click an artistic effect.

● The new effect is applied to the picture.

Create a WordArt Object

You can use the WordArt feature to turn text into interesting graphic objects to use in your Office files. For example, you can create arched text to appear over a range of data in Excel, or vertical text to appear next to a paragraph in Word. You can create text graphics that bend and twist, or display a subtle shading of color. You access the various WordArt options from the Insert tab on the Ribbon. After you convert text into a WordArt object, you can resize, move, rotate, and flip that object just as you would any other object in Office.

Create a WordArt Object

1 After typing the text you want to convert to a WordArt object, select the text.

2 Click the **Insert** tab.

3 In the Text group, click **WordArt**.

4 Click a WordArt option.

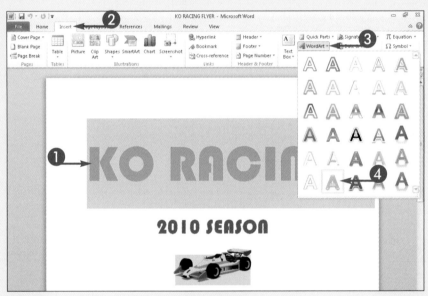

● Office converts the selected text to an object, applies the WordArt option you selected, and opens the Format tab with various Office drawing tools shown.

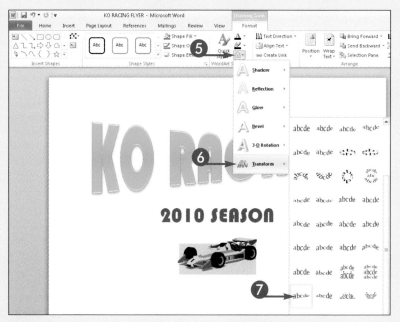

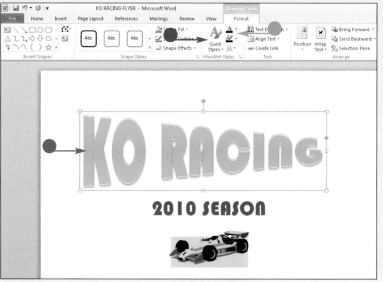

5 Click the **Text Effects** button (⬛).

6 Click **Transform**.

7 Click a transform style.

● The WordArt object is transformed.

You can resize or move the image.

Note: See the section "Resize and Move Objects" to learn more.

● You can click the **Quick Styles** button to change the text style.

● You can click these buttons to change the text outline color (⬛) and text fill color (⬛).

How do I edit my WordArt text?
To edit WordArt text, simply click the WordArt text box, select the text that you want to change, and type over it. To edit the appearance of the WordArt object, use the WordArt Styles tools, located on the Format menu on the Ribbon.

How do I remove a WordArt object?
To remove a WordArt object from your Office file, click the WordArt text box and then press Delete. Alternatively, click the WordArt text box, click the **Quick Styles** button in the Format tab, and click **Clear Word Art**. The WordArt object disappears.

Add
SmartArt

You can use the SmartArt feature to create all kinds of diagrams to illustrate concepts and processes in your Office files. For example, you might insert a diagram in a document to show the hierarchy in your company or to show the workflow in your department.

Office 2010 includes several predefined diagram types from which to choose, including

list, process, cycle, hierarchy, relationship, matrix, pyramid, and picture. In addition, you can choose from several diagram styles within each type. For example, if you choose to create a hierarchy diagram, you can choose from several different styles of hierarchy diagrams.

Add SmartArt

① Click in your file where you want to insert the diagram.

② Click the **Insert** tab.

③ Click the **SmartArt** button.

The Choose a SmartArt Graphic dialog box appears.

④ Click a category.

⑤ Click a chart style.

⑥ Click **OK**.

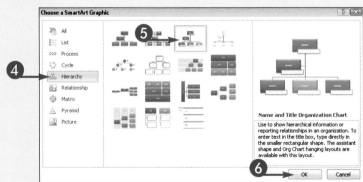

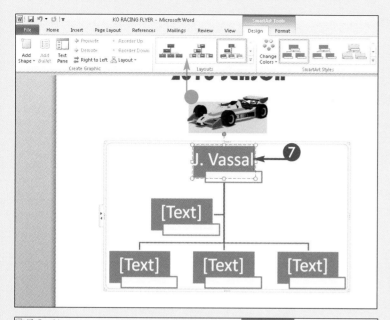

The diagram and placeholder text boxes appear, along with the Text pane.

⑦ Click in a text box and type the text for the item.

● You can change the layout here.

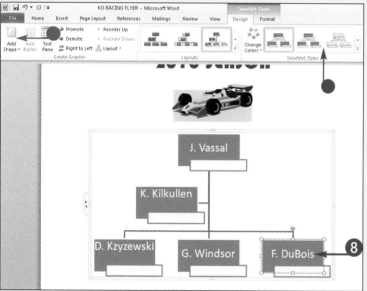

⑧ Continue typing text in each diagram text box.

● To add another text box and element to the diagram, click the **Add Shape** button.

● To change the shape style, click another shape from the SmartArt Styles group.

Simplify It

Can I resize my diagram?
Yes. You can move and resize a diagram just like any other Office object. To move or resize a diagram, see the "Resize and Move Objects" section. You can also use the controls on the Format tab to resize a diagram.

Can I change a shape's position or form?
Yes. To change the position, click the shape and then click the **Promote** or **Demote** button in the Create Graphic group on the Design tab. To change the form, click the shape, click the **Format** tab, and click the **Change Shape** button in the Shapes group.

Create a New Workspace

You can use the Office Live Web site to store and share your Office files. By default, Office Live contains one predefined workspace, called Documents, which you can use to store and share files, but you can create additional workspaces as needed. For example, you might create a workspace devoted to a particular project, a workspace for use with a specific client, or different workspaces for use with different members of your team. New workspaces can be blank or based on a template. When you create a workspace based on a template, it includes various predefined documents and other items.

Create a New Workspace

① After logging on to Office Live Workspace in your Internet browser, click the **New Workspace** link under My Workspaces.

Note: For help logging on to Office Live Workspace, see the first tip at the end of this section.

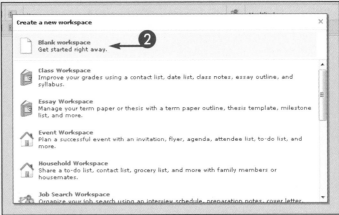

The Create a New Workspace dialog box appears.

② Click the type of workspace you want to create.

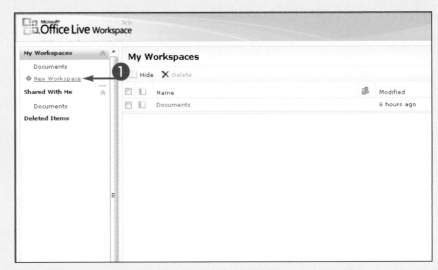

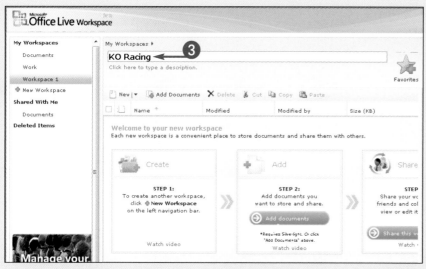

Office Live Workspace creates a new workspace based on the template you chose.

③ Type a name for the new workspace.

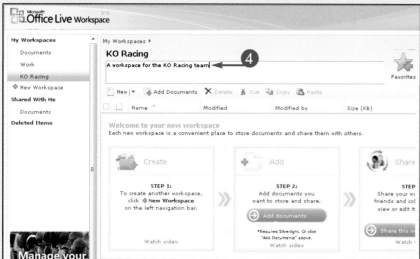

④ Type a description for the new workspace.

Simplify It

How do I log on to Office Live Workspace?

To use Office Live Workspace, you must have a Windows Live account. To obtain one, direct your Web browser to home. live.com, click the **Sign Up** link, and enter the requested information. Next, direct your browser to workspace.office. live.com, type your Windows Live ID and password, and click **Sign In**.

What workspace templates are available?

Office Live offers several workspace templates, including Class, Event, Household, Meeting, Project, and School. Each template contains specific files. For example, Household includes an announcement board, an emergency contact list, a grocery list, a household event list, and a to-do list.

Upload a File to Office Live Workspace

You can upload files that you have stored on your hard drive to Office Live Workspace. Doing so enables you to access the files from any computer connected to the Internet. For example, you might upload a file stored on the hard drive of your work computer to Office Live Workspace so that you can access it from your home computer. In addition, when you upload a file to Office Live Workspace, you can easily share that file with others. You can store as much as 5GB of files on Office Live Workspace.

Upload a File to Office Live Workspace

① Click the workspace in which you want to store the uploaded file.

② Click **Add Documents**.

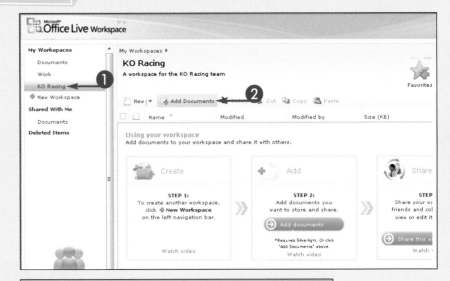

The Open dialog box appears.

③ Locate and select the file you want to upload.

④ Click **Open**.

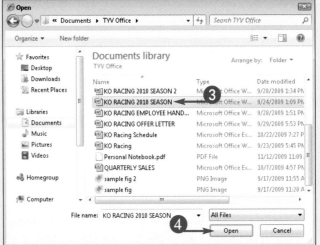

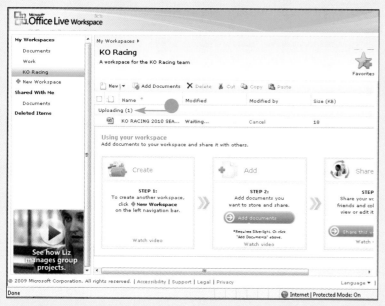

Office Live Workspace uploads the file.

● Office Live Workspace indicates the progress of the upload.

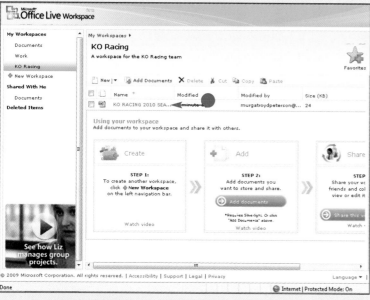

● The uploaded file appears as a clickable link.

Simplify It

Can I upload multiple files at once?
Yes. If you want to upload multiple files to a workspace at once, you can easily do so. Simply click the **Add Documents** button in Office Live Workspace to launch the Open dialog box. There, locate the folder containing the files you want to upload to your workspace; then press Ctrl as you click each file you want to include in the upload operation. Once all the desired files are selected, click the **Open** button in the Open dialog box. Office Live Workspace uploads the files.

Create a New File in Office Live Workspace

In addition to uploading files to Office Live Workspace from your computer, you can create new Word documents, Excel spreadsheets, and PowerPoint presentations from within Office Live Workspace. In addition, you can create new notes and lists, including task lists, contact lists, and event lists. (As an aside, you can also create folders in which to organize your files on Office Live Workspace.)

To create new files from within Office Live Workspace, you must first install the Office Live Update on your computer. Click the Install Office Live Update button in the Office Live Workspace window to get started.

Create a New File in Office Live Workspace

① Click the workspace in which you want to create the new file.

② Click **New**.

③ Click the type of file you want to create (in this example, **Word document**).

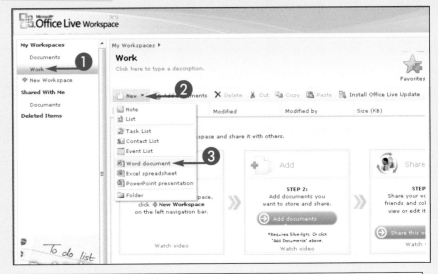

Office Live Workspace creates a new file in the appropriate program.

Note: *You may be warned that the file you have created may be unsafe. Click the* **Enable Editing** *button to proceed.*

④ Enter your data in the file.

⑤ Click the file's **Close** button (❌).

Office prompts you to save your changes.

⑥ Click **Save**.

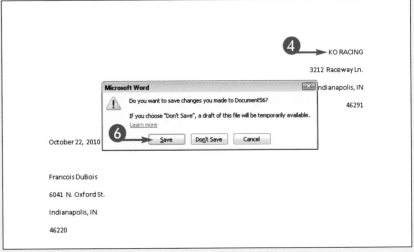

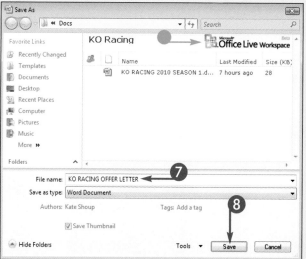

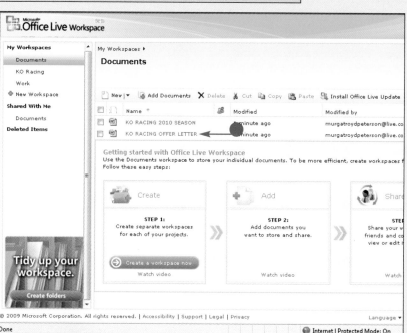

The Save As dialog box appears.

● Your file is saved in your Office Live workspace by default.

⑦ Type a name for your file.

⑧ Click **Save**.

● The file is saved in your Office Live workspace.

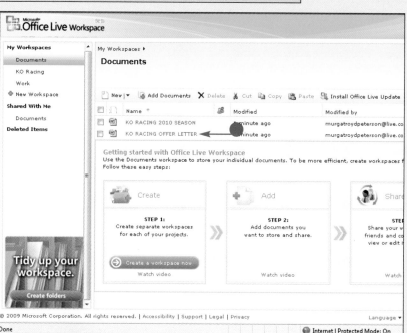

Simplify It

Is there a faster way to access Office Live Workspace?
Yes. If you use Internet Explorer as your Web browser, you can save any workspace in Office Live Workspace as a favorite. Simply click the **Favorites** button in the upper right corner of the Office Live Workspace window and click **Add** in the dialog box that appears. Next time you want to access Office Live Workspace, click the **Favorites** button in the upper left corner of your browser window, click the **Favorites** tab in the pane that appears, and locate and click the **Office Live Workspace** entry.

Edit a File in Office Live Workspace

Suppose you have saved a Word document on Office Live Workspace. You can open that document within Word to edit it; then, when you save the document, any changes you made to it are visible in Office Live Workspace. The same is true for Excel and PowerPoint files that you have saved on Office Live Workspace.

Alternatively, you can open the file from within Office Live Workspace, as described in this section. When you do, Office Live Workspace launches the appropriate program, enabling you to make the necessary edits. When you save the edits, the file is updated accordingly on Office Live Workspace.

Edit a File in Office Live Workspace

① Click the workspace containing the file you want to edit.

② Click the link for the file to open it.

● The file opens in Office Live Workspace.

③ Click the **Edit** button.

● An Open Document dialog box may appear, warning you that you should open the file only if it is from a trusted source.

Note: *Alternatively, you may be warned that the file you have created may be unsafe. Click the* ***Enable Editing*** *button to proceed.*

④ Click **OK**.

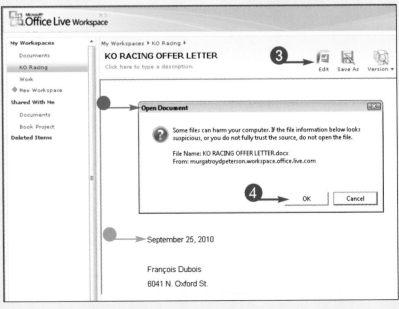

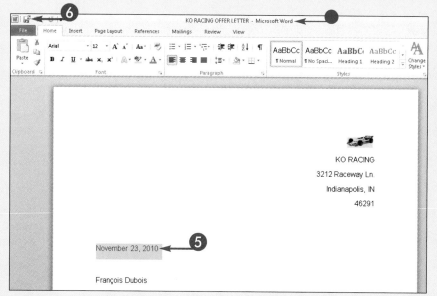

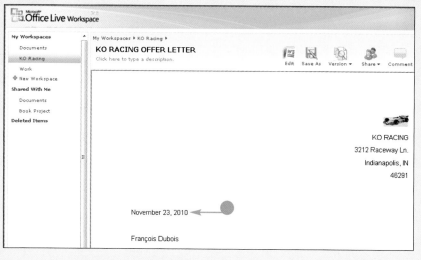

● The file opens in the appropriate Office program (in this example, Microsoft Word).

⑤ Edit the file as desired.

⑥ Click the **Save** button (📠) in the Quick Access toolbar.

Note: *The Save button in the Quick Access toolbar appears different here because the file you are working on is online.*

⑦ Click the **Close** button (✖).

● Your edits appear in the file in your Office Live workspace.

How do I view earlier versions of a file?
Office Live Workspace maintains multiple versions of files. To view previous versions of a file, open the file in Office Live Workspace, click the **Version** menu, and click the version you want to view from the list that appears.

What are the Office Live Web apps?
Office Web apps are free, scaled-down, Web-based versions of certain Microsoft Office programs. They include the Word Web app, the Excel Web app, and the PowerPoint Web app. You access and use these apps from within your Web browser.

Share a Workspace

After you set up a workspace, you can share it with others. When you do, you can specify what level of permission others may have. Users you designate as Editors can make changes to files in the workspace; users you designate as Viewers can only view the files. (Note that people with whom you share your files are not required to sign in to Office Live to view them.)

If you do not want to share an entire workspace, you can instead share individual files. Note that in order to share individual files, they must be stored in your Documents workspace.

Share a Workspace

Share an Entire Workspace

① Click the workspace you want to share.

② Click **Share**.

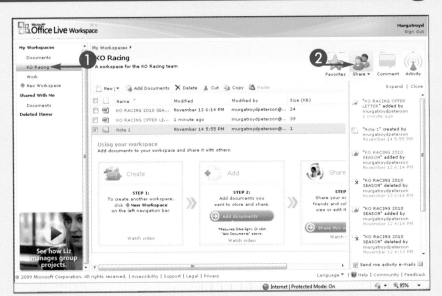

Office Live Workspace creates an e-mail invitation.

③ To allow Editors access, type the recipient's e-mail address in the **Editors** field.

④ To allow Viewers access, type the recipient's e-mail address in the **Viewers** field.

⑤ Type a message in the **Message** field.

● Select this check box to allow the recipient to preview your workspace without signing in to Office Live.

⑥ Click the **Send** button.

Office Live Workspace sends the sharing invitation.

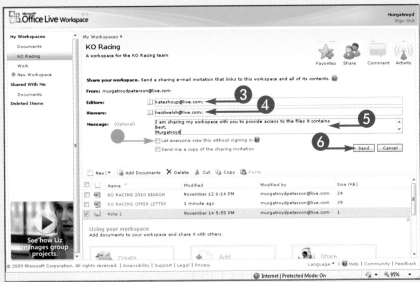

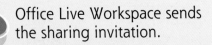

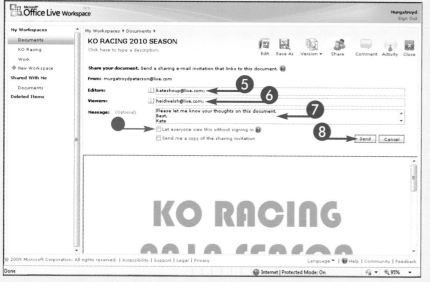

Share a File

1 Click the **Documents** workspace.

2 Select the file you want to share.

3 Click **Share**.

4 Click **Share Document**.

Office Live Workspace creates an e-mail invitation.

5 To allow Editors access, type the recipient's e-mail address in the **Editors** field.

6 To allow Viewers access, type the recipient's e-mail address in the **Viewers** field.

7 Type a message in the **Message** field.

● Select this check box to allow recipients to preview the workspace without signing in to Office Live.

8 Click **Send**.

Office Live Workspace sends the invitation.

Simplify It

How do I change sharing settings?
Open the shared workspace and click **View Sharing Details** to view users with whom this workspace is shared and change the sharing permissions associated with each user. To share with more users, click the **Share with More** button; to stop sharing, click the **Stop Sharing** button.

What does the Comment feature do?
Clicking the **Comment** button opens a Comments pane. Here, you can type comments, which are visible to anyone who has access to the workspace. To add a comment, simply type your comment text and click **Add Comment**. To close the Comment pane, click **Close**.

View Shared Workspaces

Just as you can use Office Live Workspace to share workspaces and files with other users, so, too, can others use the site to share workspaces and files with you. Shared workspaces appear under Shared With Me in the Office Live Workspace Navigation pane. Depending on what permissions you have been granted, you may be able to simply view files in a shared workspace, or you may be able to edit them. As shown here, you open files that have been shared with you the same way you do files that you have uploaded to or created on Office Live Workspace.

View Shared Workspaces

1 Under Shared With Me in the Navigation pane, click the shared workspace you want to view.

● Files in the shared workspace appear.

2 Click a file to view it.

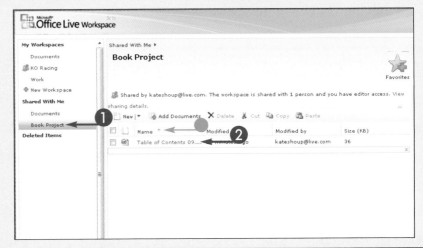

● The file opens in the Office Live Workspace window.

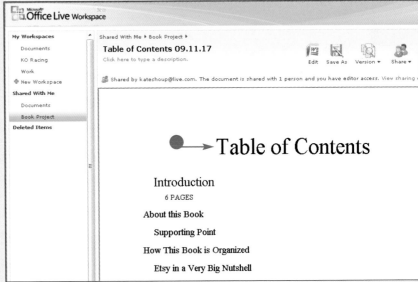

Delete a File from Office Live Workspace

You can delete files you no longer need from Office Live Workspace. Deleted files are not removed from the workspace right away, however. Instead, deleted files are moved to the Deleted Items folder.

If you find you have deleted a file in error, you can restore it. To do so, simply click the Deleted

Items folder in the Navigation pane, select the check box next to the file, and then click the Restore button. To permanently remove files in the Deleted Items folder from Office Live Workspace, open the Deleted Items folder and click Empty All Items.

Delete a File from Office Live Workspace

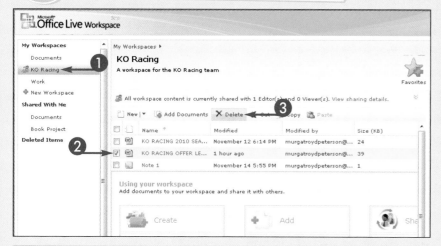

1 Click the workspace containing the file you want to delete.

2 Select the check box next to the file you want to delete.

3 Click **Delete**.

● Office Live Workspace deletes the file.

● The file is moved to the Deleted Items folder.

Part II

Word

You can use Word to tackle any project involving text, such as letters, faxes, memos, reports, manuscripts, and more. Word's versatile formatting features enable you to enhance your text documents with ease, changing the font size and color, altering the text alignment, and more. You can also add elements such as tables, headers and footers, page numbers, a table of contents, even an index. Word offers a variety of editing tools to help you make your document look its best. In this part, you learn how to build and format Word documents and tap into Word's many tools to preview, proofread, and print your documents.

Change Word's Views

Microsoft Word offers you several ways to control how you view your document. For example, the Zoom tool enables you to control the magnification of your document. You can change the zoom setting by using the Zoom slider or the Zoom buttons.

You can also choose from five different views: Print Layout, which displays margins, headers, and footers; Outline, which shows the document's outline levels; Web Layout, which displays a Web page preview of your document; Full Screen Reading, which optimizes your document for easier reading; and Draft, which omits certain elements such as headers and footers.

Change Word's Views

Use the Zoom Tool

1 Drag the **Zoom** slider on the Zoom bar.

● You can also click a magnification button to zoom in or out.

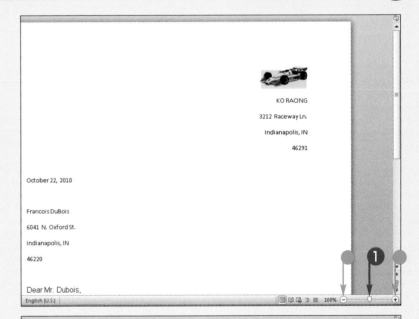

● Word applies the magnification to the document.

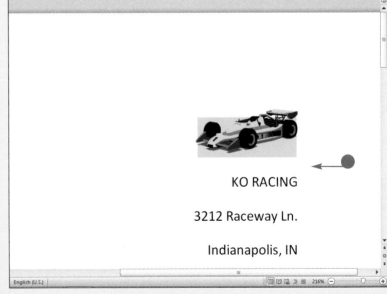

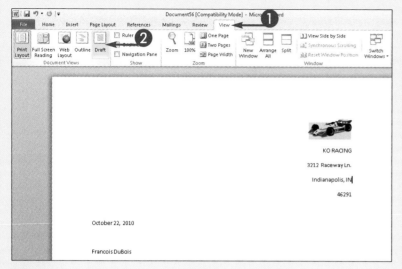

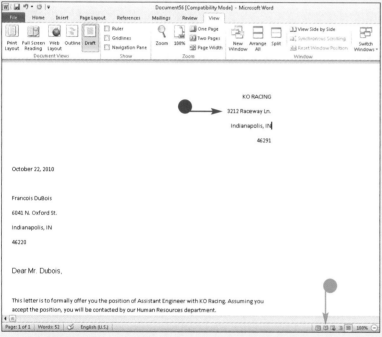

Switch Layout Views

1 Click the **View** tab on the Ribbon.

2 Click a layout view button.

Word immediately displays the new view.

● In this example, Draft view displays the text without graphics or other elements.

● You can also switch views using the View buttons at the bottom of the program window.

Simplify It

How do I move through a Word document?
Use the scroll bars to move up and down a document page. Alternatively, press the arrow keys on your keyboard to move up, down, left, and right in the document. You can also press the Page Up and Page Down keys to move to the preceding or next page in the document.

What can I do in the Outline view?
If your document's structure incorporates headings, subheadings, and body text, you can use Outline view to see and change the document structure. Switching to Outline view displays the Outlining tab, with buttons for changing heading styles and levels.

Type and Edit Text

When you launch Microsoft Word, a blank document appears, ready for you to start typing. By default, Word is set to Insert mode; when you start typing, any existing text moves over to accommodate the new text. You can press **Insert** to switch to Overtype mode; in this mode, the new text overwrites the existing text. (You may have to set up Word to allow this. To do so, click the File tab, click Options, and click Advanced. Then, under Editing Options, select the Use the Insert Key to Control Overtype Mode check box; then click OK.

Type and Edit Text

Type Text

① Start typing your text.

● Word automatically wraps the text to the next line for you.

● The insertion point, or cursor, marks the current location where text appears when you start typing.

② Press **Enter** to start a new paragraph.

● You can press **Enter** twice to add an extra space between paragraphs.

● You can press **Tab** to quickly create an indent for a line of text.

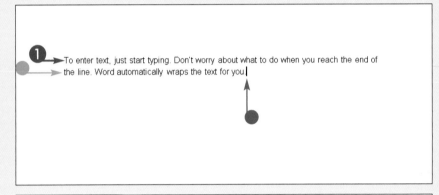

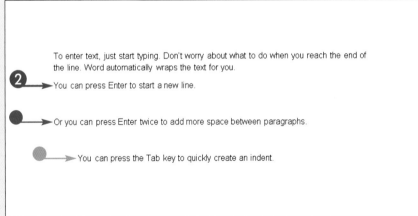

To enter text, just start typing. Don't worry about what to do when you reach the end of the line. Word automatically wraps the text for you.

You can press Enter to start a new line.

Or you can press Enter twice to add more space between paragraphs.

You can press the Tab ky to quickly create an indent.

①

To enter text, just start typing. Don't worry about what to do when you reach the end of the line. Word automatically wraps the text for you.

You can press Enter to start a new line.

Or you can press Enter twice to add more space between paragraphs.

You can press the Tab k|to quickly create an indent.

③

Edit Text

① Click in the document where you want to fix a mistake.

② Press `Backspace` to delete characters to the left of the cursor.

③ Press `Delete` to delete characters to the right of the cursor.

You can also delete selected text.

Note: *If you make a spelling mistake, Word either corrects the mistake or underlines it in red.*

Simplify It

How do I add lines to my Word documents?
If you type three or more special characters on a new line and press `Enter`, Word replaces the characters with a line of a particular style. For example, if you type three asterisks and press `Enter`, Word displays a dotted line. Use this table for more line styles that you can add:

Character	Line Style
*	Dotted line
=	Double line
~	Wavy line
#	Thick decorative line
_	Thick single line

Insert Quick Parts

Suppose you repeatedly type the same text in your documents — for example, your company name. You can add this text to Word's Quick Parts Gallery; then, the next time you need to add the text to a document, you can select it from the gallery instead of retyping it.

In addition to creating your own Quick Parts for use in your documents, you can use any of the wide variety of preset phrases included with Word. You access these preset Quick Parts from Word's Building Blocks Organizer window. (See the tip at the end of this section for more information.)

Insert Quick Parts

Add a Quick Parts Entry

1. Select the text that you want to add to the Quick Parts Gallery.

2. Click the **Insert** tab on the Ribbon.

3. Click the **Quick Parts** button.

4. Click **Save Selection to Quick Part Gallery**.

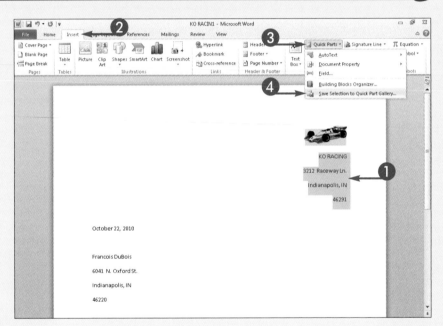

The Create New Building Block dialog box appears.

5. Type a name for the entry, or use the default name.

● You can also assign a gallery, a category, and a description for the entry.

6. Click **OK**.

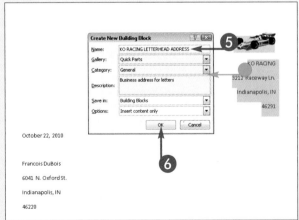

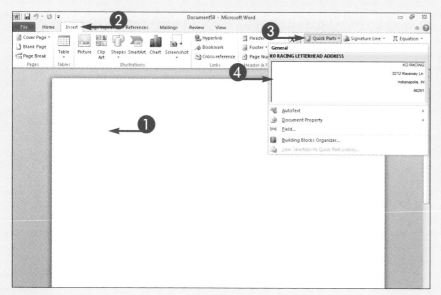

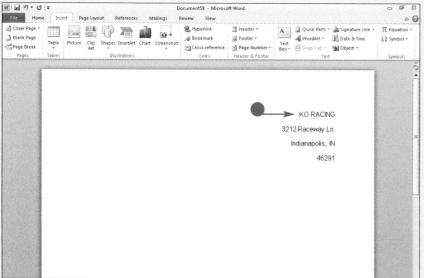

Insert a Quick Part Entry

1 Click in the text where you want to insert a Quick Part.

2 Click the **Insert** tab on the Ribbon.

3 Click the **Quick Parts** button.

4 Click the entry that you want to insert.

● Word inserts the entry into the document.

How do I insert a preset Quick Part?
Click the **Insert** tab on the Ribbon, click the **Quick Parts** button, and click **Building Blocks Organizer** to open the Building Blocks Organizer. Locate the Quick Part you want to insert (they are organized into galleries and categories), click it, and click **Insert**.

How do I remove a Quick Parts entry?
To remove a Quick Parts entry from the Building Blocks Organizer, open the Organizer (see the preceding tip for help), locate and select the entry you want to remove, click **Delete**, and click **Yes** in the dialog box that appears.

Insert Symbols

From time to time, you might need to insert a special symbol or character into your Word document, such as a mathematical symbol. You can use the Symbol palette to access a wide range of symbols, including mathematical and Greek symbols, architectural symbols, and more. For yet more symbols, open the Symbol dialog box. Here, you can view a list of recently used symbols, as well as access literally hundreds of symbols in a variety of fonts. You can also use the Symbol dialog box to insert special characters such as em dashes, copyright symbols, and so on.

Insert Symbols

① Click where you want to insert a symbol.

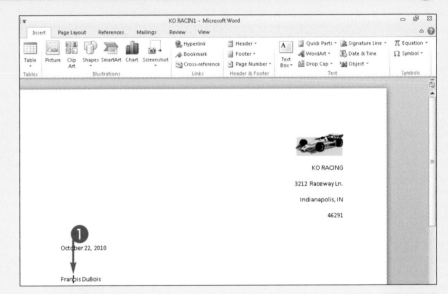

② Click the **Insert** tab.

③ Click the **Symbol** button.

④ If the symbol you want to insert appears in the Symbol palette, click it. Otherwise, click **More Symbols**.

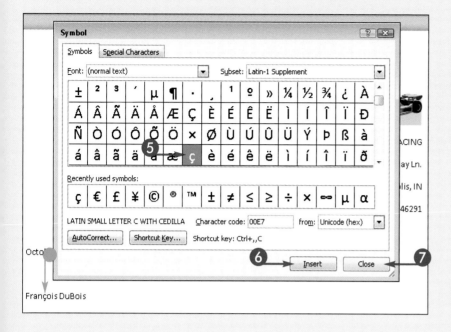

The Symbol dialog box appears.

⑤ Click the character that you want to insert.

Note: *You can click the **Font*** *and click another font to change what symbols appear in the Symbols tab. For example, the Wingdings font includes a library of character icons, such as clocks and smiley faces, whereas the Symbols font lists basic symbols.*

⑥ Click **Insert**.

● Word adds the character to the current cursor location in the document.

The dialog box remains open so that you can add more characters to your text.

⑦ When finished, click **Close**.

How do I add a special character?
To add a special character, such as an em dash, a copyright symbol, an ellipsis, or similar characters, open the Symbol dialog box (click the **Symbol** button and choose **More Symbols**) and click the **Special Characters** tab. Locate and click the character you want to add, and then click **Insert**. Click **Close** to close the dialog box.

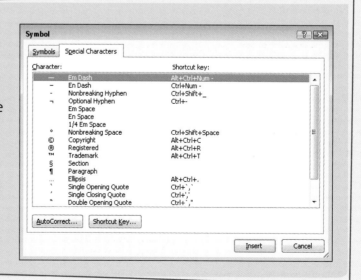

Create a Blog Post

If you keep an online blog, you can use Word to create a document to post on it. This enables you to take advantage of Word's many proofing and formatting tools. You can then post the blog entry directly from Word.

To post your blog entry, you must first set up Word to communicate with the Internet server that hosts your online blog; the first time you post a blog entry from Word, the program prompts you to register your blog account. Click Register Now, choose your blog provider in the dialog box that appears, and follow the on-screen prompts.

Create a Blog Post

Note: You must be connected to the Internet to complete this section.

① Click the **File** tab.

② Click **New**.

③ Click **Blog Post**.

④ Click **Create**.

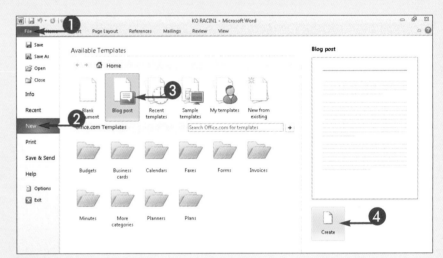

Word opens the blog post document.

⑤ Click in the title area and type a title for your post.

⑥ Click in the body of the post and type your blog entry.

⑦ When you are ready to post your blog, click the **Publish** button.

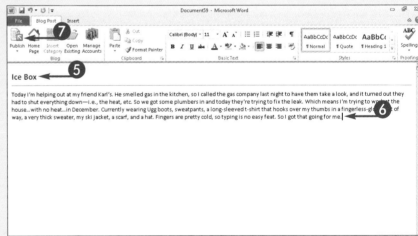

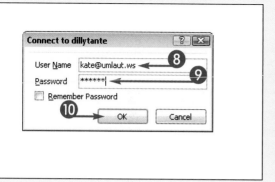

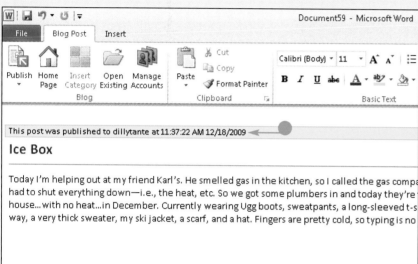

Word connects to the server that hosts your online blog.

⑧ Type the user name you have set up with your blog host.

⑨ Type your blog password.

⑩ Click **OK**.

● Word posts your blog entry online.

Simplify It

Can I edit my blog accounts from within Word?
Yes. Click the **Manage Accounts** button on the Blog Post tab when viewing a blog page in Word to open the Blog Accounts dialog box. Here, you can edit an existing account, add a new account, or delete an account that you no longer use.

Can I turn an existing Word document into a blog post?
Yes. First, open the document in Word. Then click the **File** tab, click **Share**, click **Publish as Blog Post**, and then click **Publish as Blog Post** again. Word coverts the document into a blog post.

Change the Font, Size, and Color

By default, when you type text in a Word 2010 document, the program uses an 11-point Calibri font. You can change the text font, size, and color to alter the appearance of text in a document. For example, you might change the font, size, and color of your document's title text to emphasize it. In addition, you can use Word's basic formatting commands — Bold, Italic, Underline, Strikethrough, Subscript, and Superscript — to quickly add formatting to your text. You can also change the font that Word 2010 applies by default.

Change the Font, Size, and Color

Change the Font

1 Select the text that you want to format.

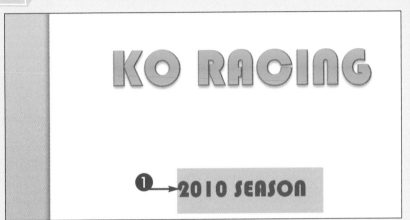

2 Click the **Home** tab on the Ribbon.

3 Click the **Font** ⏷.

4 Click a font.

Note: *With Word's Live Preview feature on, you can immediately preview any font in the list by positioning your mouse pointer over it in the Font list.*

● Word applies the font to the text.

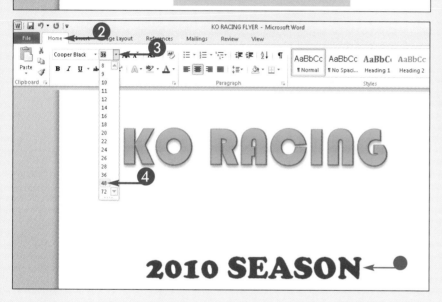

Change the Size

① Select the text that you want to format.

② Click the **Home** tab on the Ribbon.

③ Click the **Font Size** ▾.

④ Click a size.

● Word applies the font size to the text.

This example applies a 48-point font size to the text.

Note: *Another way to change the font size is to click the **Grow Font** and **Shrink Font** buttons (▲ and ▾) on the Home tab. Word increases or decreases the font size with each click of the button.*

How do I apply formatting to my text?
To apply formatting to your text, select the text you want to format, click the **Home** tab, and click the **Bold** (**B**), **Italic** (*I*), **Underline** (U̲), **Strikethrough** (a̶b̶c̶), **Subscript** (X₂), or **Superscript** (X²) button.

What is the toolbar that appears when I select text?
When you select text, Word's mini toolbar appears, giving you quick access to common formatting commands. You can also right-click selected text to display the toolbar. To use any of the tools on the toolbar, simply click the desired tool; otherwise, continue working, and the toolbar disappears.

Change the Font, Size, and Color *(continued)*

Changing the text color can go a long way toward emphasizing it on the page. For example, if you are creating an invitation, you might make the description of the event a different color to stand out from the other details. Likewise, if you are creating a report for work, you might make the title of the report a different color from the information contained in the report, or even color-code certain data in the report. Obviously, when selecting text colors, you should avoid choosing colors that make your text difficult to read.

Change the Font, Size, and Color *(continued)*

Change the Color

① Select the text that you want to format.

② Click the **Home** tab on the Ribbon.

③ Click the ⊡ next to the **Font Color** button (⬛).

④ Click a color.

● Word applies the color to the text.

This example applies a gold color to the text.

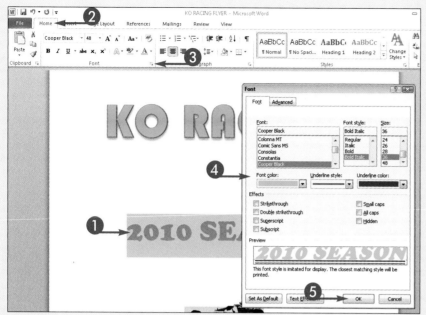

Use the Font Dialog Box

① Select the text that you want to format.

② Click the **Home** tab on the Ribbon.

③ Click the corner group button (▣) in the Font group.

   The Font dialog box appears.

④ Click the font, style, size, color, underline style, or effect that you want to apply.

⑤ Click **OK**.

● Word applies the font change.

Can I change the default font and size?
Yes. To change the default font and size, follow these steps. Display the Font dialog box. Click the font and font size that you want to set as defaults. Click the **Set As Default** button. A new dialog box appears. Specify whether the change should apply to this document only or to all documents created with the current template. Click **OK**, and click **OK** again to close the Font dialog box. The next time you create a new document, Word applies the default font and size that you specified.

Align Text

You can use Word's alignment commands to change how text and objects are positioned horizontally on a page. By default, Word left-aligns text and objects. You can also choose to center text and objects on a page (using the Center command), align text and objects to the right side of the page (using the Right Align command), or justify text and objects so that they line up at both the left and right margins of the page (using the Justify command). You can change the alignment of all the text and objects in your document or change the alignment of individual paragraphs and objects.

Align Text

1 Select the text that you want to format.

2 Click the **Home** tab on the Ribbon.

3 Click an alignment button.

Click the **Align Left** button (≣) to left-align text.

Click the **Center** button (≣) to center text.

Click the **Align Right** button (≣) to right-align text.

Click the **Justify** button (≣) to justify text between the left and right margins.

● Word applies the alignment to the text.

This example centers the text on the document page.

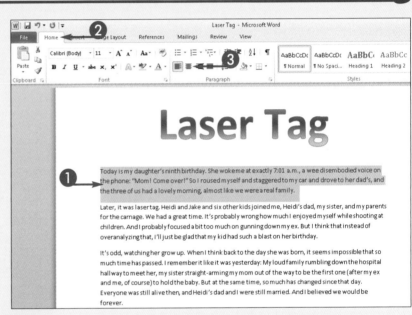

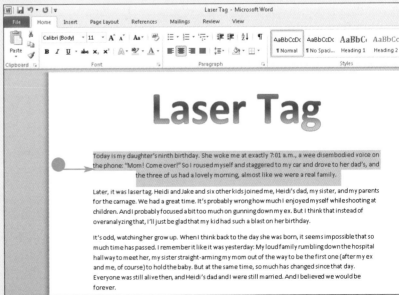

Set Line Spacing

You can adjust the amount of spacing that appears between lines of text in your paragraphs. For example, you might set 2.5 spacing to allow for handwritten edits in your printed document, or set 1.5 spacing to make paragraphs easier to read. By default, Word assigns 1.15 spacing for all new documents that you create.

You can also control how much space appears before and after each paragraph in your document. For example, you might opt to single-space the text within a paragraph, but to add space before and after the paragraph to set it apart from the paragraphs that precede and follow it.

Set Line Spacing

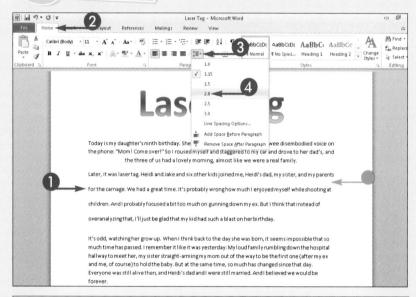

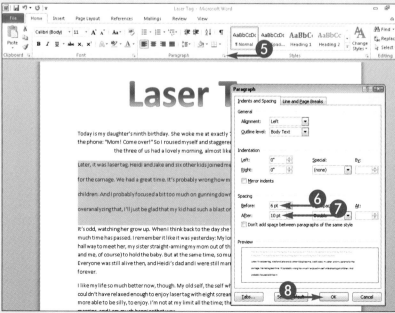

① Select the text that you want to format.

② Click the **Home** tab on the Ribbon.

③ Click the **Line Spacing** button (▤).

④ Click a line spacing option.

● Word immediately applies the new spacing.

This example applies 2.0 line spacing.

⑤ To control the spacing that surrounds a paragraph, click the corner group button (▫) in the Paragraph group.

The Paragraph dialog box opens.

⑥ Use the **Before** spin box to specify how much space should appear before the paragraph.

⑦ Use the **After** spin box to specify how much space should appear after the paragraph.

⑧ Click **OK**.

Indent Text

You can use indents as another way to control the horizontal positioning of text in a document. Indents are simply margins that affect individual lines or paragraphs. You might use an indent to distinguish a particular paragraph on a page — for example, a long quote.

Word offers several tools for setting indents. For example, the Home tab on the Ribbon contains buttons for quickly increasing and decreasing indents by a predefined amount. You can make more precise changes to indent settings in the Paragraph dialog box. Finally, you can use the Word ruler to set indents.

Indent Text

Set Quick Indents

1 Click anywhere in the paragraph you want to indent.

2 Click the **Home** tab on the Ribbon.

3 Click an indent button.

You can click the **Decrease Indent** button (▤) to decrease the indentation.

You can click the **Increase Indent** button (▤) to increase the indentation.

● Word applies the indent change.

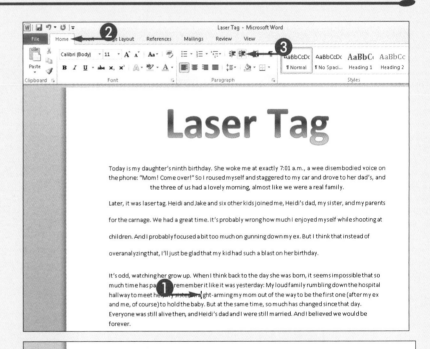

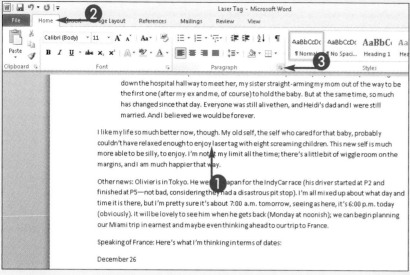

Set Precise Indents

① Click anywhere in the paragraph you want to indent.

② Click the **Home** tab on the Ribbon.

③ Click the corner group button (⬜) in the Paragraph group.

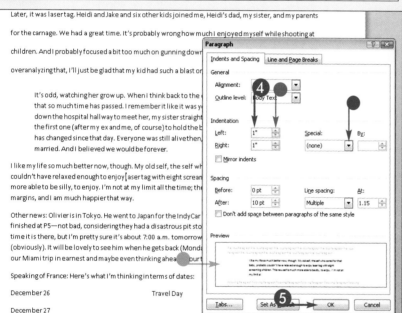

The Paragraph dialog box appears.

④ Type a specific indentation in the **Left** or **Right** indent text boxes.

● You can also click 🔼 to set an indent measurement.

● To set a specific kind of indent, you can click the **Special** 🔽 and then click an indent.

● The Preview area shows a sample of the indent.

⑤ Click **OK**.

Word applies the indent to the text.

Simplify It

How do I set indents using the Word ruler?
You can quickly set an indent using the Word ruler. To do so, simply drag the indent marker (⬚) on the ruler to the desired location. If the ruler is not visible in the Word window, position your mouse pointer over the top of the work area and pause; the ruler appears. (You can also click the **View** tab and click **Ruler** to display the ruler). The ruler contains markers for changing the left indent, right indent, first-line indent, and hanging indent. (To determine which marker is which, you can position your mouse pointer over each one; Word displays the marker's name.)

Set
Tabs

You can use tabs to create vertically aligned columns of text in your Word document. To insert a tab, simply press the `Tab` key on your keyboard; the cursor moves to the next tab stop on the page.

By default, Word creates tab stops every 0.5 inches across the page, and left-aligns the text on each tab stop. You can set your own tab stops using the ruler or the Tabs dialog box. You can also use the Tabs dialog box to change the tab alignment and specify an exact measurement between tab stops.

Set Tabs

Set Quick Tabs

❶ Position your mouse pointer over the top edge of the work area and pause to display the ruler.

⬤ You can also click the **View** tab and click **Ruler** to turn on the ruler.

❷ Click the **Tab marker** area to cycle through to the type of tab marker that you want to set.

⬚ sets a left-aligned tab.

⬚ sets a center-aligned tab.

⬚ sets a right-aligned tab.

⬚ sets a decimal tab.

⬚ sets a bar tab.

❸ Click in the ruler where you want to insert the tab.

❹ Click at the end of the text after which you want to add a tab.

❺ Press `Tab`.

❻ Type the text that should appear in the next column.

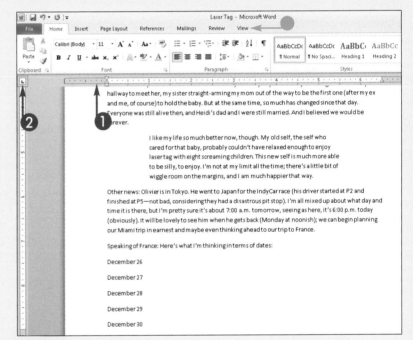

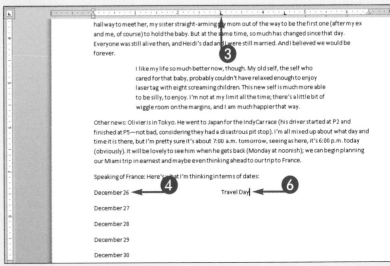

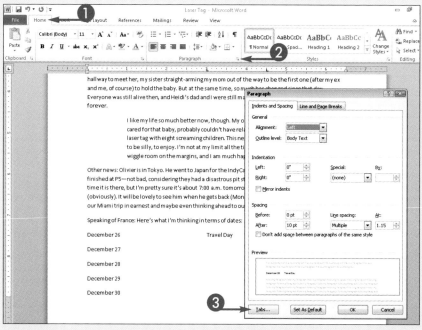

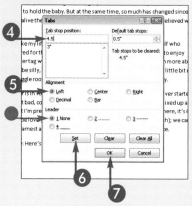

Set Precise Tabs

1 Click the **Home** tab on the Ribbon.

2 Click the corner group button (▣) in the Paragraph group.

The Paragraph dialog box appears.

3 Click **Tabs** on the Indents and Spacing tab.

The Tabs dialog box appears.

4 Click in the **Tab stop position** text box and type a new tab stop measurement.

5 Click to select a tab alignment.

● You can also select a tab leader character.

6 Click **Set**.

Word saves the new tab stop.

7 Click **OK**.

Word exits the dialog box, and you can use the new tab stops.

Simplify It

Can I remove tab stops that I no longer need?
Yes. To remove a tab stop from the ruler, drag the tab stop off of the ruler. To remove a tab stop in the Tabs dialog box, select it, and then click **Clear**. To clear every tab stop that you saved in the Tabs dialog box, click **Clear All**.

What are leader tabs?
You can use leader tabs to separate tab columns with dots, dashes, or lines. Leader tabs help readers follow the information across tab columns. You can set leader tabs using the Tabs dialog box, as shown in this section.

Set Margins

By default, Word assigns a 1-inch margin all the way around the page in every new document that you create. You can change these margin settings, however. For example, you can set wider margins to fit more text on a page, or set smaller margins to fit less text on a page. You can apply your changes to the current document only, or set them as the new default setting, to be applied to all new Word documents you create.

Set Margins Using Page Layout Tools

1. Click the **Page Layout** tab on the Ribbon.

2. Click the **Margins** button.

3. Click a margin setting.

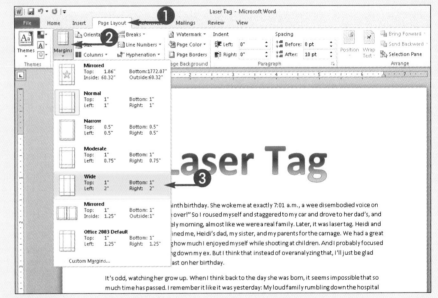

● Word applies the new settings.

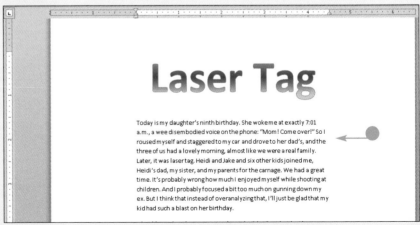

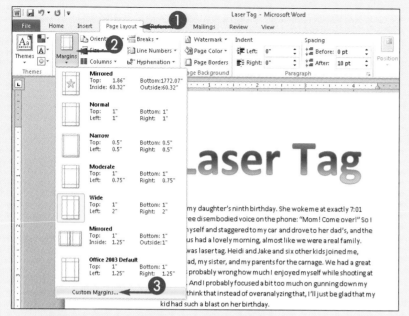

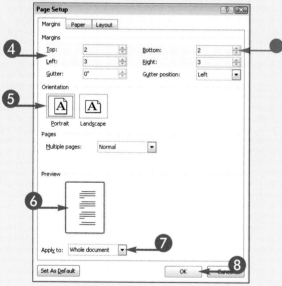

Set a Custom Margin

1 Click the **Page Layout** tab on the Ribbon.

2 Click the **Margins** button.

3 Click **Custom Margins**.

The Page Setup dialog box opens, with the Margins tab shown.

4 Type a specific margin in the **Top**, **Bottom**, **Left**, and **Right** boxes.

● You can also click 🔢 to set a margin measurement.

5 Choose a page orientation.

6 Preview the margin settings in the Preview section.

7 Click the **Apply to** 🔽 and specify whether the margin should apply to the whole document or from this point in the document forward.

8 Click **OK**.

Word immediately adjusts the margin in the document.

How do I set new default margins?
If you consistently use the same margin settings, you can choose those settings as the default for every new document that you create in Word. To do so, make the desired changes to the Margins tab of the Page Setup dialog box, and then click **Set As Default**.

Why is my printer ignoring my margin settings?
Some printers have a minimum margin in which nothing can be printed. For example, with many printers, anything less than 0.25 inches is outside the printable area. Be sure to test the margins, or check your printer documentation for more information.

Create Lists

You can set off lists of information in your documents by using bullets or numbers. Bulleted and numbered lists can help you keep your information better organized.

A bulleted list adds dots or other similar designs in front of each list item, whereas a numbered list adds sequential numbers, Roman numerals, or letters in front of each list item.

You can customize lists. For example, with bulleted lists, you can change the symbol or picture used for the bullet, the alignment of the bullet, and so on. For numbered lists, you can change the style of the number, and the font used.

Create Lists

Set Quick Lists

1. Select the text that you want to format.

2. Click the **Home** tab.

3. Click a list button.

   Click **Bullets** (≣) to create a bulleted list.

   Click **Numbering** (≣) to create a numbered list.

   Click **Multilevel List** (≣) to create a multilevel list.

Word applies the formatting to the list.

● This example shows a bulleted list.

To add more text to the list, click at the end of the line and press Enter; Word starts a new line in the list with a bullet or number.

● To end a list, press Enter twice after the last item in the list or click **Bullets** (≣), **Numbering** (≣), or **Multilevel List** (≣).

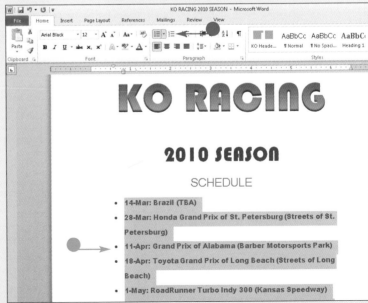

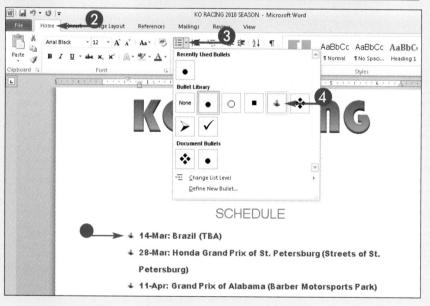

Change Bullet or Number Styles

1️⃣ Select the text that you want to format.

2️⃣ Click the **Home** tab on the Ribbon.

3️⃣ Click the **Bullets**, **Numbering**, or **Multilevel List** ▾.

4️⃣ Click a style.

⚫ Word applies the new style.

Can I customize a style?

Yes. You can create a customized style or control the positioning of bullets and numbers. Follow these steps. Click the **Bullets** or **Numbering** ▾ and then click **Define New Bullet** or **Define New Number Format**. The Define New Bullet or Define New Number Format dialog box appears. Set any options for the format and position of the bullets or numbers. Click **OK** to close the dialog box. Word applies the customized style.

Copy Formatting

Suppose you have applied a variety of formatting options to a paragraph to create a certain look — for example, you changed the font, the size, the color, and the alignment. If you want to re-create the same look elsewhere in the document, you do not have to repeat the same steps as when you applied the original formatting, again changing the font, size, color, and alignment. Instead, you can use Word's Format Painter feature to "paint" the formatting to the other text in one swift action. With the Format Painter feature, copying formatting is as easy as clicking a button.

Copy Formatting

① Select the text that contains the formatting that you want to copy.

② Click the **Home** tab on the Ribbon.

③ Click the **Format Painter** button (☑).

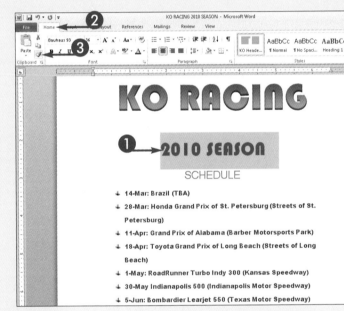

④ Click and drag over the text to which you want to apply the same formatting.

● Word immediately copies the formatting to the new text.

● To copy the same formatting multiple times, you can double-click the **Format Painter** button (☑).

You can press Esc to cancel the Format Painter feature at any time.

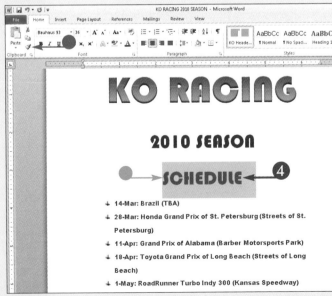

Clear Formatting

Sometimes, you may find that you have applied too much formatting to your text, making it difficult to read. Or perhaps you simply applied the wrong formatting to your text. In that case, instead of undoing all your formatting changes by hand, you can use Word's Clear Formatting command to remove any formatting you have applied to the document text. When you apply the Clear Formatting command, which is located in the Home tab on the Ribbon, Word removes all formatting applied to the text, and restores the default settings.

Clear Formatting

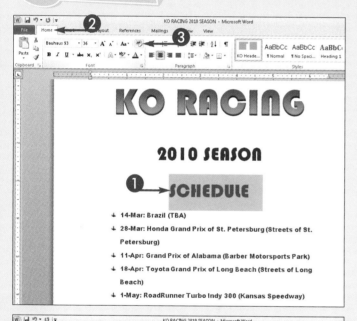

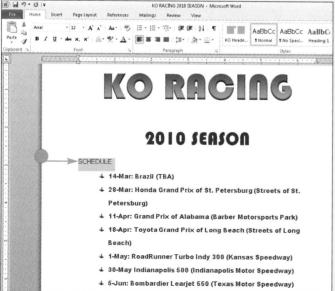

1 Select the text containing the formatting that you want to remove.

2 Click the **Home** tab on the Ribbon.

3 Click the **Clear Formatting** button (⌫).

● Word immediately removes the formatting and restores the default settings.

Format with Styles

Suppose you are writing a corporate report that requires specific formatting for every heading. Instead of assigning multiple formatting settings over and over again, you can create a style with the required formatting settings and apply it whenever you need it. A *style* is a set of text-formatting characteristics. These characteristics might include the text font, size, color, alignment, spacing, and more.

In addition to creating your own styles for use in your documents, you can apply any of Word's preset styles. These include styles for headings, normal text, quotes, and more.

Create a New Quick Style

① Format the text as desired and then select the text.

② Click the **Home** tab on the Ribbon.

③ Click the **More** button (⊡) in the Styles group.

④ Click **Save Selection as a New Quick Style**.

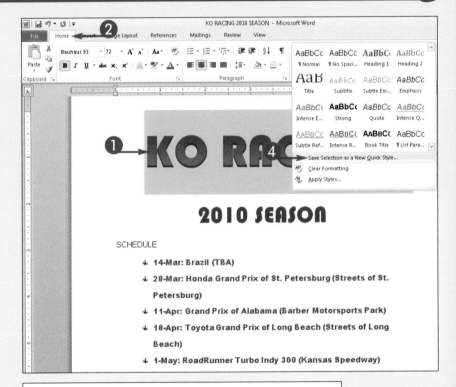

The Create New Style from Formatting dialog box appears.

⑤ Type a name for the style.

⑥ Click **OK**.

Word adds the style to the list of Quick Styles.

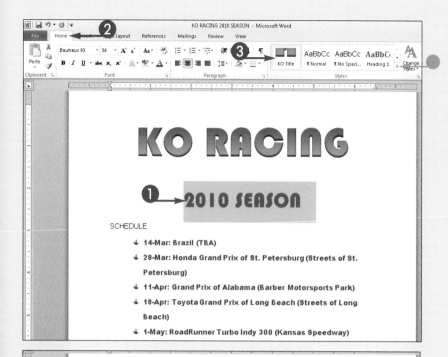

Apply a Quick Style

1 Select the text that you want to format.

2 Click the **Home** tab on the Ribbon.

3 Click a style from the Styles list.

● You can click the **More** button (⬙) to see the full palette of available styles.

● Word applies the style.

Simplify It

How do I remove a style that I no longer need?
From the Home tab, display the full Quick Styles palette, right-click the style that you want to remove, and click the **Remove from Quick Style Gallery** command. Word immediately removes the style from the Quick Styles list.

How do I customize an existing style?
Apply a style to your text. Then, with the text selected, click the **Home** tab, click the **Change Styles** button, and click the type of change that you want to make. For example, to switch fonts, click the **Fonts** option and then select another font.

Apply a Template

A *template* is a special file that stores styles and other Word formatting tools. When you apply a template to a Word document, the styles and tools in that template become available for your use with that document. Word comes with several templates preinstalled; in addition, you can create your own.

Of course, one way to apply a template to a document is to select it from the list of document types in the New screen that appears when you create a new Word document. Alternatively, you can attach a template to an existing document, as outlined here.

Apply a Template

① With the document to which you want to apply a template open in Word, click the **File** tab.

② Click **Options**.

The Word Options window opens.

③ Click **Add-Ins**.

④ Click the **Manage** ⏷.

⑤ Click **Templates**.

⑥ Click **Go**.

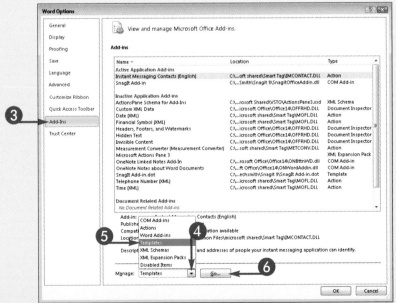

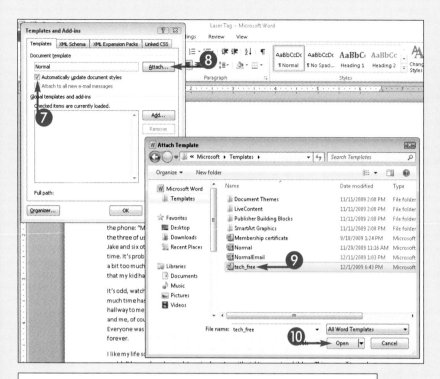

The Templates and Add-ins dialog box opens.

⑦ Click to select the **Automatically update document styles** check box.

⑧ Click **Attach**.

The Attach Template dialog box opens.

⑨ Locate and select the template you want to apply.

⑩ Click **Open**.

Word applies the template.

● The styles used in the document are updated to reflect those appearing in the template.

Laser Tag

Today is my daughter's ninth birthday. She woke me at exactly 7:01 a.m., a wee disembodied voice on the phone: "Mom! Come over!" So I roused myself and staggered to my car and drove to her dad's, and the three of us had a lovely morning, almost like we were a real family. Later, it was laser tag. Heidi and Jake and six other kids joined me, Heidi's dad, my sister, and my parents for the carnage. We had a great time. It's probably wrong how much I enjoyed myself while shooting at children. And I probably focused a bit too much on gunning down my ex. But I think that instead of overanalyzing that, I'll just be glad that my kid had such a blast on her birthday.

It's odd, watching her grow up. When I think back to the day she was born, it seems impossible that so much time has passed. I remember it like it was yesterday: My loud family rumbling down the hospital hallway to meet her, my sister straight-arming my mom out of the way to be the first one (after my ex and me, of course) to hold the baby. But at the same time, so much has changed since that day. Everyone was still alive then, and Heidi's dad and I were still married. And I believed we would be forever.

I like my life so much better now, though. My old self, the self who cared for that baby, probably couldn't have relaxed enough to enjoy laser tag with eight screaming children. This new self is much more able to be silly, to enjoy. I'm not at my limit all the time; there's a little bit of wiggle room on the margins, and I am much happier that way.

Other news: Olivier is in Tokyo. He went to Japan for the IndyCar race (his driver started at P2 and finished at P5— not bad, considering they had a disastrous pit stop). I'm all mixed up about what day and time it is there, but I'm pretty sure it's about 7:00 a.m. tomorrow, seeing as here, it's 6:00 p.m. today (obviously). It will be lovely to see him when he gets back (Monday at noonish); we can begin planning our Miami trip in earnest and maybe even thinking ahead to our trip to France.

Simplify It

Can I create my own templates?
Yes. The easiest way to create a template is to base it on an existing Word document. With the document on which you want to base your template open in Word, click the **File** tab, and click **Save As**. The Save As dialog box opens; locate and select the folder in which you want to save the template, type a name for the template in the **File Name** field, click the **Save as Type** ⊡ and choose **Word Template**, and click **Save**. Word saves the template in the folder you chose.

Assign a Theme

A *theme* is a predesigned set of color schemes, fonts, and other visual attributes. Applying a theme to a document is a quick way to add polish to it.

Because themes are shared among the Office programs, you can use the same theme in your Word document that you have applied to worksheets in Excel or slides in PowerPoint.

Note that the effect of applying a theme is more obvious if you have assigned styles such as headings to your document. The effects of themes are even more pronounced when you assign a background color to a page.

Assign a Theme

Apply a Theme

1. Click the **Page Layout** tab on the Ribbon.

2. Click the **Themes** button.

3. Click a theme.

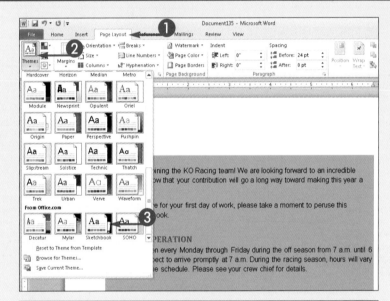

- Word immediately applies the theme to the current document.

- You can use these tools to change the formatting of the theme's colors (■), fonts (Ⓐ), and effects (◉).

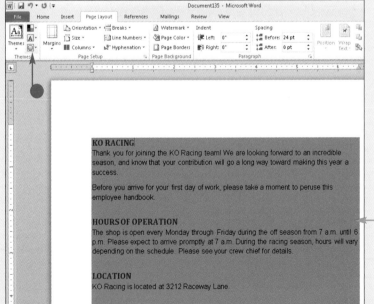

Create a Custom Theme

1. Apply a theme and edit the formatting to create the theme that you want to save.

2. Click the **Page Layout** tab on the Ribbon.

3. Click the **Themes** button.

4. Click **Save Current Theme**.

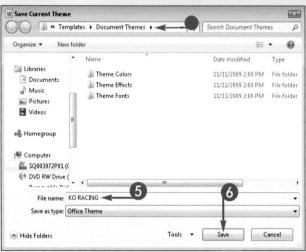

The Save Current Theme dialog box appears.

5. Type a unique name for the theme.

● By default, Word saves the theme to the Document Themes folder so that it is accessible in the Themes Gallery.

6. Click **Save**.

Word saves the theme and adds it to the list of available themes.

How can I make the effects of my theme more obvious?
As mentioned, the effects of your theme are more obvious if you have applied page styles such as headings and a background color to your document. To apply a background color, click the **Page Layout** tab on the Ribbon, click the **Page Color** button in the Page Background group, and click a color in the palette; Word applies the color you selected to the background of the page. For help applying a heading style, refer to the section "Format with Styles" in Chapter 6.

Add Borders

You can apply borders around your document text to add emphasis or make the document aesthetically appealing. You can add borders around a single paragraph, multiple paragraphs, or the entire document page. (Be aware that you should not add too many effects, such as borders, to your document because it will become difficult to read.)

Word comes with several predesigned borders, which you can apply to your document. Alternatively, you can create your own custom borders — for example, making each border line a different color or thickness. Another option is to apply shading to your text to set it apart.

Add Borders

Add a Border

1. Select the text to which you want to add a border.

2. Click the **Home** tab on the Ribbon.

3. Click the **Borders** button (▦).

4. Click a border.

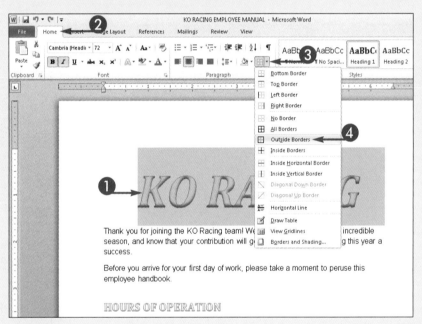

● Word applies the border to the text.

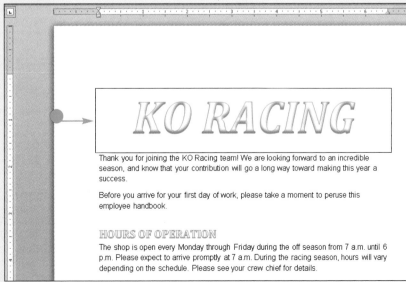

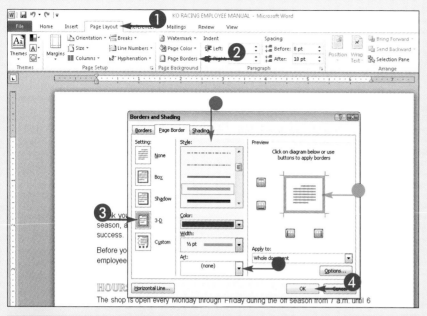

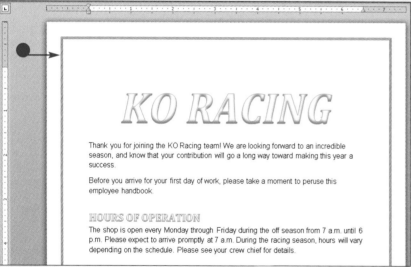

Add a Page Border

① Click the **Page Layout** tab on the Ribbon.

② Click the **Page Borders** button.

The Borders and Shading dialog box appears, and displays the Page Border tab.

③ Click the type of border that you want to add.

● You can use these settings to select a different border line style, color, and width.

● You can set a graphical border using this option.

● The Preview area displays a sample of the selections.

④ Click **OK**.

● Word applies the border to the page.

Simplify It

How do I add shading to my text?	**How do I create a custom border?**
To add shading behind a block of text, select the text, click the **Home** tab on the Ribbon, click the **Shading** button (□) in the Paragraph group, and click a color to apply.	Select the text you want to border, open the Borders and Shading dialog box, click the **Borders** tab, and choose **Custom**. Choose the settings you want to apply to the first line of the border; then click in the **Preview** area where you want the line to appear. Repeat for each line you want to add, and then click **OK**.

Create Columns

You can create columns in Word to present your text in a format similar to a newspaper or magazine. For example, if you are creating a brochure or newsletter, you can use columns to make text flow from one block to the next.

If you simply want to create a document with two or three columns, you can use one of Word's preset columns. Alternatively, you can create custom columns, choosing the number of columns you want to create in your document, indicating the width of each column, specifying whether a line should appear between them, and more.

Create Columns

Create Quick Columns

1 Select the text that you want to place into columns.

2 Click the **Page Layout** tab on the Ribbon.

3 Click the **Columns** button.

4 Click the number of columns that you want to assign.

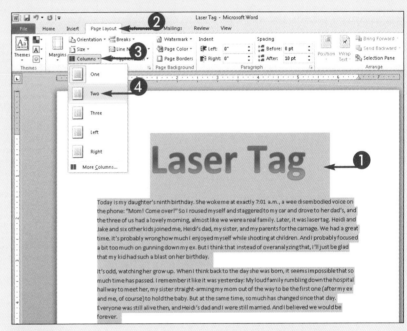

● Word places the selected text into the number of columns that you specify.

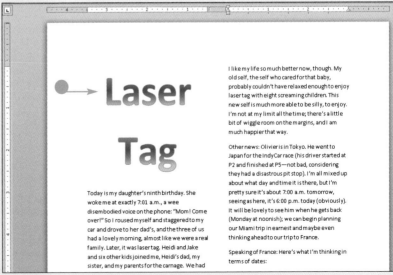

Create Custom Columns

1. Select the text that you want to place into columns.

2. Click the **Page Layout** tab on the Ribbon.

3. Click the **Columns** button.

4. Click **More Columns**.

   The Columns dialog box appears.

5. Click a preset for the type of column style that you want to apply.

   ● You can also specify the number of columns here.

   ● You can set an exact column width and spacing here.

   ● You can specify whether the columns apply to the selected text or the entire document.

   ● You can include a vertical line separating the columns.

6. Click **OK**.

   ● Word applies the column format to the selected text.

How do I wrap column text around a picture or other object?
Click the picture or other object that you want to wrap, click the **Format** tab, click the **Wrap Text** button, and then click the type of wrapping that you want to apply.

Can I create a break within a column?
Yes. To add a column break, click where you want the break to occur and then press Ctrl + Shift + Enter . To remove a break, select it and press Delete . To return to a one-column format, click the **Columns** button on the Page Layout tab, and then select the single-column format.

Insert a Table

You can use tables to present data in an organized fashion. For example, you might add a table to your document to display a list of items or a roster of classes. Tables contain columns and rows, which intersect to form *cells*. You can insert all types of data in cells, including text and graphics.

To enter text in cells, click in the cell and then type your data. As you type, Word wraps the text to fit in the cell. Press Tab to move from one cell to another. You can select table cells, rows, and columns to perform editing tasks and apply formatting.

Insert a Table

Insert a Table

① Click in the document where you want to insert a table.

② Click the **Insert** tab on the Ribbon.

③ Click the **Table** button.

④ Drag across the number of columns and rows that you want to set for your table.

● Word previews the table as you drag over cells.

● Word adds the table to the document.

⑤ Click inside a cell and type your data.

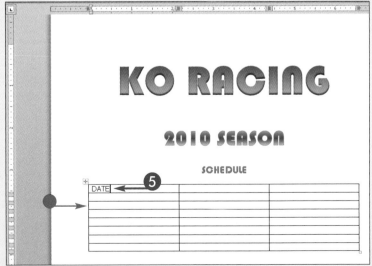

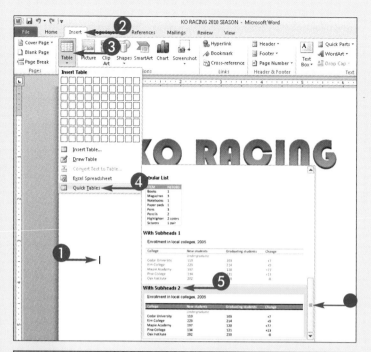

Insert a Quick Table

① Click in the document where you want to insert a table.

② Click the **Insert** tab on the Ribbon.

③ Click the **Table** button.

④ Click **Quick Tables**.

● You can use the scroll bar to scroll through the available tables.

⑤ Click the table that you want to insert.

● Word adds the table to the document.

You can click inside a cell and replace the "dummy" data with your own text.

Can I create a customized table?
Yes. You can create a customized table by drawing the table. When you do, you control the table's size and how the rows and columns appear. To draw a table, click the **Insert** tab on the Ribbon, click the **Table** button, and choose **Draw Table** from the menu that appears. Next, click in the document and drag across and down to draw an outside border for your table. Finally, click and drag to draw an internal line to delineate a row or column in your table; continue adding inner lines to build your table cells.

Apply Table Styles

When you click in a table you have added to your document, two new tabs appear on the Ribbon: Design and Layout. You can use the table styles found in the Design tab to add instant formatting to your Word tables. Word offers numerous predefined table styles, each with its own unique set of formatting characteristics, including shading, color, borders, and fonts.

The Design tab also includes settings for creating custom borders and applying custom shading. You can also use check boxes in the Table Style Options group to add a header row, emphasize the table's first column, and more.

Apply Table Styles

1 Click anywhere in the table that you want to format.

2 Click the **Design** tab on the Ribbon.

3 Click a style from the Table Styles list.

● You can click the **More** button (▼) to display the entire palette of available styles.

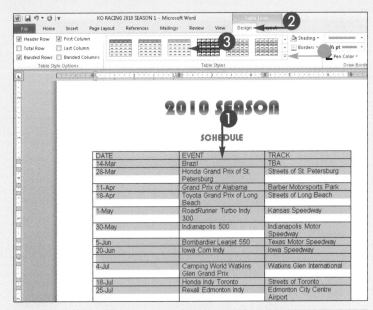

● Word applies the style.

● You can toggle table parts on or off using the Table Style Options check boxes.

● You can click these options to change the shading and borders.

Insert an Excel Spreadsheet

If Excel is installed on your computer, you can insert a new Excel spreadsheet into your Word document. You can then insert data such as text or graphics in the cells in the spreadsheet. For example, to add text, you simply click in the desired cell and begin typing; press **Tab** to move from one cell to another.

When you click in an Excel spreadsheet that you have inserted in your Word document, the Ribbon in Word changes to display various Excel tools and features. You can use these tools and features to work with any data you add to the spreadsheet.

Insert an Excel Spreadsheet

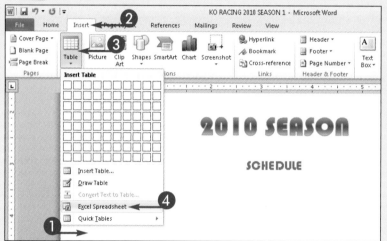

① Click in the document where you want to insert a table.

② Click the **Insert** tab on the Ribbon.

③ Click the **Table** button.

④ Click **Excel Spreadsheet**.

● An Excel spreadsheet appears, along with tools associated with the Excel program.

⑤ Click in a cell and type the data that you want to add.

● The Home tab displays tools for formatting your cells and data.

● The Formulas tab offers tools for building Excel formulas.

● You can click anywhere outside of the table to return to Word's tools and features.

Add Headers
and Footers

If you want to include text at the top or bottom of every page, such as the title of your document, your name, or the date, you can use headers and footers. Header text appears at the very top of the page above the margin; footer text appears at the very bottom of the page, below the margin.

To view header or footer text, Word must be in Print Layout view. To switch to this view, click the View tab and click the Print Layout button. Then double-click the top or bottom of the page, respectively, to view the header or footer.

Add Headers and Footers

Add a Header or Footer

1 Click the **Insert** tab.

2 Click the **Header** button to add a header, or click the **Footer** button to add a footer.

3 Click the type of header or footer that you want to add.

This example adds a header.

Word adds the header and displays the Header & Footer Tools tab.

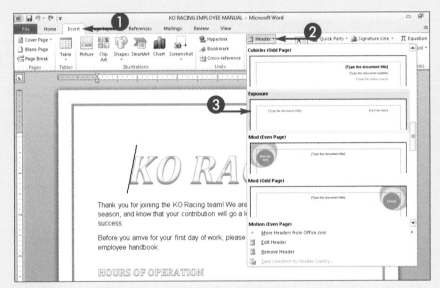

4 Click the field in the header area and type your header text.

5 If the header style you chose includes a date, click the **Date** field and choose a date from the calendar that appears.

● You can click the **Quick Parts** button to insert additional fields.

● You can insert more headers and footers using these controls.

6 Click the **Close Header and Footer** button.

Word closes the Header & Footer Tools tab.

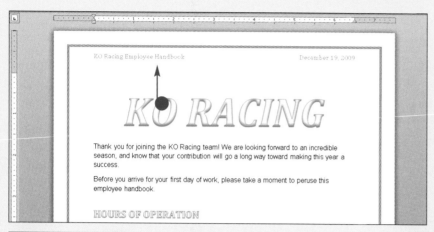

● Word displays the header or footer on the document page.

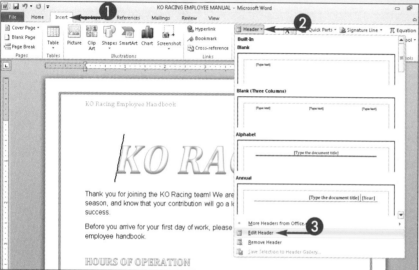

Edit a Header or Footer

① Click the **Insert** tab on the Ribbon.

② Click the **Header** or **Footer** button.

③ Click **Edit Header** or **Edit Footer**.

Word displays the Header & Footer Tools tab; you can now edit the header or footer text.

Can I omit the header or footer from the first page?
Yes. Click the **Insert** tab, click the **Header** or **Footer** button, and click **Edit Header** or **Edit Footer**. Next, select the **Different First Page** check box in the Options group. If you want to remove the header or footer for odd or even pages, click to select the **Different Odd & Even Pages** check box.

How do I remove a header or footer?
Click the **Insert** tab, click the **Header** or **Footer** button, and click the **Remove Header** or **Remove Footer** command. Word removes the header or footer from your document.

Insert Footnotes and Endnotes

You can include footnotes or endnotes in your document to identify sources or references to other materials or to add explanatory information. When you add a footnote or endnote, a small numeral or other character appears alongside the associated text, with the actual footnote or endnote appearing at the bottom of a page or the end of the document, respectively.

When you insert footnotes or endnotes in a document, Word automatically numbers them for you. As you add, delete, and move text in your document, any associated footnotes or endnotes are likewise added, deleted, or moved, as well as renumbered.

Insert Footnotes and Endnotes

Insert a Footnote

1 Click where you want to insert the footnote reference.

2 Click the **References** tab on the Ribbon.

3 Click the **Insert Footnote** button.

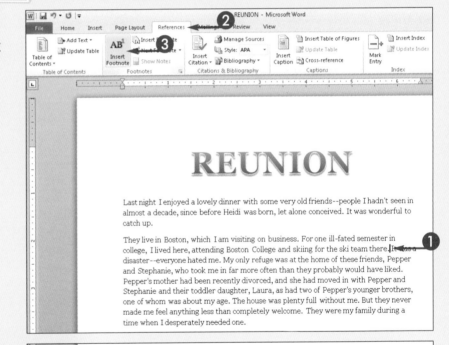

4 Type the note text.

● To return to the reference mark in the document, you can double-click the footnote number.

You can repeat these steps to add more footnotes.

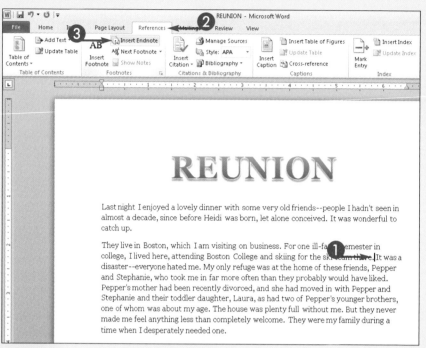

Insert an Endnote

1 Click where you want to insert the footnote reference.

2 Click the **References** tab on the Ribbon.

3 Click the **Insert Endnote** button.

4 Type your note text at the bottom of the last page of the document.

● The endnote number appears automatically.

To return to the reference mark in the document, you can double-click the endnote number.

How can I change the starting number for footnotes or endnotes in my document?

If you need to change the starting footnote or endnote number in your document — for example, if you are working on a new chapter, but you want the numbering to continue from the previous one — click the **References** tab and click the corner group button (⊡) in the Footnotes group. The Footnote and Endnote dialog box appears; click in the **Start at** text box and type a number or use the spin arrow (⬧) to set a new number. Click **Apply** to apply the changes to the document.

Insert Page Numbers and Page Breaks

If you are working on a long document, you can add page numbers to help you keep the pages in order after printing the document. Page numbers are added to the header or footer area of the document. You can choose how page numbers look on your document.

Adding page breaks can help you control what text appears on what page of the document. For example, you might add a page break at the end of one chapter to ensure that the next chapter starts on its own page. You can insert page breaks using the Ribbon or using your keyboard.

Insert Page Numbers and Page Breaks

Insert Page Numbers

① Click the **Insert** tab on the Ribbon.

② Click the **Page Number** button.

③ Click a location for the page numbers.

④ Click a page number style.

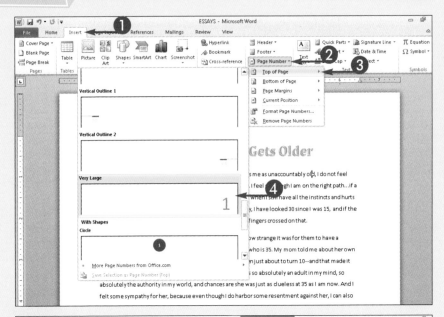

● Word assigns page numbers to your document.

⑤ Click **Close Header and Footer** to exit the header or footer area.

Note: See the "Add Headers and Footers" section to learn more.

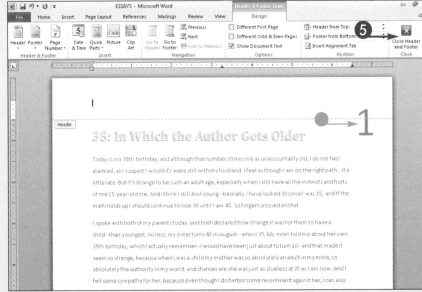

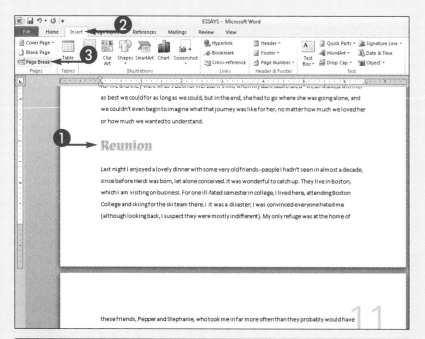

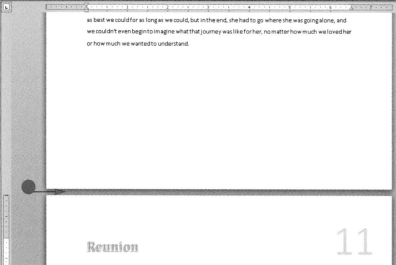

Insert Page Breaks

① Click in the document where you want to insert a page break.

② Click the **Insert** tab on the Ribbon.

③ Click the **Page Break** button.

● Word assigns the page break.

Simplify It

Is there a faster way to insert a page break?
Yes. You can use keyboard shortcuts to quickly insert a page break as you type in your document. You can insert a manual page break by pressing Ctrl + Enter. You can also insert a line break by pressing Shift + Enter.

Can I change the number style?
Yes. Click the **Page Number** button on the Insert tab, and then click **Format Page Numbers**. This opens the Page Number Format dialog box. You can change the number style to Roman numerals, alphabetical, and more. You can also include chapter numbers with your page numbers.

Mark Index Entries

If your document requires an index, you can use Word to build one. Indexes can contain main entries and subentries as well as cross-references (entries that refer to other entries).

Before you can build an index, you must mark any words or phrases in your document that

should appear in the index. When you do, Word adds a special index field, called an XE field, to the document; this field includes the marked word or phrase, as well as any cross-reference information you might have added. After you mark index entries, you can generate the index (discussed in the next section).

Mark Index Entries

Mark a Word or Phrase

1. Select the text for which you want to create an index entry.

2. Click the **References** tab.

3. Click the **Mark Entry** button.

   The Mark Index Entry dialog box opens.

● The selected text appears in the Main Entry field.

   Note: *To create an entry for a person's name, type it in the* ***Main Entry*** *field in Last Name, First Name format.*

● The Current Page radio button is selected.

● To mark just this occurrence of the text, click **Mark**.

● To mark all occurrences of the text, click **Mark All**.

● Word adds an index entry field to your document.

   Note: *To view the field, click the Home tab's* ***Show/Hide*** *button (¶).*

4. Click **Close**.

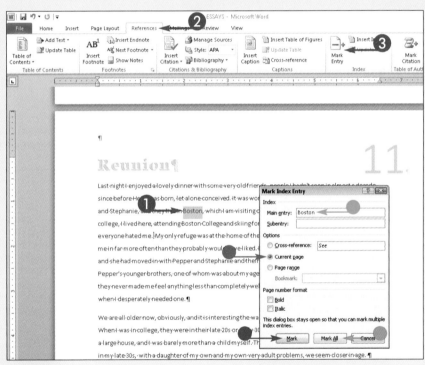

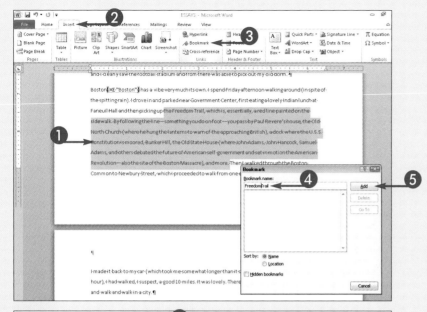

Mark a Word or Phrase that Spans a Range of Pages

1. Select the range of text to which the index entry should refer.

2. Click the **Insert** tab.

3. Click **Bookmark**.

4. In the Bookmark dialog box, type a name for the bookmark.

   Note: Do not include spaces.

5. Click **Add**.

6. Click at the end of the text you selected.

7. Click the **References** tab.

8. Click the **Mark Entry** button.

9. In the Mark Index Entry dialog box, type the word or phrase that should appear in the index.

10. Click the **Page range** radio button.

11. Click the **Bookmark** ⊡ and choose the bookmark you just created.

12. Click **Mark**.

    Word adds an XE field to your document.

13. Click **Close**.

Simplify It

Can I add a subentry?
Yes. To format selected text as a subentry, type the entry under which the text should appear in the Mark Index Entry dialog box's **Main entry** field, and then type the text in the **Subentry** field. If the text should appear as a subentry *and* a main entry, add two XE fields — one for the main entry and one for the subentry.

Can I add cross-references?
Yes. To create index entries that refer to other entries, click **Cross-reference** in the Mark Index Entry dialog box and type the word or phrase to which the entry should refer.

Generate an Index

After you mark the words and phrases in your Word document that you want to appear as index entries, including main entries, subentries, and cross-references, you can generate the index.

When you generate an index, Word searches for marked words and phrases, sorts them alphabetically, adds page-number references, and removes duplicate entries that cite the same page number.

If you do not care for the default appearance of the index, you can customize it to suit your taste. Also, if you make a change to your document after generating the index, you can update the index to reflect the change.

Generate an Index

Generate an Index

1 Click the spot in your document where you want to insert the index.

2 Click the **References** tab.

3 Click the **Insert Index** button.

The Index dialog box opens.

4 Click the **Formats** ▾ and select an index design.

● Preview the selected index design here.

5 Click the **Indented** radio button.

6 Click the **Columns** ▣ to change the number of columns per page the index will contain.

7 Click **OK**.

● Word generates the index.

Note: To delete an index entry, select the XE field (including the braces that surround it) and press Delete.

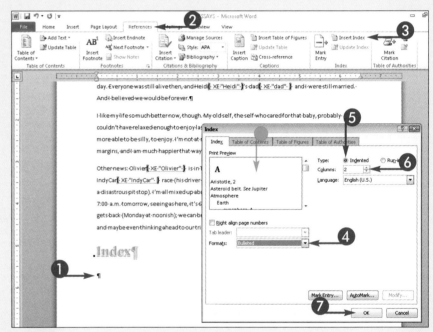

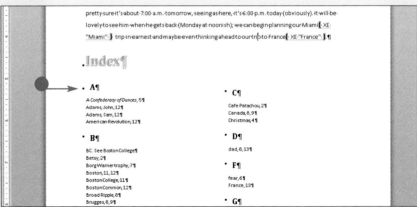

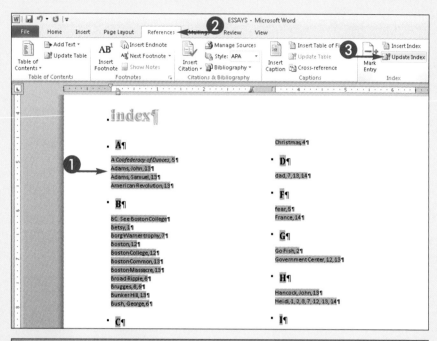

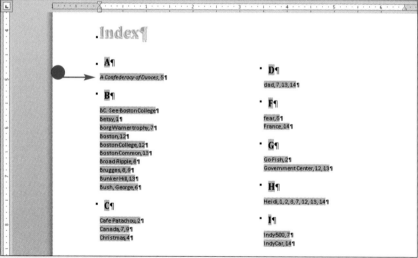

Update the Index

① After making changes to your document, click in the index.

② Click the **References** tab.

③ Click the **Update Index** button.

● Word updates the index to reflect changes to the document that have occurred since the original index was generated.

Can I customize the layout of my index?
Yes. Open the Index dialog box, click the **Formats** 🔽, choose **From Template**, and click **Modify**. The Style dialog box opens; click the index style you want to change, and again click **Modify**. Finally, select the desired options in the Formatting section.

How do I edit index entries?
Click the **Home** tab, click the **Replace** button, type the contents of the XE field that you need to replace in the **Find What** field (for example, **XE "John Adams"**), type the replacement text in the **Replace With** field (for example, **XE "Adams, John"**), and click **Replace All**.

Generate a Table of Contents

You can use Word to generate a table of contents (TOC) for your document. By default, Word generates a TOC by searching for text in your document that was formatted using one of Word's predefined heading styles. It then copies this text and pastes it into the table of contents.

Alternatively, you can create a custom TOC based on styles you choose — handy if your document uses a template that contains heading styles that are different from Word's predefined ones. Note that you can select from Word's gallery of TOC styles to establish the TOC's look and feel.

Generate a Table of Contents

Style Text as Headers

1. Select text in your document that you want to style as a header.

2. Click the **Home** tab.

- If the desired style appears in the Styles group, click it.

- If the style does not appear in the Styles group, click the **More** button (▼) and choose it from the Quick Style gallery.

- If the style does not appear in the Quick Style gallery, click the corner group button (▣) and choose it from the Styles pane, as shown here.

- Word applies the style to the selected text.

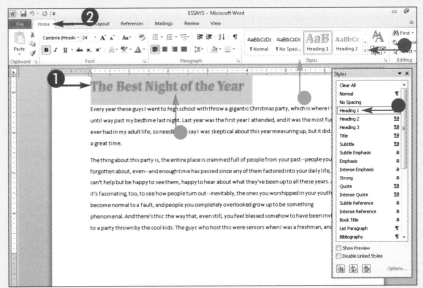

Generate a Table of Contents

1. Click the spot in your document where you want to insert a TOC.

2. Click the **References** tab.

3. Click the **Table of Contents** button.

4. Choose the desired TOC style.

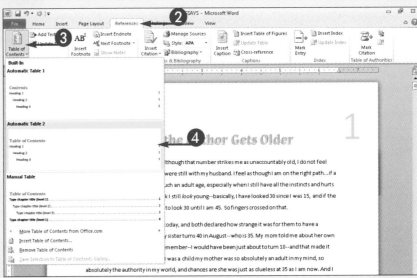

● Word generates a TOC.

Note: To delete a TOC, click the **Table of Contents** button and choose **Remove Table of Contents**.

Note: If you edit your document, you can update your TOC to reflect the changes. To do so, click the **Update Table** button in the References tab's Table of Contents group and specify whether you want to update page numbers only or the entire table.

Simplify It

How do I create a TOC from custom styles?
Click the **References** tab, click **Table of Contents**, and choose **Insert Table of Contents**. In the Table of Contents dialog box, click **Options** (●). The Table of Contents Options dialog box opens; under Available Styles, locate the top-level heading style you applied to your document; then type **1** (●) in the corresponding field to indicate that it should appear in the TOC as a level-1 heading. Repeat for additional heading styles, typing **2**, **3**, **4**, and so on to indicate their levels. Click **OK** in each dialog box to close it.

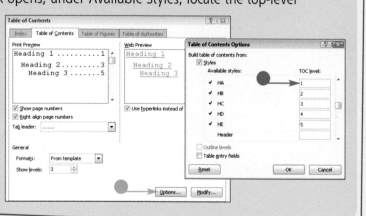

Create a Bibliography

You can use Word to generate a bibliography for your document, formatting the entries using the style of your choice — APA, MLA, The Chicago Manual of Style, and so on.

For Word to determine what entries should appear in the bibliography, you must cite sources in your document as you work. Word then collects the information from these citations to generate the bibliography. (Note that when you add a source to a document, Word saves it for use in subsequent documents.)

Create a Bibliography

Add a Citation

1 Click at the end of the text you want to cite.

2 Click the **References** tab.

3 Click the **Insert Citation** button.

4 Click **Add New Source**.

The Create Source dialog box opens.

5 Click the **Type of Source** and select the type of source you want to cite.

6 Enter the requested information.

7 Click **OK**.

Word adds a citation to your document, and adds the source to the Insert Citation menu.

Note: *To use a source from another document, click the* **Manage Sources** *button in the* **References** *tab. Then, in the Manage Sources dialog box, click the citation you want to add in the Master List, click* **Copy**, *and click* **Close**.

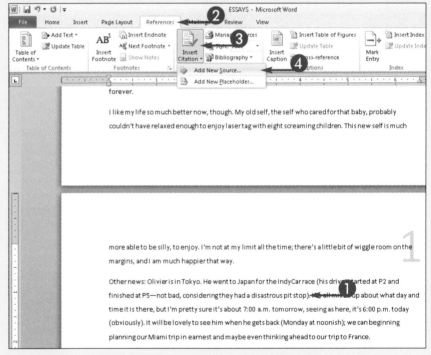

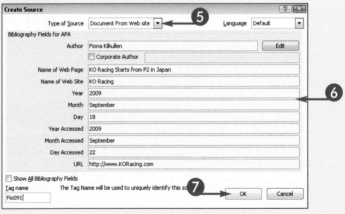

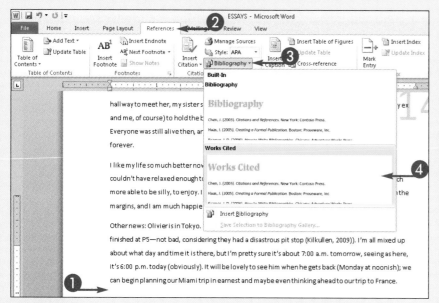

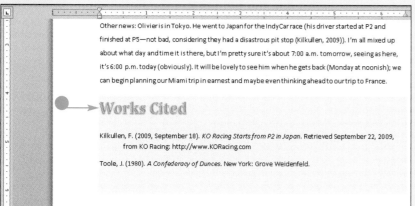

Generate the Bibliography

1. Click the spot in the document where you want the bibliography to appear (typically at the end).

2. Click the **References** tab.

3. Click the **Bibliography** button.

4. Choose one of the gallery options to insert a predesigned bibliography into your document.

● Word inserts the bibliography.

Note: *To specify which style guide you want to use, click the **References** tab, click the **Style** in the Citations & Bibliography group, and choose a style guide from the list that appears.*

What do I do if I do not have all the information I need about a citation?
If you want to add a citation to your document but you are missing some of the required information, you can create a placeholder. To do so, click the **References** tab, click **Insert Citation**, and choose **Add New Placeholder**. The Placeholder Name dialog box opens; type a name for the placeholder. Later, add citation information by clicking the **Manage Sources** button in the **References** tab to open the Manage Sources dialog box, clicking the placeholder under Current List, clicking **Edit**, and entering the necessary information.

Find and Replace Text

Suppose you want to edit a paragraph in your document that contains a specific word or phrase. Instead of scrolling through your document to locate that paragraph, you can use Word's Find tool to search for the word or phrase in the paragraph.

In addition, you can use the Replace tool to replace instances of a word or phrase with other text. For example, suppose you complete a long report, only to discover that you have misspelled the name of a product you are reviewing; you can use the Replace tool to locate and correct the misspellings.

Find and Replace Text

Find Text

① Click at the beginning of your document.

② Click the **Home** tab on the Ribbon.

③ Click the **Find** button.

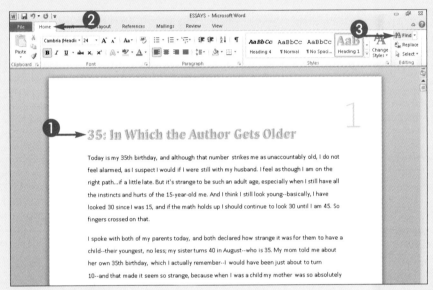

● The Navigation pane appears.

④ Type the text that you want to find and press Enter.

● Word searches the document and highlights occurrences of the text.

● Word also lists occurrences of the text in the Navigation pane.

⑤ Click an entry in the Navigation pane.

● Word selects the corresponding text in the document.

When finished, click the Navigation pane's ⊠ button.

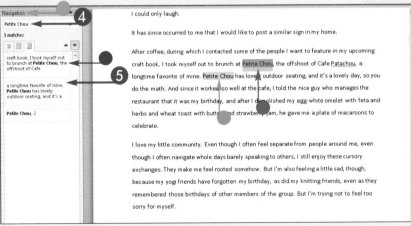

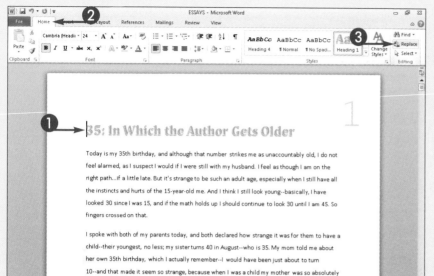

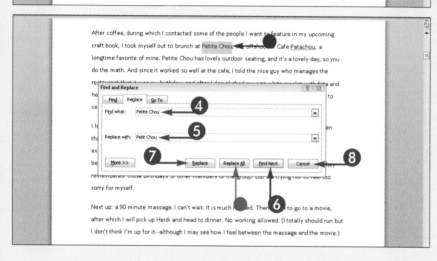

Replace Text

① Click at the beginning of your document.

② Click the **Home** tab on the Ribbon.

③ Click the **Replace** button.

The Find and Replace dialog box opens with the Replace tab shown.

④ In the **Find what** field, type the text that you want to find.

⑤ Type the replacement text in the **Replace with** field.

⑥ Click **Find Next**.

● Word locates the first occurrence.

⑦ Click **Replace** to replace the occurrence.

● To replace every occurrence in the document, you can click **Replace All**.

⑧ When finished, click **Cancel**.

Note: If Word displays a prompt box when the last occurrence is found, click OK.

Where can I find detailed search options?
Click **More** in the Find and Replace dialog box to reveal additional search options. For example, you can search for matching text case, whole words, and more. You can also search for specific formatting or special characters by clicking **Format** and **Special**.

How can I search for and delete text?
Start by typing the text you want to delete in the **Find What** field; then leave the **Replace With** field empty. When you activate the search, Word looks for the text and deletes it without adding new text to the document.

Scan Document Content

If you are working with a very long document, using the scroll bar on the right side of the screen or the Page Up and Page Down keys on your keyboard to locate a particular page in that document can be time-consuming. To rectify this, Word 2010 includes the Navigation pane. Depending on which option you choose, this pane can display all the headings in your document or a thumbnail image of each page in your document. You can then click a heading or a thumbnail image in the Navigation pane to view the corresponding page.

Scan Document Content

① Click the **View** tab on the Ribbon.

② Click to select the **Navigation Pane** check box in the Show group.

● Word displays the Navigation pane with the headings in your document listed.

● The page currently shown in the main Word window is highlighted in orange.

● You can click a heading in the Navigation pane to view the page that contains that heading.

Note: If your document contains more headings or pages than can be displayed at one time in the Navigation pane, you can use the scroll bar on the right side of the pane to move up and down through the entries in the pane. Alternatively, click ▲ and ▼ located near the top of the pane to move up and down through the entries.

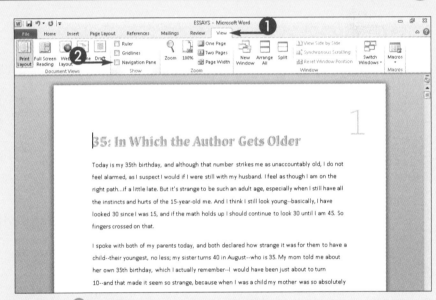

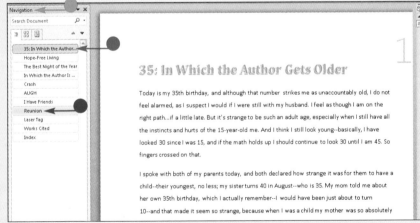

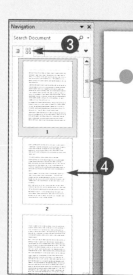

35: In Which the Author Gets Older

Today is my 35th birthday, and although that number strikes me as unaccountably old, I do not feel alarmed, as I suspect I would if I were still with my husband. I feel as though I am on the right path...if a little late. But it's strange to be such an adult age, especially when I still have all the instincts and hurts of the 15-year-old me. And I think I still look young--basically, I have looked 30 since I was 15, and if the math holds up I should continue to look 30 until I am 45. So fingers crossed on that.

I spoke with both of my parents today, and both declared how strange it was for them to have a child--their youngest, no less; my sister turns 40 in August--who is 35. My mom told me about her own 35th birthday, which I actually remember--I would have been just about to turn 10--and that made it seem so strange, because when I was a child my mother was so absolutely an adult in my mind, so absolutely the authority in my world, and chances are she was just as clueless at 35 as I am now. And I felt some sympathy for her, because even though I do harbor some resentment against her, I can also see that she couldn't possibly have known the damage

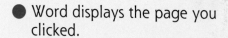

birthday latte, complete with a milk-foam heart, and it was so lovely that I took a picture of it. It reminded me of a trip we took to L.A., when we visited a cafe near our hotel, and they made lattes that featured the most amazing foamy designs, which I also felt compelled to photograph. Later in our trip, we were kicked out of said cafe for playing Go Fish with our daughter. We hadn't noticed the "No Game Playing" sign. And the whole thing was so ridiculous I could only laugh.

It has since occurred to me that I would like to post a similar sign in my home.

After coffee, during which I contacted some of the people I want to feature in my upcoming craft book, I took myself out to brunch at Petite Chou, the offshoot of Cafe Patachou, a longtime favorite of mine. Petite Chou has lovely outdoor seating, and it's a lovely day, so you do the math. And since it worked so well at the cafe, I told the nice guy who manages the restaurant that it was my birthday, and after I demolished my egg-white omelet with feta and herbs and wheat toast with butter and strawberry jam, he gave me a plate of macaroons to celebrate.

I love my little community. Even though I often feel separate from people around me, even though I often navigate whole days barely speaking to others, I still enjoy these cursory exchanges. They make me feel rooted somehow. But I'm also feeling a little sad, though, because my yogi friends have forgotten my birthday, as did my knitting friends, even as they

③ Click the **Browse the Pages in Your Document** tab.

● The Navigation pane displays thumbnail images of each page in the open document.

④ Click an image in the Navigation pane to switch to a different page.

● Word displays the page you clicked.

Simplify It

Can I view multiple heading levels in the Navigation pane?
If your document contains multiple levels of headings, you can opt to display them in the Navigation pane; alternatively, you can display top-level headings only. To specify which headings should appear in the pane, right-click a heading in the pane, choose **Show Heading Levels**, and choose the desired option from the menu that appears. Note that if you decide to display top-level headings only, you can choose to expand the outline to view subheadings beneath a top-level heading by clicking the right arrow to the left of the heading.

Check Spelling and Grammar

Word automatically checks for spelling and grammar errors. Misspellings appear underlined with a red wavy line, and grammar errors are underlined with a green wavy line. (Note that you can turn off Word's automatic Spelling and Grammar Check features, as described in the tip at the end of this section.)

In addition, you can use Word's Spelling and Grammar Check features to review your document for spelling and grammatical errors and to fix any errors that are detected.

Of course, these features are no substitute for good proofreading with your own eyes. They can catch some errors, but not all!

Check Spelling and Grammar

Correct a Mistake

1. When you encounter a spelling or grammar problem, right-click the underlined text.

   The menu that appears shows possible corrections.

2. Click a correction from the menu.

   - To ignore the error, you can click **Ignore** or click **Ignore All** for all instances of the error.

   - To add the word to the built-in dictionary, you can click **Add to Dictionary**.

Run the Spell-Checker

1. Click the **Review** tab on the Ribbon.

2. Click the **Spelling & Grammar** button.

   To check only a section of your document, you can select the section before activating the spell check.

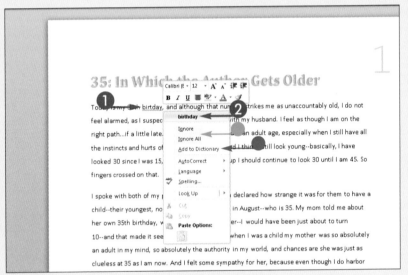

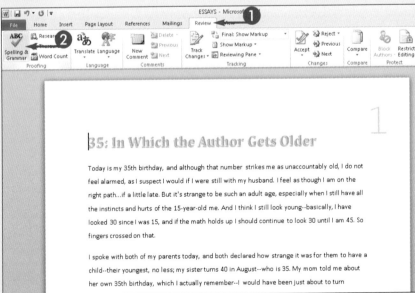

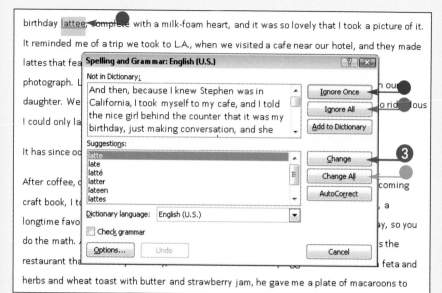

birthday lattee, complete with a milk-foam heart, and it was so lovely that I took a picture of it.

It reminded me of a trip we took to L.A., when we visited a cafe near our hotel, and they made

lattes that fea...

photograph. L...

daughter. We...

I could only la...

It has since oc...

After coffee, d...coming

craft book, I t... a

longtime favo...ay, so you

do the math. A...s the

restaurant tha...feta and

herbs and wheat toast with butter and strawberry jam, he gave me a plate of macaroons to

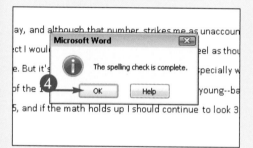

- Word searches the document for any mistakes. If it finds an error, it flags it in the document and displays the Spelling and Grammar dialog box.

③ Click **Change** to make a correction.

- To correct all of the misspellings of the same word, you can click **Change All**.

- To ignore the error one time, you can click **Ignore Once**.

- To ignore every occurrence, you can click **Ignore All** or **Ignore Rule**.

When the spell check is complete, a prompt box appears.

④ Click **OK**.

Simplify It

How do I turn the automatic spelling and grammar checking off?
To turn off the automatic Spelling and Grammar Check features, follow these steps:

① Click the **File** tab and then click **Options**.

② In the Word Options dialog box, click the **Proofing** tab.

③ Under the When Correcting Spelling and Grammar in Word options, click to deselect **Check spelling as you type**.

④ Click to deselect **Mark grammar errors as you type**.

⑤ Click **OK** to exit the Word Options dialog box.

Word turns off the automatic checking features.

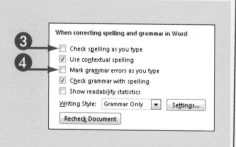

Work with AutoCorrect

As you may have noticed, Word automatically corrects your text as you type. It does this using its AutoCorrect feature, which works from a preset list of misspellings.

To speed up your text-entry tasks, you can add your own problem words — ones you commonly misspell — to the list. The next time you mistype the word, AutoCorrect fixes your mistake for you.

If you find that AutoCorrect consistently changes a word that is correct as is, you can remove that word from the AutoCorrect list. If you would prefer that AutoCorrect not make any changes to your text as you type, you can disable the feature.

Work with AutoCorrect

① Click the **File** tab.

② Click **Options**.

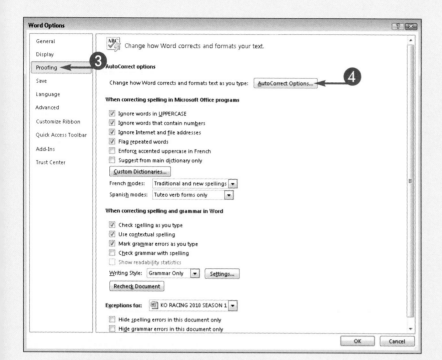

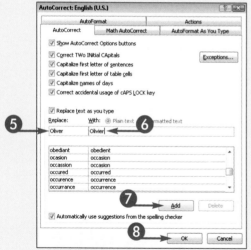

The Word Options dialog box appears.

③ Click **Proofing**.

④ Click **AutoCorrect Options**.

The AutoCorrect dialog box appears, displaying the AutoCorrect tab.

⑤ Type a common misspelling in the **Replace** text field.

⑥ Type the correct spelling in the **With** text field.

⑦ Click **Add**.

AutoCorrect adds the word to the list.

⑧ Click **OK** to exit the AutoCorrect dialog box.

⑨ Click **OK** to exit the Word Options dialog box.

The next time you misspell the word, AutoCorrect corrects it for you.

Note: *If AutoCorrect corrects text that you do not want to be changed, press* Ctrl + Z *to undo the change.*

Simplify It

How do I remove a word from the AutoCorrect list?
Open the AutoCorrect dialog box, click the **AutoCorrect** tab, click the word you want to remove, and click **Delete**. Finally, click **OK** to close the dialog box and apply your changes.

Can I customize how the AutoCorrect feature works?
Yes. Open the AutoCorrect dialog box, click the **AutoCorrect** tab, and select or deselect the check boxes as needed to enable or disable various features. To prevent AutoCorrect from replacing text as you type, deselect the **Replace text as you type** check box. Click **OK** to apply your changes.

Use Word's Thesaurus and Dictionary

If you are having trouble finding just the right word or phrase, you use Word's thesaurus to find synonyms. (You can also use this tool to find antonyms.) Word also includes a dictionary, which you can use to look up unfamiliar words in a document.

You access these tools from within Word's Research pane; this pane also offers access to

Word's translation tools and other reference-based features, such as Factiva iWorks (for news and business information), HighBeam Research (a repository of millions of newspaper, magazine, and journal articles), MSN Money, and the Thomson Gale Company Profiles site.

Use Word's Thesaurus and Dictionary

Use Word's Thesaurus

1. Select the word for which you want to find a synonym.

2. Click the **Review** tab.

3. Click the **Thesaurus** button.

   The Research task pane opens, displaying synonyms for the selected word.

4. Position your mouse pointer over the word you want to use as a replacement.

5. Click the ⏷ that appears.

6. Click **Insert**.

   Word replaces the word in your document with the one you chose in Step **6**.

● Click the **Close** button (⊠) to close the Research pane.

   Note: *You can also replace text with a synonym by right-clicking the word you want to replace and choosing the desired synonym from the menu that appears.*

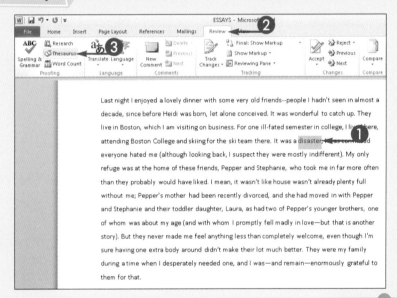

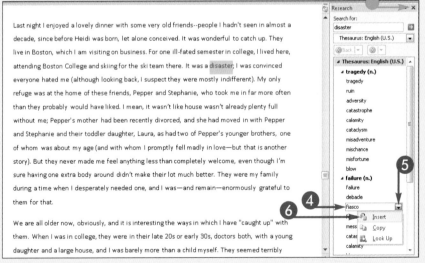

birthday, which I actually remember--I would have been just about to turn

made it seem so strange, because when I was a child my mother was so absolutely

y mind, so absolutely the authority in my world, and chances are she was just

s as I am now. And I felt some sympathy for her, because even though I do harbor

nent against her, I can also see that she couldn't possibly have known the dam

on me at the time; I can see that she really was doing her best. It just wasn't a

at's all. But I can forgive that. Really I can.

e call of the day came from Heidi, but I was in the bath, so I missed it, but she

e in her hurried little voice, the words rushing out of her, starting with "Hi Mo

which made me smile, because, obviously, who else could it be? And I'm very

my ex-husband offered to loan me Heidi for the evening so I can take her out

y family. I would have be- sad

eep in this morning but woke up

rthday bubble bath and then tall

t developments with Stephen (to

ew Stephen was in California, I to

ounter that it was my birthday, ju

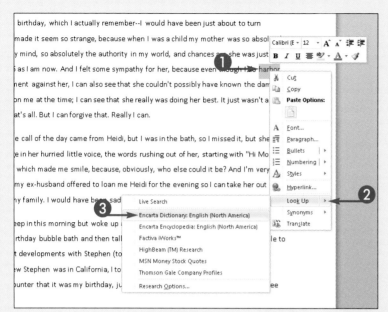

Use Word's Dictionary

1 Right-click the word you want to look up.

2 Click the right arrow (▶) next to **Look Up**.

A list of research resources appears.

3 Click **Encarta Dictionary: English (North America)**.

Word launches the Research pane.

● Word displays definitions of the word.

my sister turns 40 in August--who is 35. My mom told me about

I actually remember--I would have been just about to turn

strange, because when I was a child my mother was so absolutely

utely the authority in my world, and chances are she was just as

d I felt some sympathy for her, because even though I do harbor

, I can also see that she couldn't possibly have known the damage

e; I can see that she really was doing her best. It just wasn't all

forgive that. Really I can.

came from Heidi, but I was in the bath, so I missed it, but she left

little voice, the words rushing out of her, starting with "Hi Mom,

smile, because, obviously, who else could it be? And I'm very

offered to loan me Heidi for the evening so I can take her out to

d have been sad not to see her on my birthday.

ng but woke up at 6:15 anyway, so I rolled out of bed and treated

ath and then talked on the phone to my friend Betsy for a while to

with Stephen (to be detailed in a subsequent post). And then,

n California, I took myself to my cafe, and I told the nice girl

How do I access Word's other research tools?
As mentioned, Word's Research pane offers easy access to several research tools. To use these tools, open the Research pane, type the topic you want to research in the pane's **Search for** field (●), click the ⏷ near the top of the pane (●), and choose the desired resource from the menu that appears. The pane displays a list of links to research resources that relate to the word you typed; click one to launch your Web browser and access the resource you chose with the related article shown.

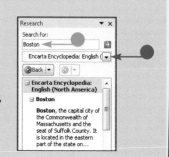

Translate Text

Word contains translation tools that enable you to quickly and easily translate words or phrases that you write in your native tongue into one of several other languages and vice versa. (Note that your ability to translate text to and from a language may be limited by your computer's operating system.)

Using Word, you can quickly translate a word or phrase in your document via the Research pane or with Word's Mini Translator tool. Word can also help if your translation needs are more robust, sending entire documents to be translated online in an instant (assuming that your computer is connected to the Internet).

Translate Text

Translate a Word or Phrase

1 Select the word or phrase that you want to translate.

2 Click the **Review** tab.

3 Click the **Translate** button.

4 Click **Translate Selected Text**.

Note: *If you are using Word's Translate function for the first time, you may be prompted to install the necessary bilingual dictionaries. Click OK.*

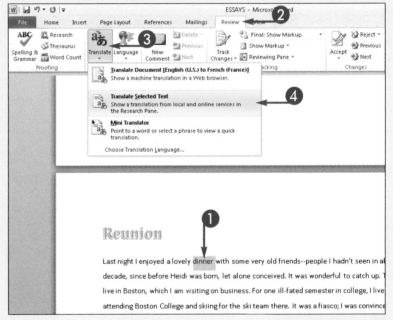

● Word launches the Research pane, with the Translation options open.

5 Click the **From** ⊡ and choose the language from which you want to translate.

6 Click the **To** ⊡ and select the language to which you want to translate.

● Word translates the selected text.

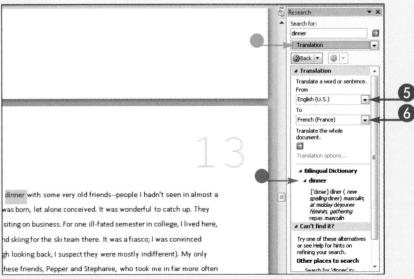

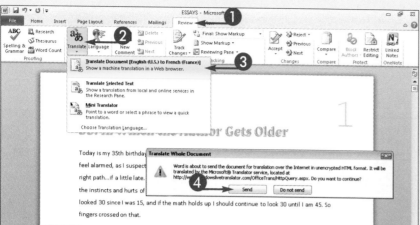

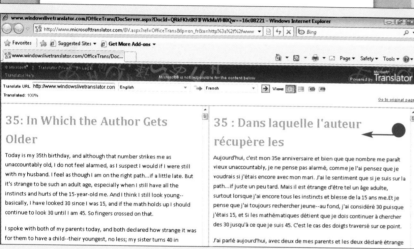

Translate a Document

1 With the document you want to translate open in Word, click the **Review** tab.

2 Click the **Translate** button.

3 Click **Translate Document**.

The Translate Whole Document dialog box opens, notifying you that your document will be sent over the Internet for translation.

4 Click the **Send** button.

● Word displays the translated text alongside the original text.

Is there a faster way to translate text?

Yes. If you only need to translate the occasional word in your documents, you can use Word's Mini Translator feature. First, however, you must enable this feature. To do so, click the **Review** tab on the Ribbon, click the **Translate** button, and select **Mini Translator** from the menu that appears. Word displays the Translation Language Options dialog box with the Mini Translator tab open; click the **Translate To** ⊡ and choose the language into which you need to translate. Then, simply position your mouse pointer over the word in question (●); Word displays a translation for the word.

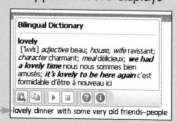

Track and Review Document Changes

If you share your Word documents with others, you can use the program's Track Changes feature to keep track of what edits others have made, including formatting changes and text additions or deletions.

The Track Changes feature uses different colors for each person's edits, making it easy to see who changed what in the document. If you like, you can change the color used for your edits.

When you review the document, you can specify whose edits you want to review, what types of edits you want to see, and whether to accept or reject the changes.

Track and Review Document Changes

Turn On Tracking

1. Click the **Review** tab on the Ribbon.

2. Click the **Track Changes** button.

Word activates the Track Changes feature.

3. Edit the document.

● Any additions to the text appear underlined and in color.

● Word marks the deleted text with a strikethrough.

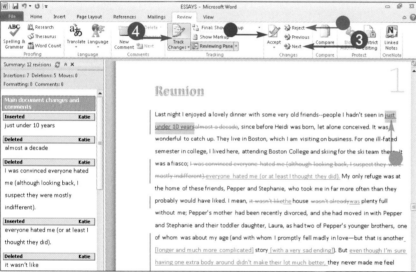

Review Changes

1 Click the **Review** tab on the Ribbon.

2 Click the **Reviewing Pane** button.

● The Reviewing pane opens.

The Reviewing pane shows each person's edits, including the user's name.

3 Click the **Next** button.

○ Word highlights the next edit in the document.

● Click the **Accept** button to add the change to the final document.

Note: *To accept all changes in the document, click the down arrow under the **Accept** button and choose **Accept All Changes in Document**.*

● Click the **Reject** button to reject the change.

4 When you complete the review, click the **Track Changes** button to turn the feature off.

Simplify It

Can I customize the markup options?
Yes. You can change the color used for your edits. To do so, click the **Review** tab, click the **Track Changes** button, and then click **Change Tracking Options**. The Track Changes dialog box opens; here, you can make changes to the tracking color, formatting, and more.

Can I control what markup elements appear in a document?
Yes. You can click the **Show Markup** button on the Review tab to select what elements you want to include in the review. For example, you may want to hide comments or review marks for a particular user.

Compare Documents

Suppose someone edits a document without first enabling the Track Changes feature. To determine what edits were made, you can run a Compare operation to compare the edited document with the original version. When you run a Compare operation, you can specify what aspects of the two documents should be compared.

The result of running a Compare operation is a third file that flags any discrepancies such that they appear exactly like edits made with Track Changes enabled. You can then choose to accept or reject each change, just as you would if Track Changes had been enabled when the document was edited.

Compare Documents

1 Click the **Review** tab on the Ribbon.

2 Click the **Compare** button.

3 Click **Compare**.

The Compare Documents dialog box opens.

4 Click 📄 next to the Original Document field.

Word launches the Open dialog box.

5 Locate and select the original document.

6 Click **Open**.

7 Repeat Steps **4** to **6**, this time clicking 📄 next to the Revised Document field.

Note: A faster way to specify which documents to compare is to click ▼ next to the Original Document and Revised Document fields and choose the desired document from the list that appears.

8 Click **OK** in the Compare Documents dialog box.

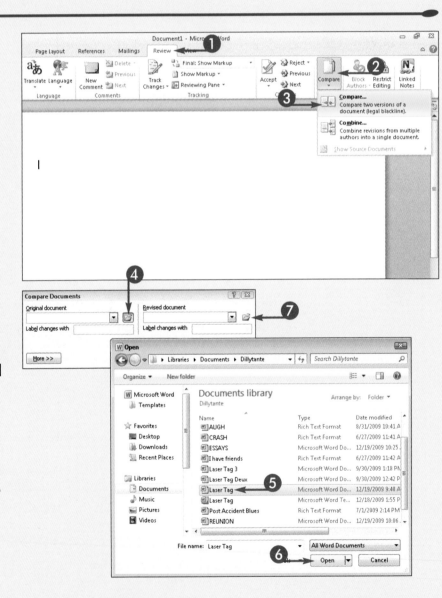

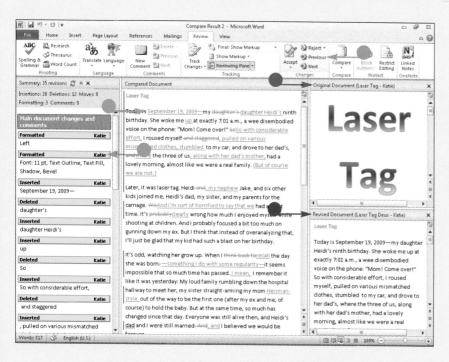

● Word compares the document, flagging discrepancies such as text additions and deletions as well as formatting changes.

● The original document appears here.

● The revised document appears here.

● Use the Reviewing pane, as well as the Next, Accept, and Reject buttons on the Review tab, to review and accept or reject the changes.

How do I customize the Compare operation?

As mentioned, you can specify what aspects of the original and revised documents should be compared. These aspects include formatting, case changes, and more. You can also specify that changes be shown in the original document or the revised document instead of in a new, third document. To do so, open the Compare Documents dialog box as described in this section, click the **More** button (after you click the More button, it changes to a Less button), select or deselect the appropriate check boxes and radio buttons, and click **OK**.

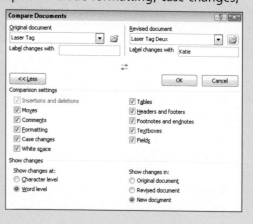

Insert Comments

You can add comments to your documents. You might add a comment to make a note to yourself about the text in a particular section of your document, or you might include a comment as a note for other users to see. For example, if you share your documents with other users, you can use comments to leave feedback about the text without typing directly in the document.

Word displays comments in a balloon (assuming you are using Print Layout view) to the right of the text or in the Reviewing pane. Comments you add are identified with your user name.

Insert Comments

Add a Comment

1. Click or select the text where you want to insert a comment.

2. Click the **Review** tab on the Ribbon.

3. Click the **New Comment** button.

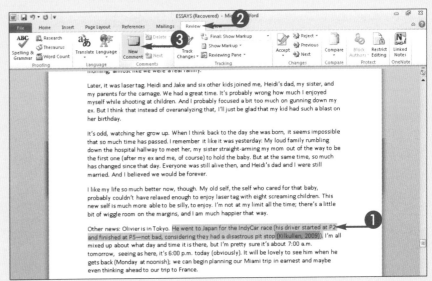

● A comment balloon appears.

4. Type your comment.

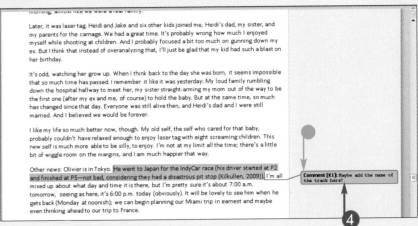

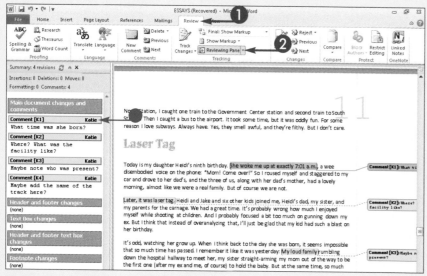

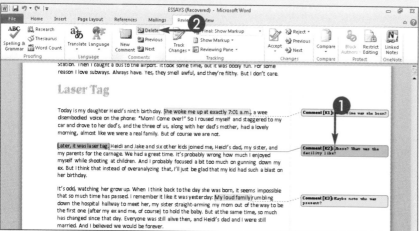

View Comments in the Reviewing Pane

1 Click the **Review** tab on the Ribbon.

2 Click the **Reviewing Pane** button.

● Word displays the Reviewing pane, and lists all of the comments associated with the document.

You can click the **Reviewing Pane** button again to hide the pane.

Delete a Comment

1 Click the comment that you want to remove.

2 Click the **Delete** button on the Review tab.

You can also right-click over a comment and click **Delete**.

Word deletes the comment.

How do I change the name used in my comments?
Click the **Review** tab, click the **Track Changes** button, and click **Change User Name** to display the Word Options dialog box. In the **User Name** text box, type a new name for your comments. Click **OK** to apply the change.

How do I respond to a comment?
You can respond to a comment by adding a new comment adjacent to the existing comment. To do so, simply click the existing comment to select it, and then click the **New Comment** button. Word inserts a new comment; add your text as you normally would.

Part III

Excel

Excel is a powerful spreadsheet program you can use to enter and organize data and to perform a wide variety of number-crunching tasks. You can use Excel strictly as a program for manipulating numerical data, or you can use it as a database program to organize and track large quantities of data. In this part, you learn how to enter data into worksheets, adjust its appearance, manage your information, tap into the power of Excel's formulas and functions to perform mathematical calculations and analysis, and create charts with your Excel data.

Enter Cell Data

You can enter data into any cell in an Excel worksheet. You can type data directly into the cell, or you can enter data using the Formula bar.

Data can be text, such as row or column labels, or numbers, which are called *values*. Values also include formulas. Excel automatically left-aligns text data in a cell and right-aligns values.

Long data entries appear truncated if you type additional data into adjoining cells. You can remedy this by resizing the column to fit the data (see "Resize Columns and Rows") or by turning on the cell's text-wrap feature (see "Turn On Text Wrapping").

Enter Cell Data

Type into a Cell

1 Click the cell into which you want to enter data.

The cell you clicked becomes the active cell. It appears highlighted, with a thicker border than the other cells.

● To add data to another worksheet in your workbook, click the worksheet tab to display the worksheet.

● To magnify your view of the worksheet, click and drag the **Zoom** slider.

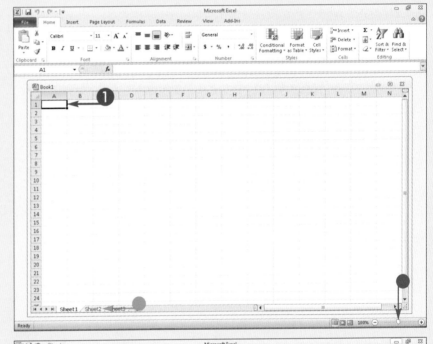

2 Type your data.

● The data appears both in the cell and in the Formula bar.

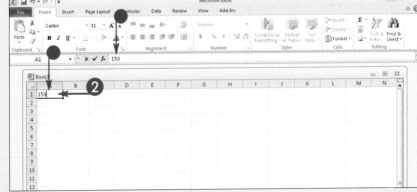

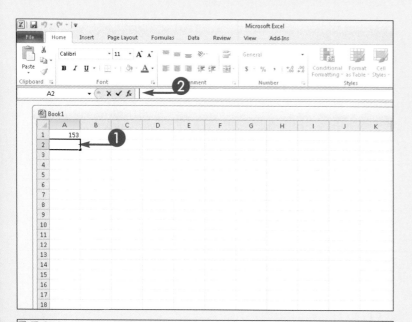

Type Data in the Formula Bar

1 Click the cell into which you want to enter data.

2 Click in the Formula bar.

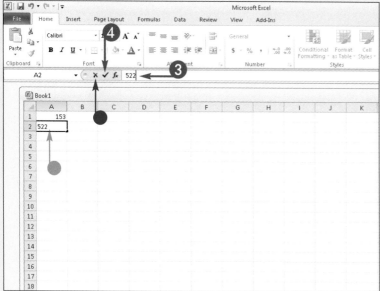

3 Type your data.

● The data appears both in the Formula bar and in the cell.

4 Click **Enter** (☑) or press Enter to enter the data.

● To cancel an entry, you can click **Cancel** (☒) or press Esc.

Simplify It

When I start typing in a cell, Excel tries to fill in the text for me. Why?
Excel's AutoComplete feature is automatic. If you repeat an entry from anywhere in the same column, AutoComplete attempts to complete the entry for you, based on the first few letters that you type. If the AutoComplete entry is correct, press Enter, and Excel fills in the text for you. If not, just keep typing the text that you want to insert into the cell. The AutoComplete feature is just one of many Excel tools that help you speed up your data-entry tasks.

Select Cells

In order to perform editing, mathematical, or formatting operations on data in an Excel worksheet, you must first select the cell or cells that contain that data. For example, you might apply formatting to data in a single cell or to data in a group, or *range*, of cells.

Selecting a single cell is easy: You just click the cell. To select a range of cells you can use your mouse or keyboard. In addition to selecting cells or ranges of cells, you can select the data contained in a cell, as described in the tip at the end of this section.

Select Cells

Select a Range of Cells

1 Click the first cell in the range of cells that you want to select.

2 Click and drag across the cells that you want to include in the range.

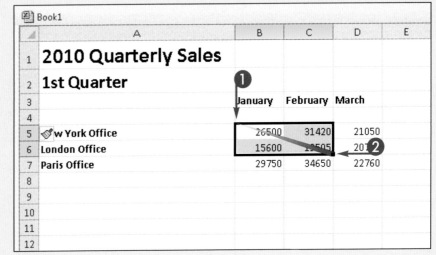

3 Release the mouse button.

● Excel selects the cells.

● To select all of the cells in the worksheet, you can click here (▱).

You can select multiple noncontiguous cells by pressing and holding **Ctrl** while clicking cells.

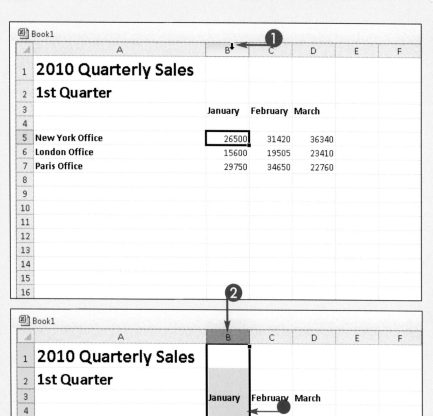

Select a Column or Row

① Position the mouse pointer over the header of the column or row that you want to select.

The ⊕ changes to ↓.

② Click the column or row.

● Excel selects the entire column or row.

To select multiple columns or rows, you can click and drag across the column or row headings.

You can select multiple noncontiguous columns or rows by pressing and holding Ctrl while clicking column or row headings.

How do I select data inside a cell?
To select data inside a cell, click the cell; then click in front of the data in the Formula bar and drag over the characters or numbers you want to select. Alternatively, click the cell and then double-click the data you want to select.

Can I use my keyboard to select a range?
Yes. Use the arrow keys to navigate to the first cell in a range. Next, press and hold Shift while using an arrow key, such as ← or ↓, to select the remaining cells' range.

Faster Data Entry with AutoFill

You can use Excel's AutoFill feature to add duplicate entries or a data series to your worksheet. This can greatly expedite data entry.

In addition to creating your own custom data lists, as described in the tip at the end of this section, you can use Excel's built-in lists of common entries to create text series — for example, to enter a list containing the days of the week or months in the year — or number series.

When you click a cell, a small fill handle appears in the lower right corner of the selector; you use this to create an AutoFill series.

AutoFill a Text Series

① Type the first entry in the text series.

② Click and drag the cell's fill handle across or down the number of cells that you want to fill.

The ✥ changes to +.

You can also use AutoFill to copy the same text to every cell that you drag over.

③ Release the mouse button.

● AutoFill fills in the text series.

● An AutoFill smart tag (▦) may appear, offering additional options that you can assign to the data.

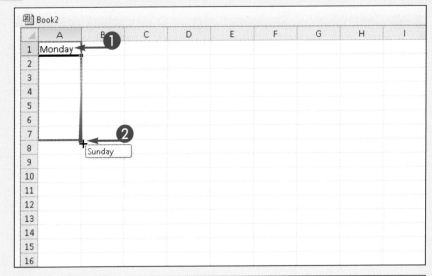

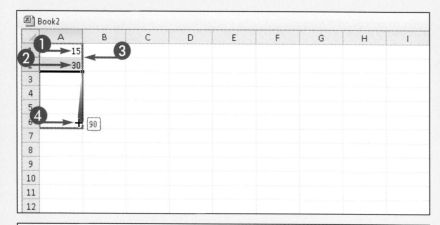

AutoFill a Number Series

1. Type the first entry in the number series.

2. In an adjacent cell, type the next entry in the number series.

3. Select both cells.

   Note: See the "Select Cells" section to learn more.

4. Click and drag the fill handle across or down the number of cells that you want to fill.

   The ⇧ changes to +.

5. Release the mouse button.

● AutoFill fills in the number series.

● An AutoFill smart tag (▦) may appear, offering additional options that you can assign to the data.

Simplify It

How do I create a custom list?
To add your own custom list to AutoFill's library, first create the custom list in your worksheet cells. Then follow these steps:

1. Select the cells containing the list that you want to save (here, a list of names).

2. Click the **File** tab and then click the **Options** button.

3. In the Options dialog box, click the **Advanced** tab.

4. Click the **Edit Custom Lists** button.

● The Custom Lists dialog box opens with the list you selected highlighted.

5. Click **Import**.

   Excel adds the series to the custom lists.

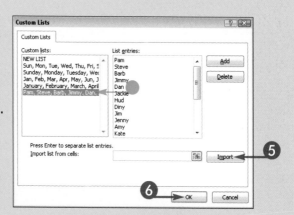

6. Click **OK**.

7. Click **OK** again to close the Options dialog box.

Turn On Text Wrapping

By default, long lines of data that you type into a cell remain on one line or are truncated if you type additional data into adjoining cells. One way to remedy this is to resize the column to fit the data (see "Resize Columns and Rows"). Another option is to turn on the cell's

text-wrapping option to make data wrap to the next line and fit into the cell without truncating the data. Note that text wrapping increases the height of the row based on the number of lines that wrap to make room.

1 Click the cell that you want to edit.

Note: *You can also apply text wrapping to multiple cells. See the "Select Cells" section, earlier in this chapter, to learn how to select multiple cells for a task.*

2 Click the **Home** tab on the Ribbon.

3 Click the **Wrap Text** button (📄).

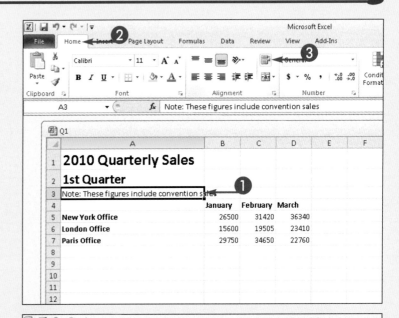

● Excel applies text wrapping to the cell.

Note: *See the section "Resize Columns and Rows" to learn how to adjust cell depth and width to accommodate your data.*

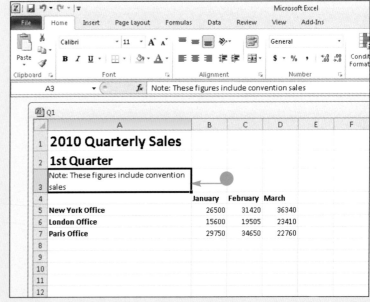

Center Data Across Columns

You can center data across a range of cells you have selected in your worksheet. For example, you might want to include a title across multiple columns of labels. You can use Excel's Merge and Center command to quickly merge the selected cells, placing the title text in the center.

You can access additional merge commands by clicking the Merge and Center ▾. These include Merge Across, which merges each selected row of cells into a larger cell; Merge Cells, which merges selected cells in multiple rows and columns into a single cell; and Unmerge Cells, which splits a cell into multiple cells.

Center Data Across Columns

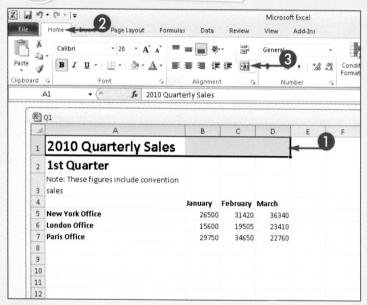

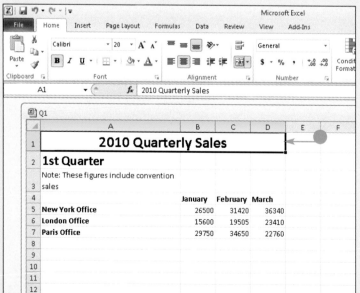

① Select the cell containing the data that you want to center, and the cells that you want to center the data across.

Note: *Refer to the "Select Cells" section to learn how to select columns and rows.*

② Click the **Home** tab on the Ribbon.

③ Click the **Merge and Center** button (▦).

You can also click the **Merge and Center** ▾ to select from several different merge commands.

● Excel merges the cells and centers the data.

Adjust Cell Alignment

By default, Excel automatically aligns text data to the left and number data to the right. Data is also aligned vertically to sit at the bottom of the cell. If you want, however, you can change the horizontal and vertical alignment of data within your worksheet cells — for example,

centering data vertically and horizontally. You might do so in order to improve the appearance of your worksheet data.

In addition to controlling the alignment of data within a cell, you can also indent data in a cell, as well as change the orientation of data in a cell.

Adjust Cell Alignment

Set Horizontal Alignment

1 Select the cells that you want to format.

2 Click the **Home** tab on the Ribbon.

3 Click an alignment button from the Alignment group.

Click the **Align Left** button (☰) to align data to the left.

Click the **Center** button (☰) to center-align the data.

Click the **Align Right** button (☰) to align data to the right.

Note: *To justify cell data, click the corner group button (▣) in the Alignment group. In the Format Cells dialog box that appears, click the* **Horizontal** *▾ and click* **Justify***.*

Excel applies the alignment to your cells.

● This example centers the text data.

Set Vertical Alignment

1 Select the cells that you want to format.

2 Click the **Home** tab on the Ribbon.

3 Click an alignment button from the Alignment group.

Click the **Top Align** button (▭) to align data to the top.

Click the **Middle Align** button (▭) to align the data in the middle.

Click the **Bottom Align** button (▭) to align data to the bottom.

Excel applies the alignment to your cells.

● This example aligns the text data to the middle of the cell.

How do I indent cell data?
To indent data, click the **Increase Indent** button (▦) on the Home tab. To decrease an indent, click the **Decrease Indent** button (▦).

Can I change the orientation of data in a cell?
Yes. For example, you might angle column labels to make them easier to distinguish from one another. To do so, select the cells you want to change, click the **Home** tab on the Ribbon, click the ▾ next to the **Orientation** button (▨), and click an orientation. Excel applies the orientation to the data in the selected cell or cells.

Change the Font and Size

You can change the font that you use for your worksheet data, along with the size of the data. For example, you may want to make the worksheet title larger than the rest of the data, or you may want to resize the font for the entire worksheet to make the data easier to read. Alternatively, you might choose to apply a specific color to certain types of data.

If you particularly like the result of applying a series of formatting options to a cell, you can copy the formatting and apply it to other cells your worksheet.

Change the Font and Size

Change the Font

1 Select the cell or data that you want to format.

2 Click the **Home** tab on the Ribbon.

3 Click the **Font** ☑.

● You can use the scroll arrows or scroll bar to scroll through all of the available fonts.

You can also begin typing a font name to choose a font.

4 Click a font.

● Excel applies the font.

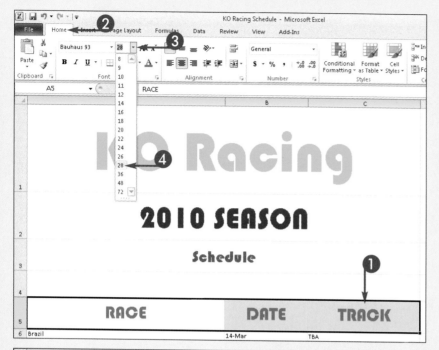

Change the Font Size

1 Select the cell or data that you want to format.

2 Click the **Home** tab on the Ribbon.

3 Click the **Font Size** ⊡.

4 Click a size.

● Excel applies the new size to the selected cell or data.

Simplify It

Can I apply multiple formatting options at once?
Yes. The Format Cells dialog box enables you to apply a new font, size, or any other basic formatting options to selected data. To open it, click the **Home** tab and click the Font group's corner group button (⊡).

Can I copy cell formatting?
Yes. Simply select the cell or range containing the formatting you want to copy, click the **Home** tab, and click the **Format Painter** button (⧉). Then click and drag over the cells to which you want to apply the formatting.

Change Number Formats

You can use number formatting to control the appearance of numerical data in your worksheet. For example, if you have a column of prices, you format the data as numbers with dollar signs and decimal points. If prices listed are in a currency other than dollars, you can indicate that as well.

Excel offers several different number categories, or styles, to choose from. These include the aforementioned Currency styles, Accounting styles, Date styles, Time styles, Percentage styles, and more. You can apply number formatting to single cells, ranges, columns, rows, or an entire worksheet.

Change Number Formats

1. Select the cell, range, or data that you want to format.

2. Click the **Home** tab on the Ribbon.

3. Click the **Number Format** ☐.

4. Click a number format.

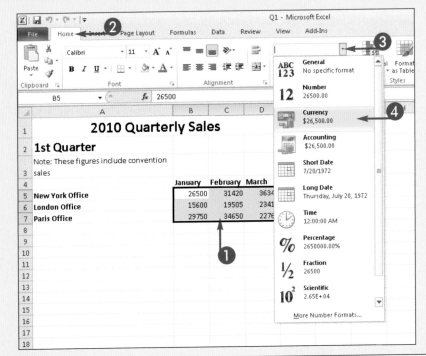

Excel applies the number format to the data.

● Click the **Accounting Number Format** button (⑤) to quickly apply dollar signs to your data. Click the button's down arrow to specify a different currency, such as Euro.

● To add percent signs to your data, click the **Percent Style** button (%).

● To apply commas to your number data, click the **Comma Style** button (☐).

● Click the corner group button (☐) to open the Format Cells dialog box, with more number-formatting options.

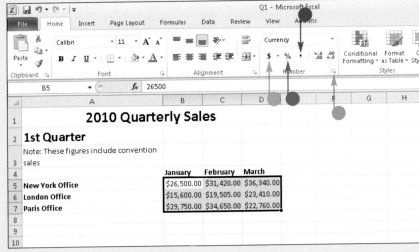

Increase or Decrease Decimals

You can control the number of decimals that appear with numeric data using the Increase Decimal and Decrease Decimal buttons. For example, you may want to increase the number of decimals shown in a cell if the data in that cell is extremely precise, such as may be the

case with worksheets tracking concentrations of various elements in a liquid. If the data in your worksheet is less precise or does not measure fractions of items — for example, in the case of a class roster — you might reduce the number of decimals shown.

Increase or Decrease Decimals

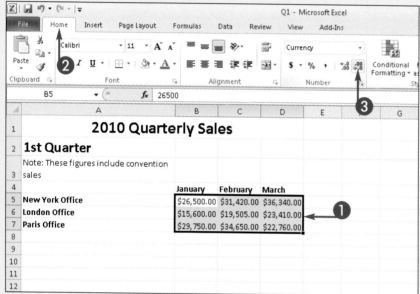

① Select the cell or range that you want to format.

② Click the **Home** tab on the Ribbon.

③ Click a decimal button.

You can click **Increase Decimal** (⬚) to increase the number of decimals.

You can click **Decrease Decimal** (⬚) to decrease the number of decimals.

Excel adjusts the number of decimals that appear in the cell or cells.

● This example removes one decimal.

● You can click **Decrease Decimal** (⬚) again to remove another decimal.

Add
Borders

By default, Excel displays a grid format to help you enter data, but the lines defining the borders of the grid do not print. You can add printable borders to your worksheet cells to help define the contents or more clearly separate the data from surrounding cells. You can also add borders to delineate different areas of your worksheet. Borders can be added to all four sides of a cell or to just one, two, or three sides. In addition to applying borders to cells in your worksheet, you can apply shading to help set apart different data.

Add Borders

Add Quick Borders

1 Select the cells that you want to format.

2 Click the **Home** tab on the Ribbon.

3 Click the ▾ next to the **Borders** button (▦).

   Note: To apply the current border selection shown, simply click the **Borders** button (▦).

4 Click a border style.

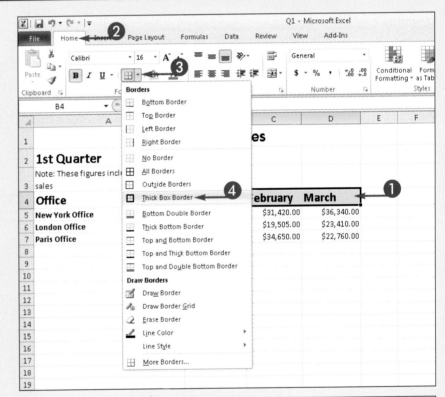

● Excel assigns the borders to the cell or cells.

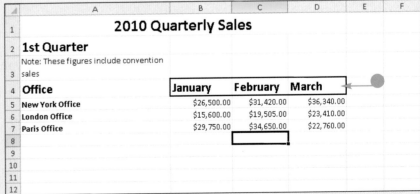

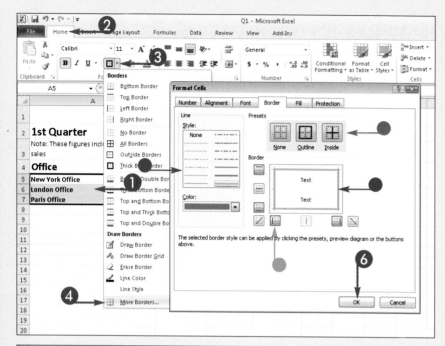

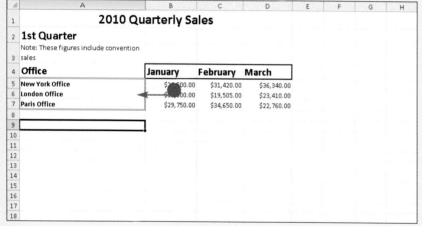

Create Custom Borders

1. Select the cells that you want to format.

2. Click the **Home** tab on the Ribbon.

3. Click the ▾ next to the **Borders** button (▦).

4. Click **More Borders**.

   The Format Cells dialog box appears with the Border tab open.

5. Click the type of border that you want to add.

● Click here to assign a preset style.

● You can use these settings to select a different border line style and color.

● You can click multiple border buttons to create a custom border.

● The Preview area displays a sample of the selections.

6. Click **OK**.

● Excel applies the border.

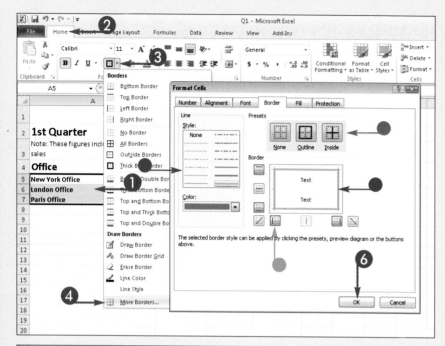

Simplify It

Can I turn worksheet gridlines on and off?
Click the **Page Layout** tab and, in the Sheet Options group, deselect the **View** check box under **Gridlines**. Note that you can also turn the gridlines on or off for printing via the **Print** check box under **Gridlines**.

Can I add color inside my worksheet cells?
Yes. Click the ▾ next to the Home tab's **Fill Color** button (▦) to display a palette of fill colors; select a color from the palette to apply that color to the selected cell. Avoid choosing colors that make it difficult to read your cell data.

Format Data with Styles

You can use Excel's styles to apply preset formatting designs to your worksheet data. You can apply table styles to a group of worksheet data, or you can apply cell styles to individual cells or ranges of cells. Note that when you apply a table style, Excel converts the data into a table.

In addition to applying styles to your worksheet, you can also change the background of your worksheet by applying an image. Applying a theme — that is, a predesigned set of formatting attributes such as color, font, and so on — is also an option.

Format Data with Styles

Format as a Table

1 Select the cells that you want to format.

2 Click the **Home** tab on the Ribbon.

3 Click the **Format as Table** button.

4 Click a table style.

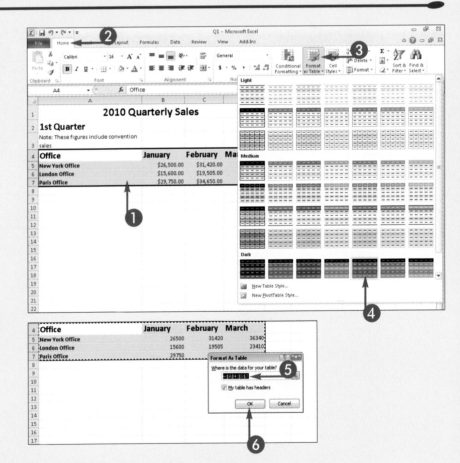

The Format As Table dialog box appears.

5 Verify the selected cells.

6 Click **OK**.

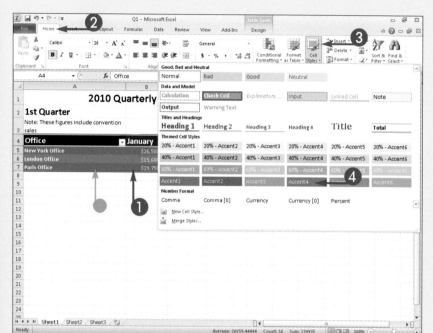

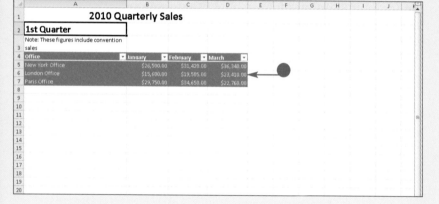

Excel applies the formatting style.

Apply a Cell Style

1 Select the cell or cells that you want to format.

2 Click the **Home** tab on the Ribbon.

3 Click the **Cell Styles** button.

4 Click a style.

Excel applies the formatting to the selected cell.

Can I add a background to my spreadsheet?
Yes. Click the **Page Layout** tab and click the **Background** button. The Sheet Background dialog box opens; locate and select the picture you want to use. When applying a background image to your worksheet, be sure the image does not distract from your cell data.

How do I apply a theme?
You can use themes to create a similar appearance among all the Office documents that you create. To apply a theme, click the **Page Layout** tab, click the **Themes** button, and select a theme from the list.

Apply Conditional Formatting

You can use Excel's Conditional Formatting tool to apply certain formatting attributes, such as bold text or a fill color, to a cell when the value of that cell meets the required condition. For example, if your worksheet tracks weekly sales, you might set up Excel's Conditional Formatting tool to alert you if a sales figure falls below

what is required for you to break even. In addition to using preset conditions, you can create your own. To help you distinguish the degree to which various cells meet your conditional rules, you can also use color scales and data bars.

Apply Conditional Formatting

Apply a Conditional Rule

1. Select the cell or range to which you want to apply conditional formatting.

2. Click the **Home** tab on the Ribbon.

3. Click the **Conditional Formatting** button.

4. Click **Highlight Cells Rules**.

5. Click the type of rule that you want to create.

   A rule dialog box appears.

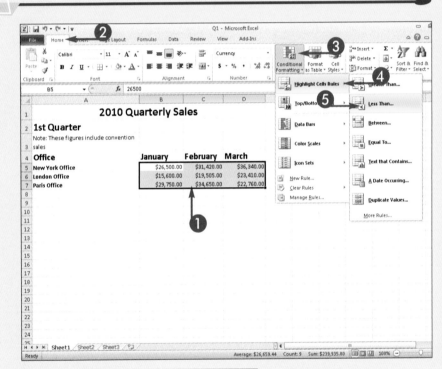

6. Specify the values that you want to assign for the condition.

7. Click **OK**.

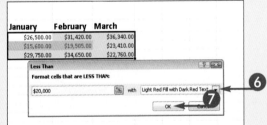

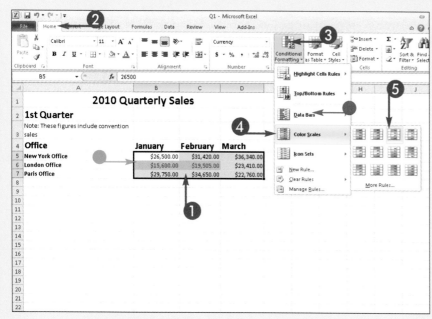

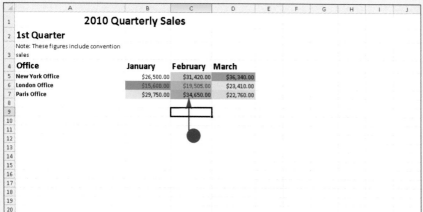

● If the value of a selected cell meets the condition, Excel applies the conditional formatting.

Apply a Color Scale

① Select the cell or range that contains the conditional formatting.

② Click the **Home** tab on the Ribbon.

③ Click the **Conditional Formatting** button.

④ Click **Color Scales**.

⑤ Click a color scale.

● You can apply color bars instead by clicking **Data Bars**.

● Excel applies the color scale to the conditional formatting.

Simplify It

How do I create a new rule for conditional formatting?
Click the **Conditional Formatting** button on the Home tab and then click **New Rule** to open the New Formatting Rule dialog box. Here, you define the condition of the rule as well as what formatting you want to apply when the condition is met.

How do I remove conditional formatting from a cell?
Select the data that contains the formatting you want to remove, click the **Conditional Formatting** button on the Home tab, and then click **Manage Rules**. Next, click the rule you want to remove, click **Delete Rule**, and click **OK**.

Add Columns and Rows

You can add columns and rows to your worksheets to include more data. For example, you might need to add a column or row in the middle of several existing columns or rows to add data that you left out the first time you created the workbook.

With Excel, you can add columns and rows in a few different ways: using the Insert button on the Ribbon or using the Insert dialog box.

You are not limited to inserting new columns and rows one at a time; if you want, you can insert multiple new columns and rows at once.

Add Columns and Rows

Add a Column

1. Click the heading of the column to the right of where you want to insert a new column.

2. Click the **Home** tab on the Ribbon.

3. Click the **Insert** 🔽.

4. Click **Insert Sheet Columns**.

   You can also right-click a column heading and click **Insert**.

● Excel adds a column.

● A smart tag icon (🗇) may appear when you insert a column; click it to view a list of options that you can apply.

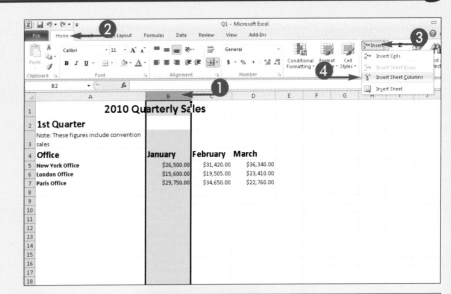

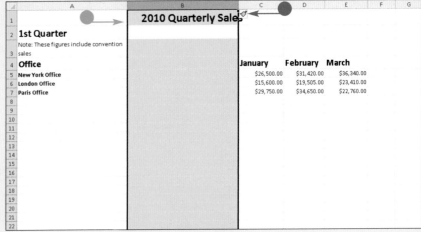

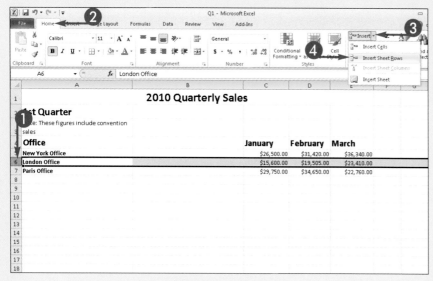

Add a Row

1 Click the heading of the row below where you want to insert a new row.

2 Click the **Home** tab on the Ribbon.

3 Click the **Insert** ⊡.

4 Click **Insert Sheet Rows**.

You can also right-click a row heading and click **Insert**.

● Excel adds a row.

● A smart tag icon (⬚) may appear, and you can click the icon to view a list of options that you can assign.

Can I insert multiple columns and rows?

Yes. First, select two or more columns and rows in the worksheet; then activate the **Insert** command as described in this section. Excel adds the same number of new columns and rows as the number you originally selected.

Can I insert columns or rows using the Insert dialog box?

Yes. Click a cell, click the **Insert** ⊡ on the Home tab, and click **Insert Cells** to open the Insert dialog box. Then click **Entire Row** or **Entire Column** and click **OK**. Excel adds a row or column above or to the left of the active cell.

Resize Columns and Rows

By default, long lines of data that you type into a cell remain on one line or are truncated if you type additional data into adjoining cells. One way to remedy this is to enable the text-wrapping (refer to the section "Turn On Text Wrapping" for details). Another option is to resize the column to fit the data. In addition to resizing your worksheet's columns to accommodate text, you can also resize columns to make the worksheet more aesthetically appealing. Note that just as you can resize columns in your worksheet, so, too, can you resize worksheet rows.

Resize Columns and Rows

① Position the mouse pointer over the border of the heading of the column or row that you want to resize.

The pointer changes to ✛.

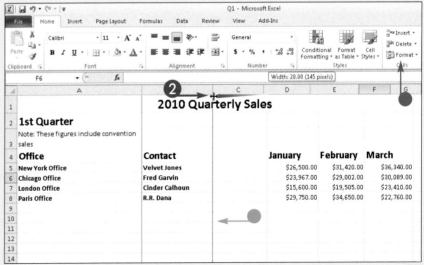

② Click and drag the border to the desired size.

● A dotted line marks the new border of the column or row as you drag.

③ Release the mouse button.

Excel resizes the column or row.

● You can also click the **Format** button on the Home tab, and then click **AutoFit Selection** to quickly resize a highlighted column to fit existing text.

Freeze a Column or Row

You can freeze portions of your worksheet to keep them visible as you scroll to view other data. This is especially handy in large worksheets. For example, you might freeze a column or row to keep the labels in view as you scroll to other areas of your worksheet to view

the data in that column or row. You cannot scroll the area that you freeze, but you can scroll the unfrozen areas of the worksheet. When you are finished viewing these other areas of your worksheet, you can quickly unfreeze the column or row you froze.

Freeze a Column or Row

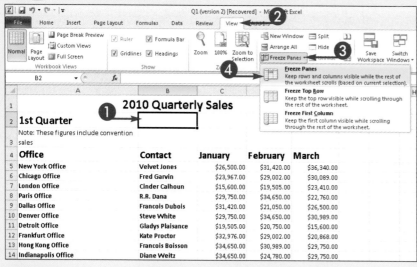

1 Click the cell to the right of the column or below the row that you want to freeze.

2 Click the **View** tab on the Ribbon.

3 Click the **Freeze Panes** ⊡.

4 Click **Freeze Panes**.

You can also choose to freeze a row of column headings or a column of row titles.

● Excel freezes the areas above or to the left of the selected cell (depending on whether you are scrolling up and down or left and right).

● To unlock the columns and rows, click the **Freeze Panes** ⊡, and then click **Unfreeze Panes**.

Name a Range

You can assign distinctive names to the cells and ranges of cells that you work with in a worksheet. (A *range* is simply a rectangular group of related cells; a range can also consist of a single cell.) Assigning names to cells and ranges makes it easier to identify their contents.

Naming ranges can also help you when deciphering formulas. (Formulas are discussed later in this book.) Note that when it comes to naming ranges, you must follow some rules, as discussed in the tip at the end of this section.

Name a Range

Assign a Range Name

1. Select the cells comprising the range that you want to name.

2. Click the **Formulas** tab on the Ribbon.

3. Click the **Define Name** button.

   The New Name dialog box opens.

4. Type a name for the selected range in the **Name** field.

   ● You can add a comment or note about the range here. For example, you might indicate what data the range contains.

5. Click **OK**.

   Note: *Another way to name a range is to select the cells in the range, click in the **Name** field to the left of the Formula bar, type the desired name, and press* Enter.

   ● Excel assigns the name to the cells.

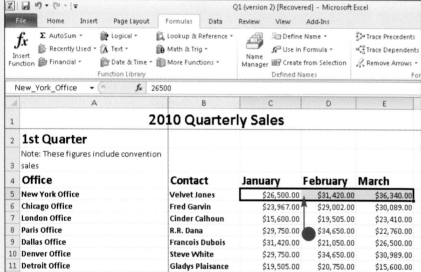

Go to a Range

1 Click the **Name** ☑.

2 Click the name of the range of cells to which you want to move.

● Excel selects the cells in the range.

Simplify It

What are the rules for naming ranges?
Range names must start with a letter, an underscore (_), or a backslash (\). Apart from that, you can use any character, uppercase or lowercase, or any punctuation or keyboard symbol except a hyphen or space. (You can substitute these with a period or underscore.)

How do I edit a range name?
Use the Name Manager feature to edit existing range names, change the cells referenced by a range, and so on. To open the Name Manager, click the **Name Manager** button on the Formulas tab.

Delete Data or Cells

You can delete Excel data that you no longer need. When you decide to delete data, you can choose whether you want to remove the data from the cells but keep the cells in place or delete the cells entirely. When you delete a cell's contents, Excel removes only the data.

When you delete a cell entirely, Excel removes the cell as well as its contents, with the existing cells in your worksheet shifting over to fill any gap in the worksheet structure. In addition to deleting single cells, you can delete whole rows or columns.

Delete Data or Cells

Delete Data

1 Select the cell or cells containing the data that you want to remove.

2 Press Delete.

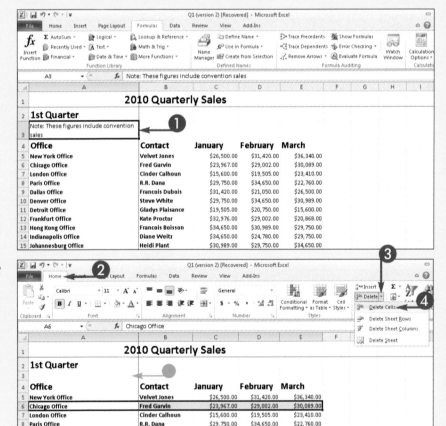

● Excel deletes the data from the cell, but the cell remains.

Delete Cells

1 Select the cell or cells that you want to remove.

2 Click the **Home** tab.

3 Click the **Delete** ⬝.

4 Click **Delete Cells**.

You can also right-click the selected cells and then click the **Delete** command.

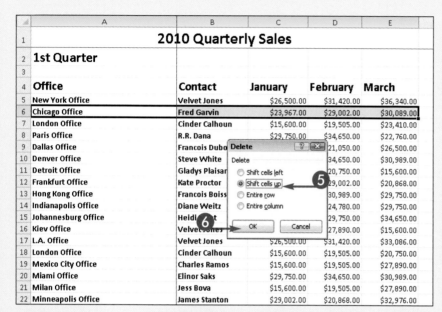

The Delete dialog box appears.

⑤ Click a deletion option.

⑥ Click **OK**.

● Excel removes the cells and their content from the worksheet.

Other cells shift over or up to fill the void of any cells that you remove from your worksheet.

Simplify It

How do I delete a whole column or row?
To delete a column or row, click the column's or row's heading to select it; then click the **Delete** button in the Home tab. When you do, Excel deletes any existing data within the selected column or row and moves subsequent columns or rows to fill the space left by the deletion.

Can I remove a cell's formatting without removing the content?
Yes. Select the cell you want to edit, click the **Home** tab, click the **Clear** button (🖉), and choose **Clear Formats** to remove the cell's formatting.

Add a Worksheet

By default, when you create a new workbook in Excel, it contains three worksheets. This may be adequate in some cases, but if your workbook requires additional worksheets in which to enter more data, you can easily add them. For example, if your workbook contains data about products your company sells, you might add worksheets for each product category.

When you add a new worksheet, Excel gives it a default name. To help you better keep track of your data, you can rename your new worksheet. For help, see the next section, "Name a Worksheet."

Add a Worksheet

① Click the **Insert Worksheet** button (⊞).

You can also right-click a worksheet tab and click **Insert** to open the Insert dialog box, where you can choose to insert a worksheet.

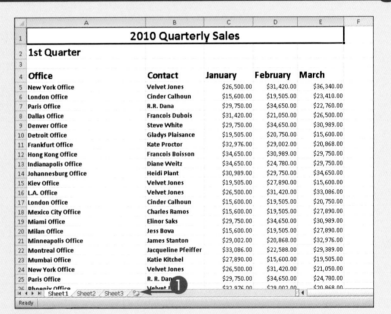

● Excel adds a new worksheet and gives it a default worksheet name.

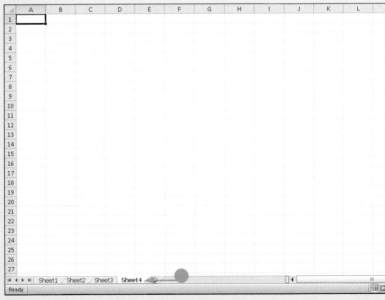

Name a Worksheet

When you create a new workbook, Excel assigns default names to each worksheet in the workbook. Likewise, Excel assigns a default name to each worksheet you add to an existing workbook. (For more information about adding worksheets to a workbook, refer to the preceding section, "Add a Worksheet.")

To help you identify their content, you can change the names of your Excel worksheets to something more descriptive. For example, if your workbook contains four worksheets, each detailing a different sales quarter, then you can give each worksheet a unique name, such as Quarter 1, Quarter 2, and so on.

Name a Worksheet

	A	B	C	D	E	F
1		2010 Quarterly Sales				
2	1st Quarter					
3						
4	Office	Contact	January	February	March	
5	New York Office	Velvet Jones	$26,500.00	$31,420.00	$36,340.00	
6	London Office	Cinder Calhoun	$15,600.00	$19,505.00	$23,410.00	
7	Paris Office	R.R. Dana	$29,750.00	$34,650.00	$22,760.00	
8	Dallas Office	Francois Dubois	$31,420.00	$21,050.00	$26,500.00	
9	Denver Office	Steve White	$29,750.00	$34,650.00	$30,989.00	
10	Detroit Office	Gladys Plaisance	$19,505.00	$20,750.00	$15,600.00	
11	Frankfurt Office	Kate Proctor	$32,976.00	$29,002.00	$20,868.00	
12	Hong Kong Office	Francois Boisson	$34,650.00	$30,989.00	$29,750.00	
13	Indianapolis Office	Diane Weitz	$34,650.00	$24,780.00	$29,750.00	
14	Johannesburg Office	Heidi Plant	$30,989.00	$29,750.00	$34,650.00	
15	Kiev Office	Velvet Jones	$19,505.00	$27,890.00	$15,600.00	
16	L.A. Office	Velvet Jones	$26,500.00	$31,420.00	$33,086.00	
17	London Office	Cinder Calhoun	$15,600.00	$19,505.00	$20,750.00	
18	Mexico City Office	Charles Ramos	$15,600.00	$19,505.00	$27,890.00	
19	Miami Office	Elinor Saks	$29,750.00	$34,650.00	$30,989.00	
20	Milan Office	Jess Bova	$15,600.00	$19,505.00	$27,890.00	
21	Minneapolis Office	James Stanton	$29,002.00	$20,868.00	$32,976.00	
22	Montreal Office	Jacqueline Pfeiffer	$33,086.00	$22,588.00	$29,389.00	
23	Mumbai Office	Katie Kitchel	$27,890.00	$15,600.00	$19,505.00	
24	New York Office	Velvet Jones	$26,500.00	$31,420.00	$21,050.00	
25	Paris Office	R. R. Dana	$29,750.00	$34,650.00	$24,780.00	
26	Phoenix Office	Velvet Jones	$32,976.00	$29,002.00	$20,868.00	

Sheet1 Sheet2 Sheet3 Sheet4
Ready

1 Double-click the worksheet tab that you want to rename.

Excel highlights the current name.

You can also right-click the worksheet name and click **Rename**.

	A	B	C	D	E	F
1		2010 Quarterly Sales				
2	1st Quarter					
3						
4	Office	Contact	January	February	March	
5	New York Office	Velvet Jones	$26,500.00	$31,420.00	$36,340.00	
6	London Office	Cinder Calhoun	$15,600.00	$19,505.00	$23,410.00	
7	Paris Office	R.R. Dana	$29,750.00	$34,650.00	$22,760.00	
8	Dallas Office	Francois Dubois	$31,420.00	$21,050.00	$26,500.00	
9	Denver Office	Steve White	$29,750.00	$34,650.00	$30,989.00	
10	Detroit Office	Gladys Plaisance	$19,505.00	$20,750.00	$15,600.00	
11	Frankfurt Office	Kate Proctor	$32,976.00	$29,002.00	$20,868.00	
12	Hong Kong Office	Francois Boisson	$34,650.00	$30,989.00	$29,750.00	
13	Indianapolis Office	Diane Weitz	$34,650.00	$24,780.00	$29,750.00	
14	Johannesburg Office	Heidi Plant	$30,989.00	$29,750.00	$34,650.00	
15	Kiev Office	Velvet Jones	$19,505.00	$27,890.00	$15,600.00	
16	L.A. Office	Velvet Jones	$26,500.00	$31,420.00	$33,086.00	
17	London Office	Cinder Calhoun	$15,600.00	$19,505.00	$20,750.00	
18	Mexico City Office	Charles Ramos	$15,600.00	$19,505.00	$27,890.00	
19	Miami Office	Elinor Saks	$29,750.00	$34,650.00	$30,989.00	
20	Milan Office	Jess Bova	$15,600.00	$19,505.00	$27,890.00	
21	Minneapolis Office	James Stanton	$29,002.00	$20,868.00	$32,976.00	
22	Montreal Office	Jacqueline Pfeiffer	$33,086.00	$22,588.00	$29,389.00	
23	Mumbai Office	Katie Kitchel	$27,890.00	$15,600.00	$19,505.00	
24	New York Office	Velvet Jones	$26,500.00	$31,420.00	$21,050.00	
25	Paris Office	R. R. Dana	$29,750.00	$34,650.00	$24,780.00	
26	Phoenix Office	Velvet Jones	$32,976.00	$29,002.00	$20,868.00	

1st Quarter Sheet2 Sheet3 Sheet4
Ready

2 Type a new name for the worksheet.

3 Press Enter.

Excel assigns the new worksheet name.

Change Page Setup Options

You can assign various settings related to page setup settings to your Excel worksheets. These include settings for changing the worksheet's orientation, margins, paper size, and more. For example, if your workbook data is too wide to fit on a standard sheet of paper, you might change the page orientation from Portrait, which is the default in Excel, to Landscape in order to fit more data on the page horizontally. You can also use Excel's page-setup settings to insert your own page breaks to control the placement of data on a printed page.

Change Page Setup Options

Change the Page Orientation

1 Click the **Page Layout** tab on the Ribbon.

2 Click the **Orientation** button.

3 Click **Portrait** or **Landscape**.

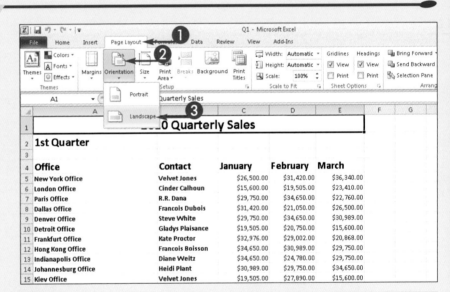

Excel applies the new orientation. This example applies Landscape.

● Excel marks the edge of the page with a dotted line.

● You can click the **Margins** button to set up page margins.

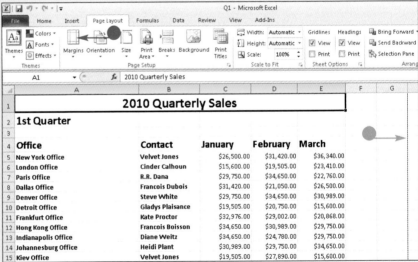

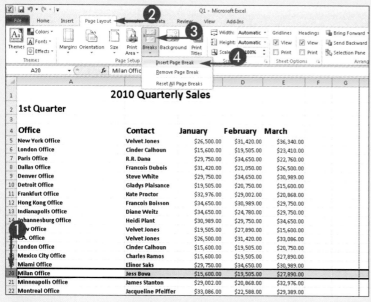

Insert a Page Break

1 Select the row above which you want to insert a page break.

2 Click the **Page Layout** tab on the Ribbon.

3 Click the **Breaks** button.

4 Click **Insert Page Break**.

Excel inserts a page break.

● Excel marks the edge of the page with a dotted line.

Simplify It

How do I print just a portion of a worksheet?
To print only a portion of a worksheet, select the cells that you want to print, click the **Page Layout** tab on the Ribbon, click the **Print Area** button, and click **Set Print Area**. Then print as normal.

How do I print a spreadsheet with gridlines?
By default, the gridlines that you see on a worksheet do not print with the cell data. To turn on gridlines for printing, select the **Print** check box under **Gridlines** on the Page Layout tab. A check mark in the check box indicates that the feature is on.

Move and Copy Worksheets

You can move a worksheet within a workbook to rearrange the worksheet order. For example, you may want to position the worksheet that you use most often as the first worksheet in the workbook, or you might move a worksheet you rarely view to be the last worksheet in the workbook.

In addition to moving worksheets within a workbook, you can copy them. You might copy a worksheet to use it as a starting point for data that is new, yet similar. When you copy a worksheet, Excel assigns it a default name: the original worksheet's name followed by a number, starting with (2).

Move and Copy Worksheets

① Click the tab of the worksheet that you want to move or copy.

② Move or copy the worksheet to the desired spot.

To move the worksheet, drag it to a new position in the list of worksheets. (The ⊿ changes to ⊾.)

To copy the worksheet, press and hold Ctrl and drag the worksheet copy to a new position in the list of worksheets. (The ⊿ changes to ⊾.)

● A small black triangle icon keeps track of the worksheet's location in the group while you drag.

③ Release the mouse button.

● Excel moves or copies the worksheet. (Here, the worksheet was moved.)

9	Denver Office	Steve White	$29,750.00
10	Detroit Office	Gladys Plaisance	$19,505.00
11	Frankfurt Office	Kate Proctor	$32,976.00
12	Hong Kong Office	Francois Boisson	$34,650.00
13	Indianapolis Office	Diane Weitz	$34,650.00
14	Johannesburg Office	Heidi Plant	$30,989.00
15	Kiev Office	Velvet Jones	$19,505.00
16	L.A. Office	Velvet Jones	$26,500.00
17	London Office	Cinder Calhoun	$15,600.00
18	Mexico City Office	Charles Ramos	$15,600.00
19	Miami Office	Elinor Saks	$29,750.00
20	Milan Office	Jess Bova	$15,600.00
21	Minneapolis Office	James Stanton	$29,002.00
22	Montreal Office	Jacqueline Pfeiffer	$33,086.00
23	Mumbai Office	Katie Kitchel	$27,890.00
24	Phoenix Office	Velvet Jones	$32,976.00
25	Rio Office	Murgatroyd Peterso	$34,298.00
26	San Francisco Office	Betsy Shoun	$18,939.00

⊣ ◂ ▸ ▸⊦ | 1st Quarter | 2nd Quarter | 3rd Quarter | 4th Quarter

Ready

8	Dallas Office	Francois Dubois	$31,420.00
9	Denver Office	Steve White	$29,750.00
10	Detroit Office	Gladys Plaisance	$19,505.00
11	Frankfurt Office	Kate Proctor	$32,976.00
12	Hong Kong Office	Francois Boisson	$34,650.00
13	Indianapolis Office	Diane Weitz	$34,650.00
14	Johannesburg Office	Heidi Plant	$30,989.00
15	Kiev Office	Velvet Jones	$19,505.00
16	L.A. Office	Velvet Jones	$26,500.00
17	London Office	Cinder Calhoun	$15,600.00
18	Mexico City Office	Charles Ramos	$15,600.00
19	Miami Office	Elinor Saks	$29,750.00
20	Milan Office	Jess Bova	$15,600.00
21	Minneapolis Office	James Stanton	$29,002.00
22	Montreal Office	Jacqueline Pfeiffer	$33,086.00
23	Mumbai Office	Katie Kitchel	$27,890.00
24	Phoenix Office	Velvet Jones	$32,976.00
25	Rio Office	Murgatroyd Peterso	$34,298.00
26	San Francisco Office	Betsy Shoun	$18,939.00

⊣ ◂ ▸ ▸⊦ | 2nd Quarter | 1st Quarter | 3rd Quarter | 4th Quarter

Ready

Delete a Worksheet

You can delete a worksheet that you no longer need in your workbook. For example, you might delete a worksheet that contains outdated data or information about a product that your company no longer sells.

When you delete a worksheet, Excel prompts you to confirm the deletion unless the

worksheet is blank, in which case it simply deletes the worksheet.

You should always check the worksheet's contents before deleting it to avoid removing any important data. As soon as you delete a worksheet, Excel permanently removes it from the workbook file.

Delete a Worksheet

4	Office	Contact	January	February	March
5	New York Office	Velvet Jones	$26,500.00	$31,420.00	$36,340.00
6	London Office	Cinder Calhoun	$15,600.00	$19,505.00	$23,410.00
7	Paris Office	R.R. Dana	$29,750.00	$34,650.00	$22,760.00
8	Dallas Office	Francois Dubois	$31,420.00	$21,050.00	$26,500.00
9	Denver Office	Steve White	$29,750.00	$34,650.00	$30,989.00
10	Detroit Office	Gladys Plaisance	$19,505.00	$20,750.00	$15,600.00
11	Frankfurt Office	Kate Proctor	$32,976.00	$29,002.00	$20,868.00
12	Hong Kong Office	Francois Boisson	$34,650.00	$30,989.00	$29,750.00
13	Indianapolis Office	Diane Weitz	$34,650.00	$24,780.00	$29,750.00
14	Johannesburg Office	Heidi Plant	$30,989.00	$29,750.00	$34,650.00
15	Kiev Office		$19,505.00	$27,890.00	$15,600.00
16	L.A. Office		$6,500.00	$31,420.00	$33,086.00
17	London Office		$15,600.00	$19,505.00	$20,750.00
18	Mexico City Office		$15,600.00	$19,505.00	$27,890.00
19	Miami Office		$29,750.00	$34,650.00	$30,989.00
20	Milan Office		$15,600.00	$19,505.00	$27,890.00
21	Minneapolis Office		$29,002.00	$20,868.00	$32,976.00
22	Montreal Office		$33,086.00	$22,588.00	$29,389.00
23	Mumbai Office		$27,890.00	$15,600.00	$19,505.00
24	Phoenix Office		$32,976.00	$29,002.00	$20,868.00
25	Rio Office		$34,298.00	$20,868.00	$29,535.00
26	San Francisco Office		$18,939.00	$27,890.00	$32,751.00

Menu items: Insert..., Delete, Rename, Move or Copy..., View Code, Protect Sheet..., Tab Color, Hide, Unhide..., Select All Sheets

Tabs: 2nd Quarter / 1st Quarter / 1st Quarter (2) / 3rd Quarter / 4th Quarter

Ready

Microsoft Excel

⚠ Data may exist in the sheet(s) selected for deletion. To permanently delete the data, press Delete.

③ → [Delete] [Cancel]

① Right-click the worksheet tab.

② Click **Delete**.

*Note: You can also click the **Delete** ⊡ on the Home tab and then click **Delete**.*

If the worksheet contains any data, Excel prompts you to confirm the deletion.

③ Click **Delete**.

Excel deletes the worksheet.

Find and Replace Data

Suppose you want to locate a particular number, formula, word, or phrase in your Excel worksheet. Rather than using the scroll bars in the Excel program window to scroll through your worksheet and locate that information, you can use Word's Find tool.

In addition to using the Find tool to find data, you can use the Replace tool to replace instances of text or numbers with other data. For example, suppose you discover that you have consistently misspelled the name of a product in your worksheet; you can use the Replace tool to locate and correct the misspellings.

Find and Replace Data

Find Data

1. Click the **Home** tab on the Ribbon.

2. Click the **Find & Select** button.

3. Click **Find**.

   The Find and Replace dialog box appears, displaying the Find tab.

4. Type the data that you want to find.

5. Click **Find Next**.

● Excel searches the worksheet and finds the first occurrence of the data.

   You can click **Find Next** again to search for the next occurrence.

6. When finished, click **Close** to close the dialog box.

   Note: Excel may display a prompt box when the last occurrence is found. Click OK.

Replace Data

1. Click the **Home** tab on the Ribbon.

2. Click the **Find & Select** button.

3. Click **Replace**.

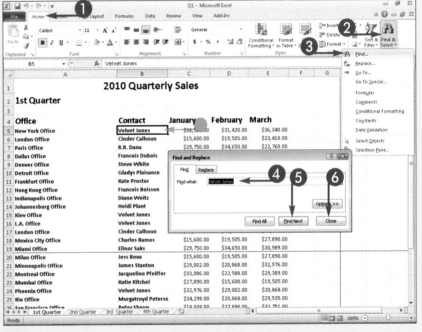

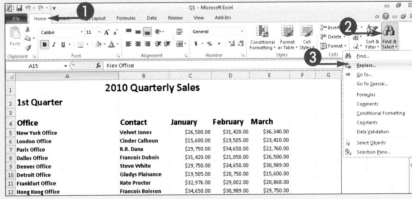

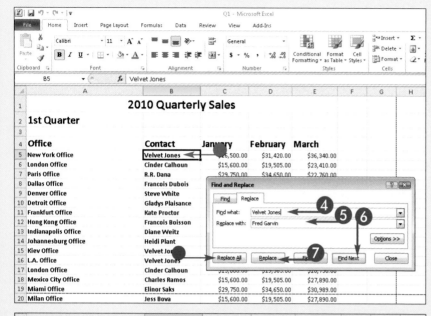

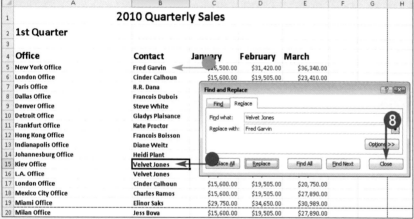

The Find and Replace dialog box appears, displaying the Replace tab.

④ Type the data that you want to find.

⑤ Type the replacement data.

⑥ Click **Find Next**.

● Excel locates the first occurrence of the data.

⑦ Click **Replace** to replace it.

● You can click **Replace All** to replace every occurrence in the worksheet.

● Excel replaces the data with the text you typed.

● Excel selects the next instance of the data.

⑧ When finished, click **Close**.

Note: Excel may display a prompt box when the last occurrence is found. Click OK.

Where can I find detailed search options?
Click the **Options** button in the Find and Replace dialog box to reveal additional search options. For example, you can search by rows or columns, matching data, and more. You can also search for specific formatting or special characters using Format options.

How can I search for and delete data?
Start by typing the text in the **Find what** field; then leave the **Replace with** field empty. When you activate the search, Excel looks for the data and deletes it without adding new data to the worksheet.

Sort Data

You can sort your Excel data to reorganize the information. This technique is particularly useful when using Excel to create database tables. A *database table* is a list of related information. Tables contain *fields* — typically columns — to break the list into manageable pieces. Rows contain each record in your list of data. Each entry in the list is called a *record*.

For example, you might want to sort a client table to list the names alphabetically. Ascending sorts list records from A to Z or from lowest number to highest number; descending sorts list records from Z to A or from highest number to lowest number.

Sort Data

Perform a Quick Sort

1. Click in the field name, or heading, that you want to sort.

2. Click the **Home** tab on the Ribbon.

3. Click the **Sort & Filter** button.

4. Click an ascending or descending sort command.

● Excel sorts the records.

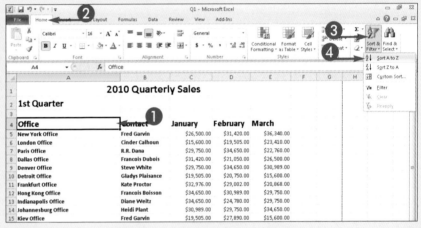

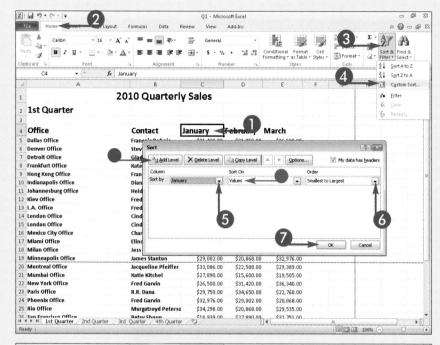

Perform a Custom Sort

1. Click in the worksheet you want to sort.

2. Click the **Home** tab on the Ribbon.

3. Click the **Sort & Filter** button.

4. Click **Custom Sort**.

   The Sort dialog box appears.

5. Click the first **Sort by** ☑ and select the primary field to sort by.

● By default, the Sort On field is set to Values. To sort on another setting, you can click the **Sort On** ☑ and choose a setting.

6. Click the **Order** ☑ to sort the field in ascending or descending order.

● To specify additional sort fields, click **Add Level** and repeat Steps **5** and **6**.

7. Click **OK**.

● Excel sorts the data.

Can I sort data in rows?
Yes. Although most database tables place related data in columns, some place this data in rows. If the data in your table that you want to sort is across a row rather than down a column, you can activate the Sort Left to Right option. To do so, click in the worksheet you want to sort, click the **Home** tab, click the **Sort & Filter** button, and choose **Custom Sort** to open the Sort dialog box. Then click the **Options** button. In the Sort Options dialog box that appears, click **Sort Left to Right**.

Filter Data

If you are using Excel as a database, you can use an AutoFilter to view only portions of your data. When you sort data, the entire table is sorted. (Refer to the previous section, "Sort Data," to learn how to sort data in Excel.) In contrast, when you apply an AutoFilter, only certain records are shown based on criteria you set. Any records that do not match the criteria are hidden. For example, you might set up an AutoFilter to display only those data records containing a particular value in the ZIP code field.

Filter Data

① Select the field names for the data you want to filter.

② Click the **Home** tab on the Ribbon.

③ Click the **Sort & Filter** button.

④ Click **Filter**.

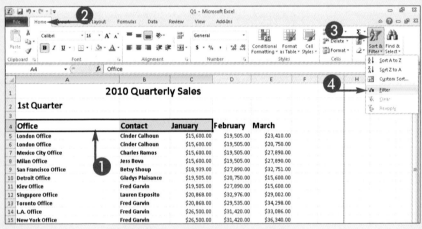

● Excel adds drop-down arrow buttons (⏷) to your field names.

⑤ Click a field's ⏷.

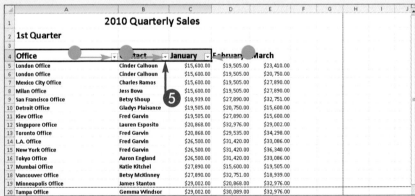

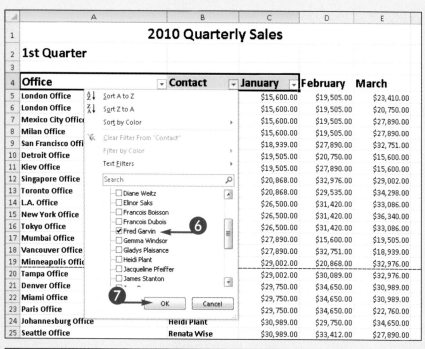

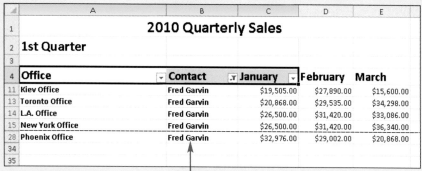

6 Click the data you want to use as a filter.

7 Click **OK**.

● Excel filters the table.

To view all the records again, click the **Sort & Filter** button in the Home tab and choose **Clear**.

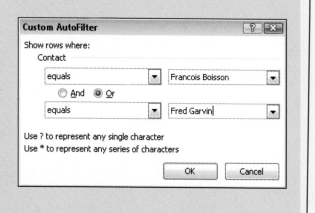

Simplify It

Can I customize a filter?
Yes. To customize a filter, click ⊡ next to the field by which you want to filter, click **Text Filters** or **Number Filters**, and then click **Custom Filter** to open the Custom AutoFilter dialog box. In this dialog box, you can customize the filter by selecting operators and values to apply on the filtered data. In this case, a custom filter has been set to display all records whose Contact field contains the value Francois Boisson or Fred Garvin. To learn more about customizing AutoFilters, see Excel's help files.

Track and Review Worksheet Changes

If you share your Excel workbooks with others, you can use the program's Track Changes feature to help you keep track of what edits others have made, including formatting changes and data additions or deletions.

The Track Changes feature uses different colors for each person's edits, making it easy to see who changed what in the workbook. If you want, you can change the color used for your edits.

When you review the workbook, you can specify whose edits you want to review, what types of edits you want to see, and whether to accept or reject the changes.

Track and Review Worksheet Changes

Turn On Tracking

1. Click the **Review** tab on the Ribbon.

2. Click the **Track Changes** ▾.

3. Click **Highlight Changes**.

   The Highlight Changes dialog box appears.

4. Select the **Track changes while editing** check box.

   This option automatically creates a shared workbook file if you have not already activated the Share Workbook feature.

   ● You can select options to choose when, by whom, or where you track changes.

   ● You can leave this check box selected to view changes in the file.

5. Click **OK**.

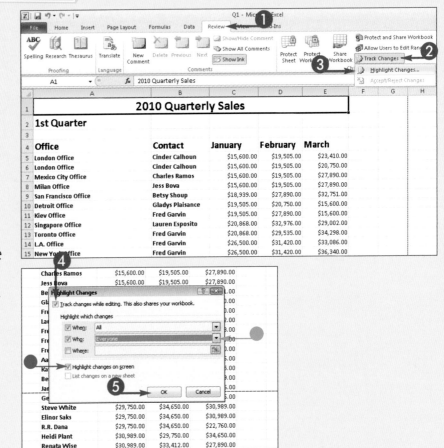

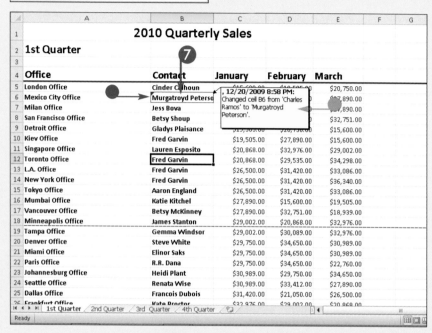

Excel prompts you to save the workbook.

6 Click **OK**.

Excel activates the tracking feature.

7 Edit your worksheet.

● Excel highlights any cells that contain changes.

● To view details about a change, position the mouse pointer over the highlighted cell.

Simplify It

What does the Share Workbook feature do?
The Share Workbook feature enables multiple users to work in a workbook at the same time. You use the Advanced tab of the Share Workbook dialog box to change various Share Workbook settings, such as when files are updated to reflect one user's changes and what should happen when changes made by two or more users conflict. You can also use this dialog box to remove a user from the shared workbook (click the **Editing** tab to access this option). To open this dialog box, click the **Share Workbook** button on the Ribbon.

continued

Track and Review Workbook Changes *(continued)*

Reviewing edits made to a worksheet is simple. When you start the reviewing process, Excel automatically locates and highlights the first edit in the worksheet and gives you the option to accept or reject the edit. After you make your selection, Excel automatically locates and selects the next edit, and so on. You can accept or reject edits one at a time or accept or reject all edits in the worksheet at once.

When the review is complete, you can turn the tracking feature off if you want to. Subsequent edits made to the worksheet are not tracked.

Track and Review Workbook Changes *(continued)*

Review Changes

1. Click the **Review** tab on the Ribbon.

2. Click **Track Changes**.

3. Click **Accept/Reject Changes**.

Excel prompts you to save the file.

4. Click **OK**.

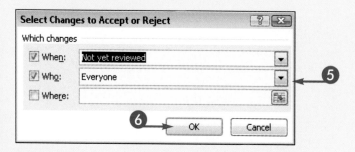

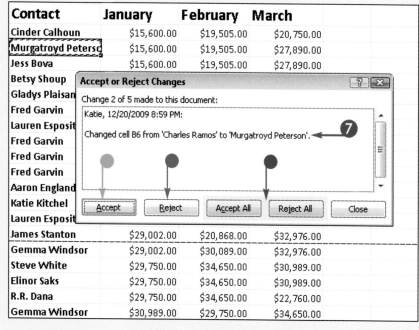

Contact	January	February	March
Cinder Calhoun	$15,600.00	$19,505.00	$20,750.00
Murgatroyd Peterson	$15,600.00	$19,505.00	$27,890.00
Jess Bova	$15,600.00	$19,505.00	$27,890.00
Betsy Shoup			
Gladys Plaisan			
Fred Garvin			
Lauren Esposit			
Fred Garvin			
Fred Garvin			
Fred Garvin			
Aaron England			
Katie Kitchel			
Lauren Esposit			
James Stanton	$29,002.00	$20,868.00	$32,976.00
Gemma Windsor	$29,002.00	$30,089.00	$32,976.00
Steve White	$29,750.00	$34,650.00	$30,989.00
Elinor Saks	$29,750.00	$34,650.00	$30,989.00
R.R. Dana	$29,750.00	$34,650.00	$22,760.00
Gemma Windsor	$30,989.00	$29,750.00	$34,650.00

The Select Changes to Accept or Reject dialog box appears.

⑤ Click options for which changes you want to view.

⑥ Click **OK**.

The Accept or Reject Changes dialog box appears.

⑦ Specify an action for each edit.

● You can click **Accept** to add the change to the final worksheet.

● To reject the change, you can click **Reject**.

● You can click one of these options to accept or reject all of the changes at the same time.

Note: *To turn off Track Changes, click the **Review** tab, click the **Track Changes** button, and choose **Highlight Changes**. In the Highlight Changes dialog box, deselect the **Track changes while editing** check box and click **OK**.*

Can I password-protect shared workbooks?
Yes. First, however, you must disable sharing; deselect **Allow Changes by More Than One User at a Time** in the Share Workbook dialog box's Editing tab (see the preceding tip for help opening this dialog box). Next, click the **Review** tab, click **Protect Workbook**, and set a password in the dialog boxes that appear. Then re-share the workbook by reselecting **Allow Changes by More Than One User at a Time** in the Share Workbook dialog box. Finally, click **Protect Shared Workbook** in the **Review** tab, select **Sharing with track changes**, and enter the password you set.

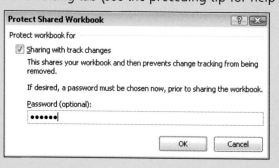

Insert a Comment

You can add comments to your worksheets. You might add a comment to make a note to yourself about a particular cell's contents, or you might include a comment as a note for other users to see. For example, if you share your workbooks with other users, you can use comments to leave feedback about the data without typing directly in the worksheet.

When you add a comment to a cell, Excel displays a small red triangle in the upper right corner of the cell until you choose to view it. Comments you add are identified with your user name.

Insert a Comment

Add a Comment

1 Click the cell to which you want to add a comment.

2 Click the **Review** tab on the Ribbon.

3 Click the **New Comment** button.

You can also right-click the cell and choose **Insert Comment**.

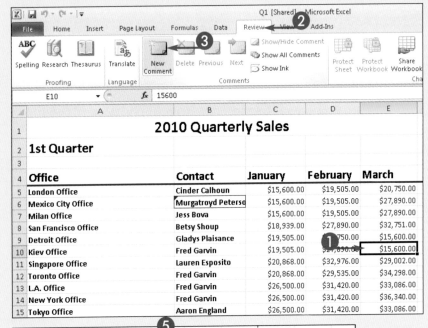

A comment balloon appears.

4 Type your comment text.

5 Click anywhere outside the comment balloon to deselect the comment.

	January	February	March		
	$15,600.00	$19,505.00	$20,750.00		
	$15,600.00	$19,505.00	$27,890.00		
	$15,600.00	$19,505.00	$27,890.00		
	$18,939.00	$27,890.00	$32,751.00		
	$19,505.00	$20,750.00	$15,600.00		
	$19,505.00	$27,890.00	$15,600.00		
	$20,868.00	$32,976.00	$29,002.00		
	$20,868.00	$29,535.00	$34,298.00		
	$26,500.00	$31,420.00	$33,086.00		
	$26,500.00	$31,420.00	$36,340.00		
	$26,500.00	$31,420.00	$33,086.00		
	$27,890.00	$15,600.00	$19,505.00		
	$27,890.00	$32,751.00	$18,939.00		
	$29,002.00	$20,868.00	$32,976.00		

● Cells that contain comments display a tiny red triangle in the corner.

	January	February	March		
	$15,600.00	$19,505.00	$20,750.00		
	$15,600.00	$19,505.00	$27,890.00		
	$15,600.00	$19,505.00	$27,8●00		
	$18,939.00	$27,890.00	$32,751.00		
	$19,505.00	$20,750.00	$15,600.00		
	$19,505.00	$27,890.00	$15,600.00		
	$20,868.00	$32,976.00	$29,002.00		
	$20,868.00	$29,535.00	$34,298.00		
	$26,500.00	$31,420.00	$33,086.00		
	$26,500.00	$31,420.00	$36,340.00		
	$26,500.00	$31,420.00	$33,086.00		
	$27,890.00	$15,600.00	$19,505.00		
	$27,890.00	$32,751.00	$18,939.00		
	$29,002.00	$20,868.00	$32,976.00		

Katie:
Fred: I'm concerned about the drop between February and March. Please explain.

View a Comment

1 Position the mouse pointer over the cell.

● The comment balloon appears, displaying the comment.

How do I remove a comment?
To remove a comment, right-click the cell containing the comment and choose **Delete Comment** from the shortcut menu that appears. Alternatively, click the comment to select it and click the **Delete** button in the Review tab's Comments area.

How do I view all the comments in a worksheet?
If a worksheet contains several comments, you can view them one after another by clicking the **Next** button in the Review tab's Comments area. To view a comment you have already seen, click the **Previous** button. Alternatively, display all comments at once by clicking the **Show All Comments** button.

Understanding Formulas

You can use formulas, which you can build using mathematical operators, values, and cell references, to perform all kinds of calculations on your Excel data. For example, you can add the contents of a column of monthly sales totals to determine the cumulative sales total.

If you are new to writing formulas, this section explains the basics of building your own formulas in Excel. You learn about the correct way to structure formulas in Excel, how to reference cell data in your formulas, which mathematical operators are available for your use, and more.

Formula Structure

Ordinarily, when you write a mathematical formula, you write the values and the operators, followed by an equal sign, such as 2 + 2 =. In Excel, formula structure works a bit differently. All Excel formulas begin with an equal sign (=), such as = 2 + 2. The equal sign tells Excel to recognize any subsequent data as a formula rather than as a regular cell entry.

Referencing Cells

In addition to entering specific values in your Excel formulas, you can also reference data in cells — for example, adding the contents of two cells together. Every cell in a worksheet has a unique address, called a *cell reference*, composed of the cell's column letter and row number. Cell D5, for example, identifies the fifth cell down in column D. You can also assign your own names to cells — for example, naming a cell that contains a figure totaling weekly sales "Sales."

Cell Ranges

A group of related cells in a worksheet is called a *range*. Excel identifies a range by the cells in the upper left and lower right corners of the range, separated by a colon. For example, range A1:B3 includes cells A1, A2, A3, B1, B2, and B3. You can also assign names to ranges to make it easier to identify their contents. Range names must start with a letter, underscore, or backslash, and can include uppercase and lowercase letters. Spaces are not allowed.

Mathematical Operators

You can use mathematical operators in Excel to build formulas. Basic operators include the following:

Operator	Operation	Operator	Operation
+	Addition	=	Equal to
-	Subtraction	<	Less than
*	Multiplication	≤	Less than or equal to
/	Division	>	Greater than
%	Percentage	≥	Greater than or equal to
^	Exponentiation	< >	Not equal to

Operator Precedence

Excel performs operations from left to right, but gives some operators precedence over others:

First	All operations enclosed in parentheses
Second	Exponential equations
Third	Multiplication and division
Fourth	Addition and subtraction

When you are creating equations, the order of operations determines the results. For example, suppose you want to determine the average of values in cells A2, B2, and C2. If you enter the equation $= A2 + B2 + C2/3$, Excel first divides the value in cell C2 by 3, and then adds that result to $A2 + B2$ — yielding the wrong answer. The correct way to write the formula is $= (A2 + B2 + C2)/3$.

Reference Operators

You can use Excel's reference operators to control how a formula groups cells and ranges to perform calculations. For example, if your formula needs to include the cell range D2:D10 and cell E10, you can instruct Excel to evaluate all the data contained in these cells using a reference operator. Your formula might look like this: $= SUM(D2:D10,E10)$.

Operator	Example	Operation
:	= SUM(D3:E12)	Range operator. Evaluates the reference as a single reference, including all of the cells in the range from both corners of the reference.
,	= SUM(D3:E12,F3)	Union operator. Evaluates the two references as a single reference.
[space]	= SUM(D3:D20 D10:E15)	Intersect operator. Evaluates the cells common to both references.
[space]	= SUM(Totals Sales)	Intersect operator. Evaluates the intersecting cell or cells of the column labeled Totals and the row labeled Sales.

Create a Formula

You can write a formula to perform a calculation on data in your worksheet. In Excel, all formulas begin with an equal sign (=) and contain the cell references of the cells that contain the relevant data. (Note that in addition to referring to cells in the current worksheet, you can also build formulas that refer to cells in other worksheets.) For example, the formula for adding the contents of cells C3 and C4 together is =C3+C4. You create formulas in the Formula bar; formula results appear in the cell to which you assign a formula.

Create a Formula

① Click in the cell to which you want to assign a formula.

② Type =.

● Excel displays the formula in the Formula bar and in the active cell.

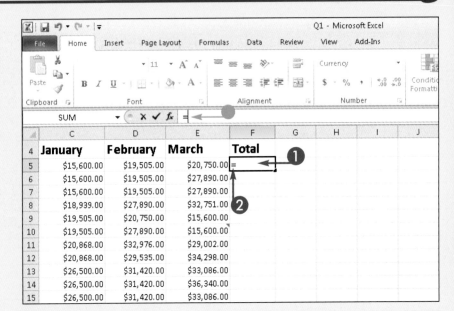

③ Click the first cell that you want to reference in the formula.

● Excel inserts the cell reference into the formula.

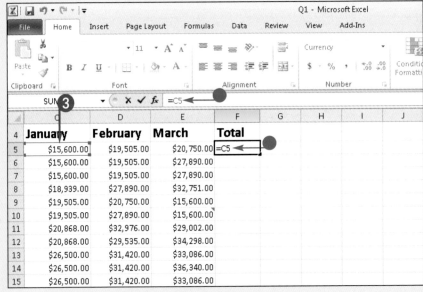

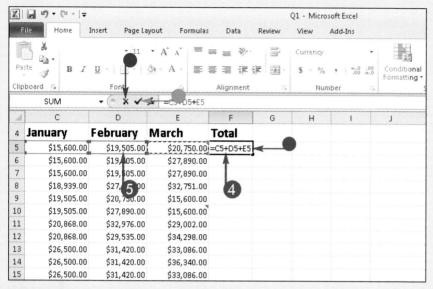

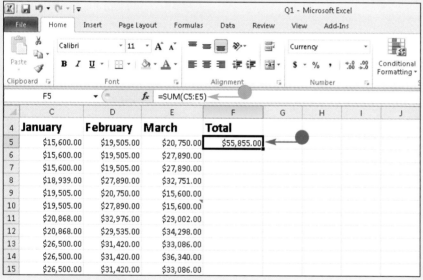

④ Type an operator.

⑤ Click the next cell that you want to reference in the formula.

● Excel inserts the cell reference into the formula.

⑥ Repeat Steps **4** and **5** until all the necessary cells and operators have been added.

⑦ Press Enter.

● You can also click **Enter** (☑) on the Formula bar to accept the formula.

● You can click **Cancel** (☒) to cancel the formula.

● The formula results appear in the cell.

To view the formula in the Formula bar, you can simply click in the cell.

● The Formula bar displays any formula assigned to the active cell.

Note: *If you change a value in a cell referenced in your formula, the formula results automatically update to reflect the change.*

How do I edit a formula?
To edit a formula, click in the cell containing the formula and make any corrections in the Formula bar. Alternatively, double-click in the cell to make edits to the formula from within the cell itself. When finished, press Enter or click **Enter** (☑) on the Formula bar.

How do I reference cells in other worksheets?
To reference a cell in another worksheet, specify the worksheet name followed by an exclamation mark and then the cell address (for example, Sheet2!D12 or Sales!D12). If the worksheet name includes spaces, enclose the sheet name in single quote marks, as in 'Sales Totals'!D12.

Apply Absolute and Relative Cell References

By default, Excel uses *relative cell referencing*. That is, it treats the location of cells that you include in formulas as relative rather than absolute. If you copy a formula to a new location, the cell references in that formula adjust accordingly.

If you want to refer to a particular cell regardless of where the formula appears, you can assign an absolute cell reference. For example, suppose you have a formula that refers to a discount rate disclosed in cell G10. Even if you move that formula, it must always reference cell G10 — meaning cell G10 should be absolute.

Apply Absolute and Relative Cell References

Assign Absolute References

1. Click in the cell containing the formula that you want to change.

2. Select the cell reference in the Formula bar.

3. Press **F4**.

   Note: *You can also type dollar signs in the Formula bar to make a reference absolute.*

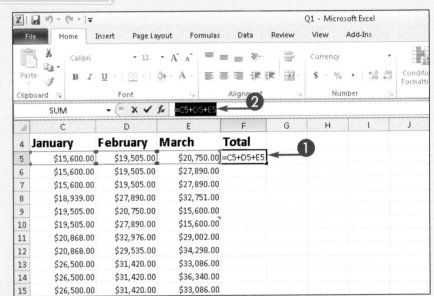

- Excel enters dollar signs ($) before each part of the cell reference, making the cell reference absolute.

  Note: *You can continue pressing* **F4** *to cycle through mixed, relative, and absolute references.*

4. Press **Enter** or click **Enter** (☑).

   Excel assigns the changes to the formula.

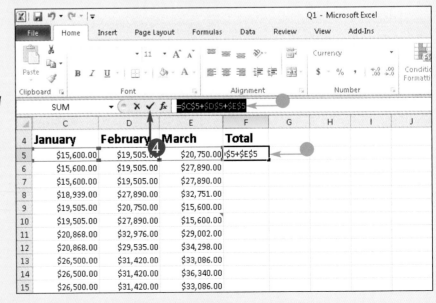

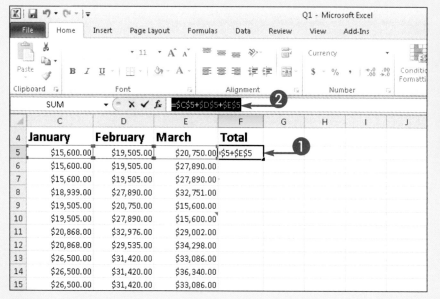

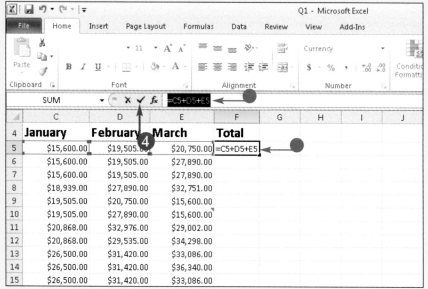

Assign Relative References

1. Click in the cell containing the formula that you want to change.

2. Select the cell reference.

3. Press F4 as many times as needed to cycle to relative addressing (that is, remove the dollar signs).

    Note: You can press F4 multiple times to cycle through mixed, relative, and absolute references.

    Note: You can also delete the dollar sign characters in the Formula bar to make a reference relative.

4. Press Enter or click **Enter** (☑).

● Excel assigns the changes to the formula.

When would I use mixed cell references?
You are not limited to using relative and absolute references; you can also use mixed references. You use mixed referencing to reference the same row or column, but different relative cells within. For example, referencing $C6 keeps the column absolute whereas the row remains relative. If the mixed reference is C$6, the column is relative but the row is absolute. You can press F4 while writing a formula to cycle through absolute, mixed, and relative cell referencing, or you can type the dollar signs ($) as needed.

Understanding Functions

If you are looking for a speedier way to enter formulas, you can use any one of a wide variety of functions. *Functions* are ready-made formulas that perform a series of operations on a specified range of values.

Excel offers more than 300 functions, grouped into 12 categories, that you can use to perform mathematical calculations on your worksheet data.

Functions use arguments to indicate what cells contain the values you want to calculate. Functions can refer to individual cells or to ranges of cells. This section explains the basics of working with functions.

Function Elements

All functions must start with an equal sign (=). Functions are distinct in that each one has a name. For example, the function that sums data is called SUM, and the function for averaging values is called AVERAGE. You can create functions by typing them directly into your worksheet cells or Formula bar; alternatively, you can use the Insert Function dialog box to select and apply functions to your data.

Constructing Arguments

Arguments are enclosed in parentheses. When applying a function to individual cells in a worksheet, you can use a comma to separate the cell addresses, as in =SUM(A5,B5,C5). When applying a function to a range of cells, you can use a colon to designate the first and last cells in the range, as in =SUM(B5:E12). If your range has a name, you can insert the name, as in =SUM(Sales).

Types of Functions

Excel groups functions into 12 categories, each of which includes a variety of functions:

Category	Description
Financial	Includes functions for calculating loans, principal, interest, yield, and depreciation.
Date & Time	Includes functions for calculating dates, times, and minutes.
Math & Trig	Includes a wide variety of functions for calculations of all types.
Statistical	Includes functions for calculating averages, probabilities, rankings, trends, and more.
Lookup & Reference	Includes functions that enable you to locate references or specific values in your worksheets.
Database	Includes functions for counting, adding, and filtering database items.
Text	Includes text-based functions to search and replace data and other text tasks.
Logical	Includes functions for logical conjectures, such as if-then statements.
Information	Includes functions for testing your data.
Engineering	Offers many kinds of functions for engineering calculations.
Cube	Enables Excel to fetch data from SQL Server Analysis Services, such as members, sets, aggregated values, properties, and KPIs.
Compatibility	Use these functions to keep your workbook compatible with earlier versions of Excel.

Common Functions

The following table lists some of the more popular Excel functions that you might use with your own spreadsheet work.

Function	Category	Description	Syntax
SUM	Math & Trig	Adds values	= SUM(number1,number2,...)
INT	Math & Trig	Rounds down to the nearest integer	= INT(number)
ROUND	Math & Trig	Rounds a number specified to a specified number of digits	= ROUND(number,number_digits)
ROUNDDOWN	Math & Trig	Rounds a number down	= ROUNDDOWN(number,number_digits)
COUNT	Statistical	Counts the number of cells in a range that contain data	= COUNT(value1,value2,...)
AVERAGE	Statistical	Averages a series of arguments	= AVERAGE(number1,number2,...)
MIN	Statistical	Returns the smallest value in a series	= MIN(number1,number2,...)
MAX	Statistical	Returns the largest value in a series	= MAX(number1,number2,...)
MEDIAN	Statistical	Returns the middle value in a series	= MEDIAN(number1,number2,...)
PMT	Financial	Finds the periodic payment for a fixed loan	= PMT(interest_rate,number_of_periods,present_value,future_value,type)
RATE	Financial	Returns an interest rate	= RATE(number_of_periods,payment,present_value,future_value,type,guess)
TODAY	Date & Time	Returns the current date	= TODAY()
IF	Logical	Returns one of two results that you specify based on whether the value is true or false	= IF(logical_text,value_if_true,value_if_false)
AND	Logical	Returns true if all of the arguments are true, false if any is false	= AND(logical1,logical2,...)
OR	Logical	Returns true if any argument is true, false if all arguments are false	= OR(logical1,logical2,...)

Apply a Function

You can use functions to speed up your Excel calculations. *Functions* are ready-made formulas that perform a series of operations on a specified range of values.

You use the Insert Function dialog box to look for a particular function from among Excel's 300-plus available functions. Functions are divided into 12 categories: Financial, Date &

Time, Math & Trig, Statistical, Lookup & Reference, Database, Text, Logical, Information, Engineering, Cube, and Compatibility.

After you have selected your function, you build the formula using the Function Arguments dialog box. Functions use arguments to indicate what cells contain the values you want to calculate.

Apply a Function

1 Click in the cell to which you want to assign a function.

2 Click the **Formulas** tab on the Ribbon.

3 Click the **Insert Function** button.

● Excel inserts an equal sign to denote a formula.

Excel launches the Insert Function dialog box.

4 Click the **Or select a category** ⊡ and choose a function category.

● A list of functions in the selected category appears.

5 Click the function that you want to apply.

● A description of the selected function appears here.

6 Click **OK**.

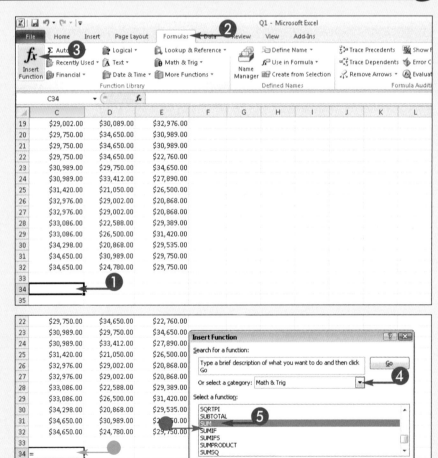

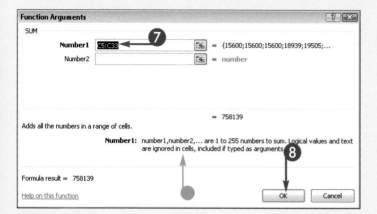

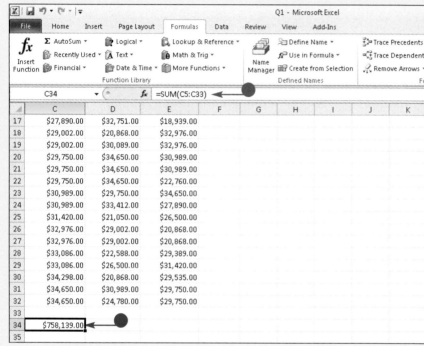

The Function Arguments dialog box appears.

⑦ Select the cells for each argument required by the function.

If you select a cell or range of cells directly in the worksheet, Excel automatically adds the references to the argument.

You can also type a range or cell address (or range or cell name) into the various text boxes.

● The dialog box displays additional information about the function here.

⑧ When you finish constructing the arguments, click **OK**.

● Excel displays the function results in the cell.

● The function appears in the Formula bar.

Can I edit a function?
Yes. To edit a function, click the cell containing the function that you want to edit, click the **Formulas** tab, and click the **Insert Function** button. Excel displays the function's Function Arguments dialog box, where you can change the cell references or values as needed.

How can I find help with a particular function?
Click the **Help on this function** link in either the Insert Function or Function Arguments dialog box to access Excel's help files to find out more about the function. The function help includes an example of the function being used and tips about how to use the function.

Total Cells with AutoSum

One of the most popular Excel functions is the AutoSum function. AutoSum automatically totals the contents of cells. For example, you can quickly total a column of sales figures.

One way to use AutoSum is to select a cell and let the function guess which surrounding cells you want to total. Alternatively, you can specify exactly which cells to sum.

In addition to using AutoSum to total cells, you can simply select a series of cells in your worksheet; Excel displays the total of the cells' contents in the status bar, along with the number of cells you selected and an average of their values.

Total Cells with AutoSum

Use AutoSum to Total Cells

1 Click in the cell where you want to insert a sum total.

2 Click the **Formulas** tab on the Ribbon.

3 Click the **AutoSum** button.

● If you click the **AutoSum** ☐, you can select another common function, such as Average.

You can also click the **AutoSum** button (Σ) on the Home tab.

● AutoSum generates a formula to total the adjacent cells.

4 Press Enter or click **Enter** (☑).

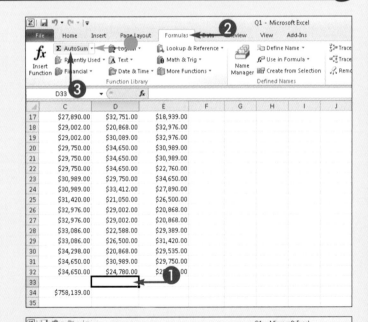

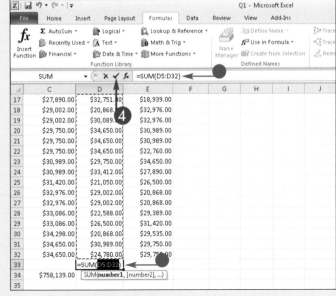

	C	D	E	F	G	H	I
17	$27,890.00	$32,751.00	$18,939.00				
18	$29,002.00	$20,868.00	$32,976.00				
19	$29,002.00	$30,089.00	$32,976.00				
20	$29,750.00	$34,650.00	$30,989.00				
21	$29,750.00	$34,650.00	$30,989.00				
22	$29,750.00	$34,650.00	$22,760.00				
23	$30,989.00	$29,750.00	$34,650.00				
24	$30,989.00	$33,412.00	$27,890.00				
25	$31,420.00	$21,050.00	$26,500.00				
26	$32,976.00	$29,002.00	$20,868.00				
27	$32,976.00	$29,002.00	$20,868.00				
28	$33,086.00	$22,588.00	$29,389.00				
29	$33,086.00	$26,500.00	$31,420.00				
30	$34,298.00	$20,868.00	$29,535.00				
31	$34,650.00	$30,989.00	$29,750.00				
32	$34,650.00	$24,780.00	$29,750.00				
33		$763,015.00 ←					
34	$758,139.00						
35							

● Excel displays the AutoSum result in the cell.

Contact	January	February	March	Total
Cinder Calhoun	$15,600.00	$19,505.00	$20,750.00	
Murgatroyd Peterso	$15,600.00	$19,505.00	$27,890.00	
Jess Bova	$15,600.00	$19,505.00	$27,890.00	
Betsy Shoup	$18,939.00	$27,890.00	$32,751.00	
Gladys Plaisance	$19,505.00	$20,750.00	$15,600.00	
Fred Garvin	$19,505.00	$27,890.00	$15,600.00	
Lauren Esposito	$20,868.00	$32,976.00	$29,002.00	
Fred Garvin	$20,868.00	$29,535.00	$34,298.00	
Fred Garvin	$26,500.00	$31,420.00	$33,086.00	
Fred Garvin	$26,500.00	$31,420.00	$36,340.00	
Aaron England	$26,500.00	$31,420.00	$33,086.00	
Katie Kitchel	$27,890.00	$15,600.00	$19,505.00 ←	
Lauren Esposito	$27,890.00	$32,751.00	$18,939.00	
James Stanton	$29,002.00	$20,868.00	$32,976.00	
Gemma Windsor	$29,002.00	$30,089.00	$32,976.00	
Steve White	$29,750.00	$34,650.00	$30,989.00	
Elinor Saks	$29,750.00	$34,650.00	$30,989.00	
R.R. Dana	$29,750.00	$34,650.00	$22,760.00	
Gemma Windsor	$30,989.00	$29,750.00	$34,650.00	
Francois Dubois	$30,989.00	$33,41_.00	$_,890.00	
Francois Dubois	$31,420.00	$21,050.00	$26,500.00	
Kate Proctor	$32,976.00	$29,002.00	$20,868.00	

3rd Quarter / 4th Quarter

Average: $26,785.71   Count: 7   Sum: $187,500.00

Total Cells without Applying a Function

① Click a group of cells whose values you want to total.

Note: To sum noncontiguous cells, press and hold Ctrl *while clicking the cells.*

● Excel adds the contents of the cells, displaying the sum in the status bar along the bottom of the program window.

● Excel also counts the number of cells you have selected.

● Excel also displays an average of the values in the selected cells.

Simplify It

Can I select a different range of cells to sum?
AutoSum takes its best guess when determining which cells to total. If it guesses wrong, simply click the cells you want to add together before pressing Enter or clicking **Enter** (☑).

Can I apply AutoSum to both rows and columns at the same time?
Yes. Simply select both the row and column of data that you want to sum, along with a blank row and column to hold the results. When you apply the AutoSum function, Excel sums the row and column and displays the results in the blank row and column.

Audit a Worksheet for Errors

On occasion, you may see an error message, such as #DIV/0!, in your Excel worksheet. If you do, you should double-check your formula references to ensure that you referenced the correct cells. Locating the source of an error is difficult, however — especially in larger worksheets. Fortunately, if an error occurs in your worksheet, you can use Excel's Formula Auditing tools — namely, Error Checking and Trace Error — to examine and correct formula errors. (For more information on types of errors and how to resolve them, see the table on the next page.)

Audit a Worksheet for Errors

Apply Error Checking

① Click the **Formulas** tab on the Ribbon.

② Click the **Error Checking** button.

● Excel displays the Error Checking dialog box and highlights the first cell containing an error.

③ To fix the error, click **Edit in Formula Bar**.

● To find help with an error, you can click here to open the help files.

● To ignore the error, you can click **Ignore Error**.

● You can click **Previous** and **Next** to scroll through all of the errors on the worksheet.

④ Make edits to the cell references in the Formula bar.

⑤ Click **Resume**.

When the error check is complete, a prompt box appears.

⑥ Click **OK**.

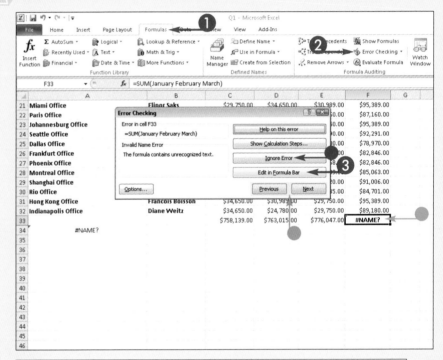

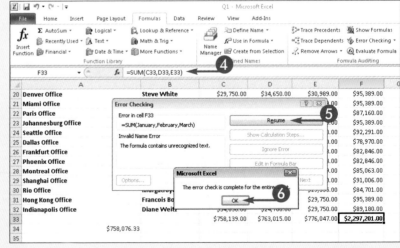

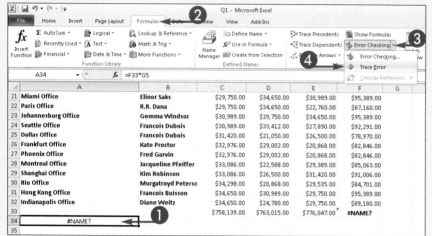

Trace Errors

1 Click in the cell containing the error that you want to trace.

2 Click the **Formulas** tab on the Ribbon.

3 Click the **Error Checking** 🔽.

4 Click **Trace Error**.

	A	B	C	D	E	F	G
21	Miami Office	Elinor Saks	$29,750.00	$34,650.00	$30,989.00	$95,389.00	
22	Paris Office	R.R. Dana	$29,750.00	$34,650.00	$22,760.00	$87,160.00	
23	Johannesburg Office	Gemma Windsor	$30,989.00	$29,750.00	$34,650.00	$95,389.00	
24	Seattle Office	Francois Dubois	$30,989.00	$33,412.00	$27,890.00	$92,291.00	
25	Dallas Office	Francois Dubois	$31,420.00	$21,050.00	$26,500.00	$78,970.00	
26	Frankfurt Office	Kate Proctor	$32,976.00	$29,002.00	$20,868.00	$82,846.00	
27	Phoenix Office	Fred Garvin	$32,976.00	$29,002.00	$20,868.00	$82,846.00	
28	Montreal Office	Jacqueline Pfeiffer	$33,086.00	$22,588.00	$29,389.00	$85,063.00	
29	Shanghai Office	Kim Robinson	$33,086.00	$26,500.00	$31,420.00	$91,006.00	
30	Rio Office	Murgatroyd Peterson	$34,298.00	$20,868.00	$29,535.00	$84,701.00	
31	Hong Kong Office	Francois Boisson	$34,650.00	$30,989.00	$29,750.00	$95,389.00	
32	Indianapolis Office	Diane Weitz	$34,650.00	$24,780.00	$29,750.00	$89,180.00	
33			$758,139.00	$763,015.00	$776,047.00	#NAME?	
34	#NAME?						
35							

● Excel displays trace lines from the current cell to any cells referenced in the formula.

You can make changes to the cell contents or changes to the formula to correct the error.

Note: *Click the **Remove Arrows** button on the Ribbon to turn off the trace lines.*

Simplify It

What kinds of error messages does Excel display for formula errors?
Different types of error values appear in cells when an error occurs:

Error	Problem	Solution
######	The cell is not wide enough to contain the value	Increase the column width
#DIV/0!	Dividing by zero	Edit the cell reference or value of the denominator
#N/A	Value is not available	Ensure that the formula references the correct value
#NAME?	Does not recognize text in a formula	Ensure that the name referenced is correct
#NULL!	Specifies two areas that do not intersect	Check for an incorrect range operator or correct the intersection problem
#NUM!	Invalid numeric value	Check the function for an unacceptable argument
#REF!	Invalid cell reference	Correct cell references
#VALUE!	Wrong type of argument or operand	Double-check arguments and operands

Add a Watch Window

Suppose you want to view a cell containing a formula at the top of your worksheet while making changes to data referenced in the formula at the bottom of the worksheet. To do so, you can create a watch window. This displays the cell containing the formula, no matter where you scroll. You can also use a watch window to view cells in other worksheets or in a linked workbook. You can position your watch window anywhere on-screen or dock the window to appear with the toolbars at the top of the program window.

Add a Watch Window

① Click the **Formulas** tab on the Ribbon.

② Click the **Watch Window** button.

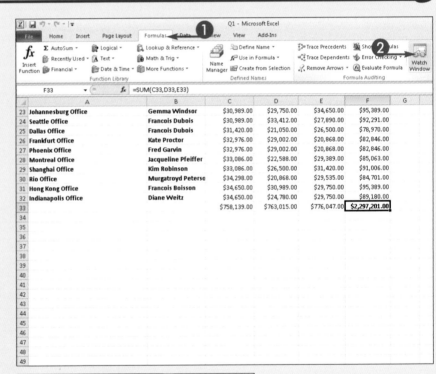

The Watch Window opens.

③ Click **Add Watch**.

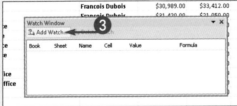

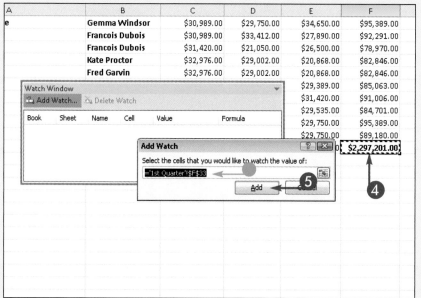

The Add Watch dialog box appears.

④ Select the cell or range that you want to watch.

● You can also type the cell reference.

⑤ Click **Add**.

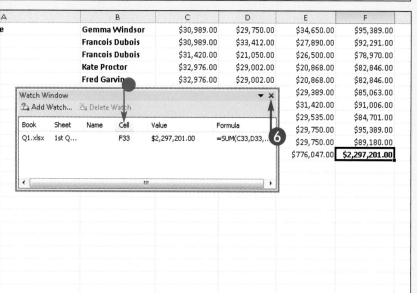

Note: You can add multiple cells to the watch window.

● Excel adds the cells to the watch window, including any values or formulas within the cells.

If you scroll away from the original cells, the watch window continues to display the cell contents.

To return to the original cell, you can double-click the cell name.

⑥ Click the **Close** button (⊠) to close the watch window.

How do I remove and add cells in the watch window?
To remove a cell from the watch window, click the cell name, and then click the **Delete Watch** button in the watch window. Excel removes the cell from the window. To add more cells, click the **Add Watch** button and select the cell that you want to add to the window.

How can I move and resize the watch window?
To move the watch window, click and drag the window's title bar. To resize the columns within the watch window, position the mouse pointer over a column in the watch window, and drag to resize the column.

Create a Chart

You can quickly convert your spreadsheet data into easy-to-read charts. You can choose from a wide variety of chart types to suit your needs, including column, line, pie, bar, area, scatter, stock, surface, doughnut, bubble, and radar charts. Excel makes it easy to determine exactly what type of chart works best for your data.

(Note that these charts are different from the charts you can create using Excel's SmartArt tool, as discussed in the tip at the end of this section.)

After you create a chart, you can use the Chart Tools on the Ribbon to fine-tune the chart to best display and explain the data.

Create a Chart

1. Select the range of data that you want to chart.

   You can include any headings and labels, but do not include subtotals or totals.

2. Click the **Insert** tab on the Ribbon.

3. Click a chart type from the Charts group.

4. Click a chart style.

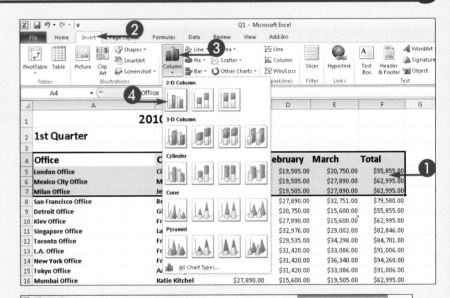

- Excel creates a chart and places it in the worksheet.

- You can click the **Design** tab to find tools for controlling design elements in the chart, such as the chart layout, style, and type.

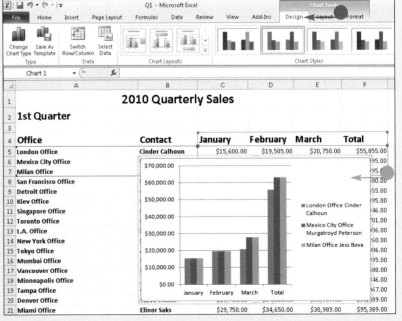

● You can click the **Layout** tab to find tools for controlling how the chart elements are positioned on the chart.

● You can click the **Format** tab to find tools for formatting various chart elements, including chart text and shapes.

Can I select noncontiguous data to include in a chart?
Yes. To select noncontiguous cells and ranges, select the first cell or range and then press and hold Ctrl while selecting additional cells and ranges.

How do I create an organizational chart in Excel?
You can add an organizational chart to track the hierarchy of an organization or a process. When you insert an organizational chart, Excel creates four shapes to which you can add your own text; you can add additional shapes and branches to the chart as needed. To create an organizational chart, click the **Insert** tab and then click the **SmartArt** button.

Move and Resize Charts

After creating a chart, you may decide that it would look better if it were a different size or located elsewhere on the worksheet. For example, you may want to reposition the chart at the bottom of the worksheet or make the chart larger so it is easier to read.

Moving or resizing a chart is like moving or resizing any other type of Office object. When you select a chart, handles appear around that chart; you use these handles to make the chart larger or smaller. Moving the chart is a matter of selecting it and then dragging it to the desired location.

Move and Resize Charts

Resize a Chart

① Click an empty area of the chart.

● Excel selects the chart and surrounds it with handles.

② Position the mouse pointer over a handle.

The ⬚ changes to ⬚.

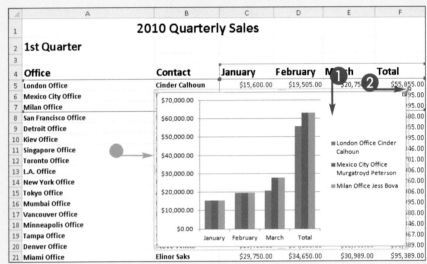

③ Click and drag a handle to resize the chart.

● A frame appears, representing the chart as you resize it on the worksheet.

④ Release the mouse button.

Excel resizes the chart.

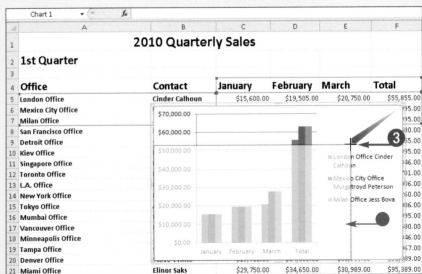

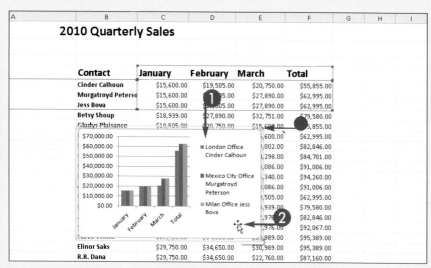

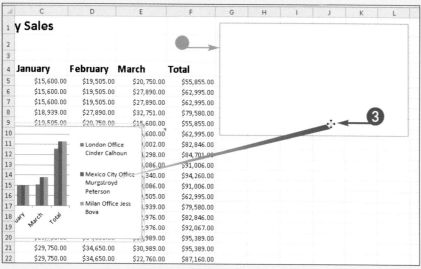

Move a Chart

① Click an empty area of the chart.

● Excel selects the chart and surrounds it with handles.

② Position the mouse pointer over an empty area of the chart.

The ⮜ changes to ⬍.

③ Click and drag the chart to a new location on the worksheet.

● A frame appears, representing the chart as you move it on the worksheet.

④ Release the mouse button.

Excel moves the chart.

Simplify It

Can I move a chart to its own worksheet?
Yes. Select the chart, click the **Design** tab, and click the **Move Chart** button. The Move Chart dialog box opens; click **New Sheet** and click **OK**. Excel adds a new worksheet to the workbook and places the chart in that worksheet.

How do I delete a chart that I no longer want?
To remove an embedded chart, click the chart and press Delete. If your chart appears on its own worksheet, you can delete the worksheet by right-clicking its tab in the bottom left corner of the screen, clicking **Delete**, and clicking **Delete** again to confirm.

Change the Chart Type

Suppose you create a column chart but quickly realize your data would be better presented in a line chart. Fortunately, Excel makes it easy to change the chart type in order to present your data in a different way. Chart types include column, line, pie, bar, area, scatter, stock, surface, doughnut, bubble, and radar charts. (Note that these charts are different from the charts you can create using Excel's SmartArt tool.) You select a new chart type from the Design tab on the Ribbon. To make this tab available, you must click the chart to select it.

Change the Chart Type

1 Click an empty area of the chart to select the chart.

2 Click the **Design** tab on the Ribbon.

3 Click the **Change Chart Type** button.

The Change Chart Type dialog box appears.

4 Click a new chart type.

5 Click a chart style.

6 Click **OK**.

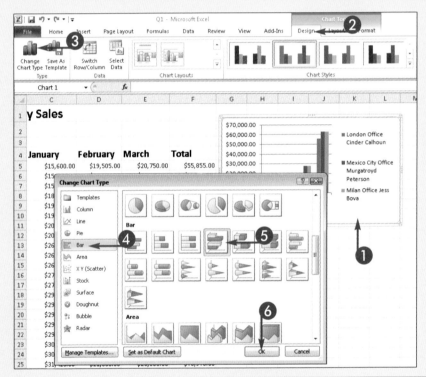

● Excel changes the chart to the chart type that you selected.

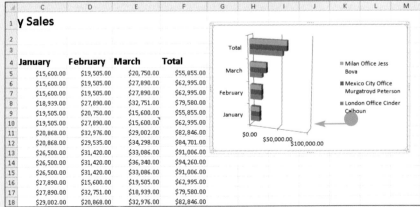

Change the Chart Style

You can change the chart style to change the appearance of a chart. You can choose from a wide variety of preset styles to find just the look you want. For example, you might prefer a brighter color scheme for the chart to make it stand out, or you might want the elements of the chart, such as the columns or pie slices, to appear 3D.

You access the various preset chart styles from the Design tab. To make this tab visible, simply click in the chart whose style you want to change.

Change the Chart Style

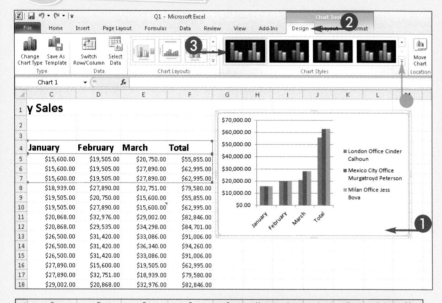

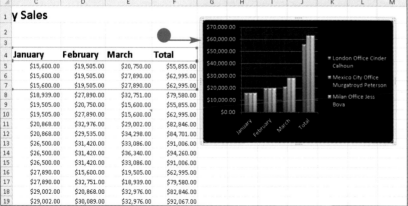

① Click an empty area of the chart to select the chart.

② Click the **Design** tab on the Ribbon.

③ Click a new chart style from the Chart Styles group.

● Click the **More** button (⊡) to view the full palette of styles.

● Excel applies the new style to the existing chart.

Change the Chart Layout

You can change the chart layout to change how chart elements are positioned. You can use Excel's preset chart-layout options to further customize your chart's appearance. For example, you may prefer to show a legend on the top of the chart rather than on the side. Or, if you want to include a title for the chart, you might prefer for it to appear above the chart rather than below it.

You access the various preset chart layouts from the Design tab. To make this tab visible, simply click in the chart whose layout you want to change.

Change the Chart Layout

① Click an empty area of the chart to select the chart.

② Click the **Design** tab on the Ribbon.

③ Click a new layout from the Chart Layouts group.

⬤ You can click the **More** button (⬚) to view the full palette of layouts.

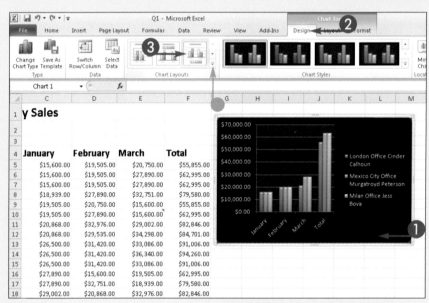

⬤ Excel applies the new layout to the existing chart.

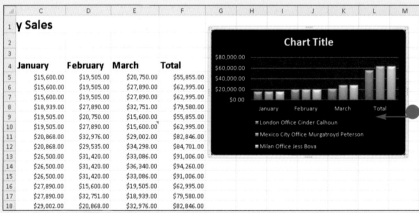

Add Axis Titles

Axes are used to show the scale of all of the values in a chart. The x-axis is the horizontal value display in a chart, and the y-axis is the vertical value display.

You can add titles to the axes on your chart to identify your chart data, positioning them as

desired. If your chart already has axis titles, you can change them.

You access options for axis titles from the Layout tab. To display this tab, simply click in the chart whose axes you want to change.

Add Axis Titles

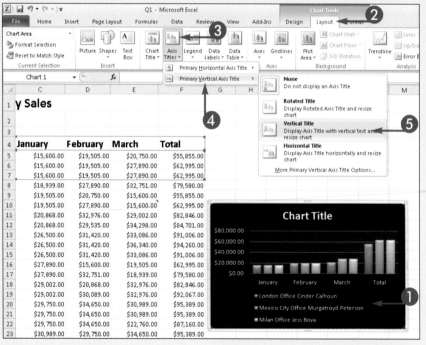

1 Click an empty area of the chart to select the chart.

2 Click the **Layout** tab on the Ribbon.

3 Click the **Axis Titles** button.

4 Click the **Primary Horizontal Axis Title** or **Primary Vertical Axis Title**.

5 Click an axis option.

● Excel adds the axis title to the chart.

6 Select the placeholder text and type over it with your own title text.

7 Click anywhere outside the axis title to deselect it.

Format Chart Objects

You can change the formatting of any element, or *object*, in a chart, such as the background pattern for the plot area or the color of a data series. To do so, you use the Format dialog box, which you access from the Format tab on the Ribbon. (To display this tab, simply click the object in the chart that you want to format.) The settings in this dialog box change depending on what object you select. This section covers changing the data series and data labels; you can apply these same techniques to format other chart objects.

Format Chart Objects

Format Data Series Objects

① Click the data series object that you want to edit.

● Excel automatically selects all corresponding objects in the series.

② Click the **Format** tab on the Ribbon.

③ Click the **Format Selection** button.

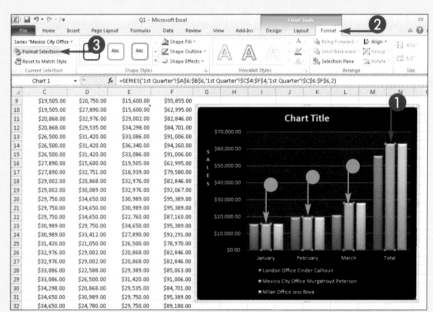

The Format Data Series dialog box appears.

④ Click the type of formatting that you want to change.

⑤ Change the desired settings.

⑥ Click **Close** to apply the changes.

● Excel applies your changes.

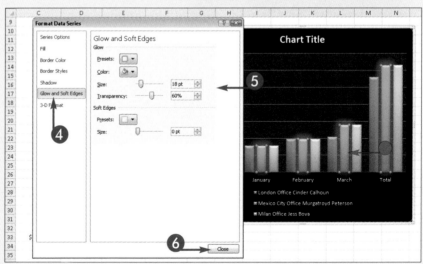

Format Data Labels

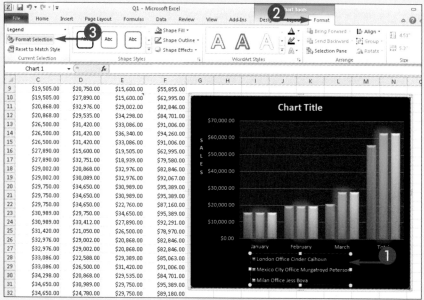

① Click the data label that you want to format.

② Click the **Format** tab on the Ribbon.

③ Click the **Format Selection** button.

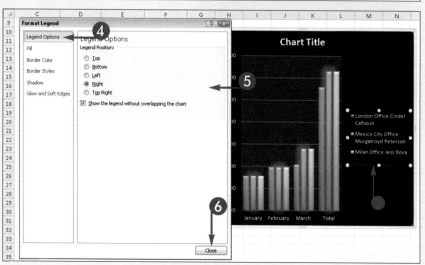

The Format Legend dialog box appears.

④ Click the type of formatting that you want to change.

⑤ Change the desired settings.

⑥ Click **Close** to apply the changes.

● Excel applies your changes.

How do I change the font for my chart text?
The quickest way to change the font is to select the chart element that contains text and then right-click the element to display the mini toolbar. From there, you can change the font, font size, font color, and font alignment, as well as apply bold and italics formatting.

How do I print my chart?
To print only the chart — not any worksheet data around it — click the chart to select it, click the **File** tab, and then click **Print**. The Print dialog box appears; ensure that the **Selected Chart** option is selected, and then click **Print**.

Add
Gridlines

As long as your chart is not a pie chart, you can add gridlines to it. You might add gridlines to a chart to make it easier to interpret. You add gridlines to a chart via the Layout tab on the Ribbon; to display this tab, simply click in the chart to which you want to apply gridlines.

Note that the Layout tab includes several chart objects that you can turn on or off in your chart; although this section shows how to turn on gridlines, you can use this same technique to display other objects.

Add Gridlines

① Click an empty area in the chart that you want to edit.

② Click the **Layout** tab on the Ribbon.

③ Click the **Gridlines** button.

④ Click the type of gridlines that you want to add.

Select **Primary Horizontal Gridlines** to add horizontal gridlines.

Select **Primary Vertical Gridlines** to add vertical gridlines.

⑤ Click a gridline option.

Excel adds the gridlines to the chart.

● This example adds horizontal gridlines.

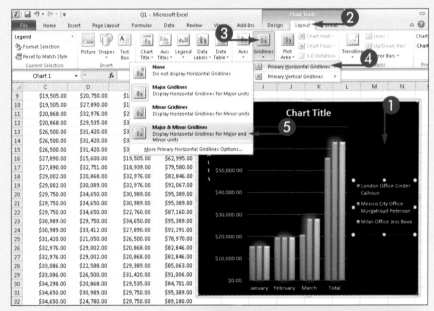

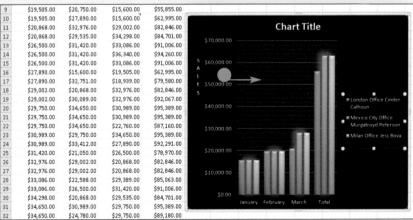

Change the Chart Data

Whenever you change data referenced in your chart, Excel automatically updates the chart data. If you are dealing with a large spreadsheet, however, locating the data you need to change can be difficult. Fortunately, Excel includes a special tool to help you do just that: the Select Data button on the Design tab.

(To display the Design tab, simply click the chart whose data you want to edit.) When you click the Select Data button, Excel highlights the data in the worksheet and launches the Select Data Source dialog box, where you can edit chart data as needed.

Change the Chart Data

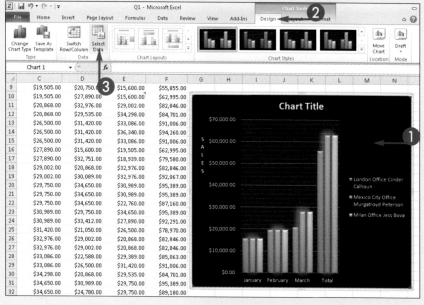

① Select the chart that you want to edit.

② Click the **Design** tab on the Ribbon.

③ Click the **Select Data** button.

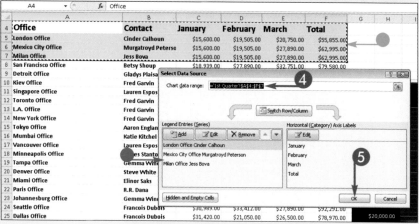

● Excel highlights the source data in the worksheet with a dashed border and displays the Select Data Source dialog box.

④ Edit the data range here, or click and drag the corner handle of the source range to add or subtract cells.

● You can edit the series or axis labels using these options.

⑤ Click **OK**.

Excel updates the chart.

Use Sparklines to View Data Trends

New in Excel 2010 are sparklines. Simple cell-sized graphics, *sparklines* show data trends, helping to bring meaning and context to the data they describe.

There are three types of sparklines: Line sparklines, which display a simple line chart within a single cell; Column sparklines, which display a simple column chart within a single cell; and Win/Loss sparklines, which display a win/loss chart in a single cell. To access sparkline options, you click the Insert tab on the Ribbon.

After you insert a sparkline, Excel displays the Sparkline Tools tab. Here, you can change the look and feel of the sparkline.

Use Sparklines to View Data Trends

1 Select the data for which you want to create a sparkline.

2 Click the **Insert** tab on the Ribbon.

3 In the Sparklines group, choose the type of sparkline you want to create.

In this example, **Column** is chosen.

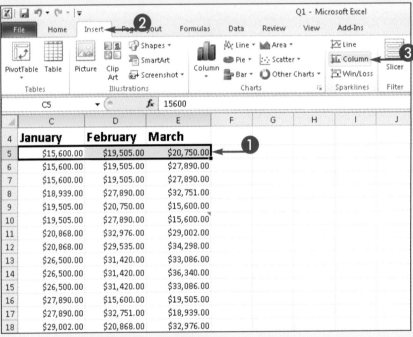

The Create Sparklines dialog box opens.

● The Data Range field already includes the data you selected in Step **1**.

4 Click the cell in your spreadsheet where you want to insert the sparkline.

A dotted line appears around the selected cell.

5 Click **OK**.

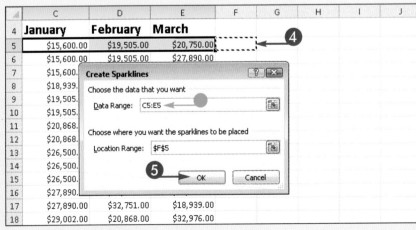

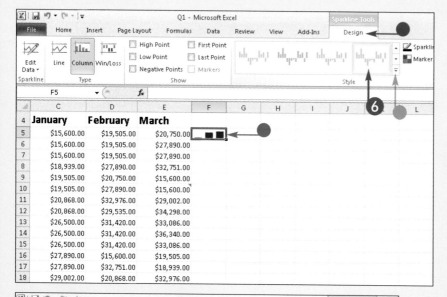

● Excel inserts the sparkline.

● Excel displays the Sparkline Tools tab. Here, you can choose a different type of sparkline, change the sparkline style and color, and more.

⑥ To change the style of the sparkline, click a style in the Style group.

● To view more styles, click the **More** button (⊡).

● Excel changes the sparkline style.

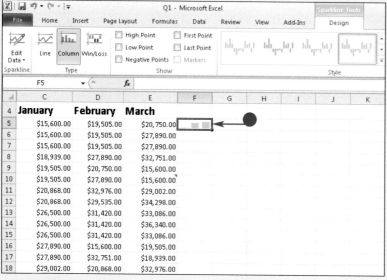

Simplify It

Can I edit my sparkline data?
Yes. To edit your sparkline data, simply edit the value in any cell to which your sparkline data refers. Excel updates the sparkline to reflect your changes. Alternatively, click the cell containing the sparkline. Excel displays the Design tab; click the **Edit Data** button to display the Edit Sparklines dialog box. Here, you can change the data range or the cell in which the sparkline graphic appears. When you finish, click **OK**.

Edit Sparklines

Choose the data that you want

Data Range: A5:E5

Choose where you want the sparklines to be placed

Location Range: F5

OK   Cancel

Part IV

PowerPoint

PowerPoint is a presentation program you can use to convey all kinds of messages to an audience. You can use PowerPoint to create slide shows to present ideas to clients, explain a concept or procedure to employees, or teach a class. In this part, you learn how to create slide shows; add text, tables, charts, video clips, and pictures to your slide show; and package your show

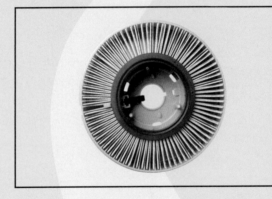

on a CD-ROM or output it as a movie file. You also learn how to add special effects, including animations, sound effects, and transitions to make your slide show lively and engaging.

Create a Photo Album Presentation

You can quickly turn any collection of digital photos on your computer into a slide show presentation in PowerPoint. For example, you might compile your photos from a recent vacation into a presentation. Alternatively, you might gather your favorite photos of a friend or loved one in a presentation. To liven up the presentation, you can include captions with your photos. You can also vary the layout of slides, including having one (the default), two, three, or more photos per slide. You can then share the presentation with others, or e-mail the file to family and friends.

Create a Photo Album Presentation

1 Click the **Insert** tab on the Ribbon.

2 Click **Photo Album**.

3 Click **New Photo Album**.

The Photo Album dialog box appears.

4 Click the **File/Disk** button.

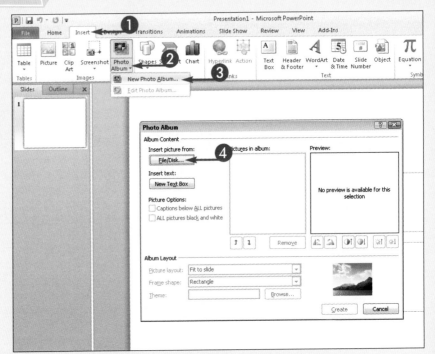

The Insert New Pictures dialog box appears.

5 Navigate to the folder or drive containing the digital pictures that you want to use.

6 Click the pictures that you want to use.

To use multiple pictures, you can press and hold Ctrl while clicking the pictures that you want to use.

7 Click **Insert**.

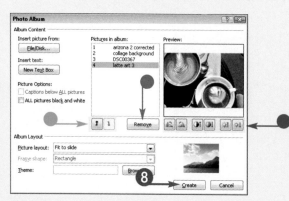

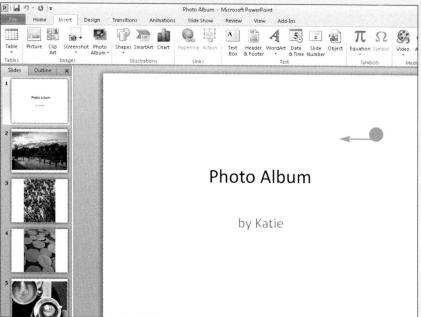

● You can change the picture order using these buttons.

● To remove a picture, you can click it in the Pictures in Album list and then click **Remove**.

● You can use the tool buttons to change the picture orientation, contrast, and brightness levels.

8 Click **Create**.

● PowerPoint creates the slide show as a new presentation file.

Note: *The first slide in the show is a title slide, containing the title "Photo Album" and your user name.*

Simplify It

How do I fit multiple pictures onto a single slide?
By default, PowerPoint displays one picture per slide, but you can use the Picture Layout setting in the Photo Album dialog box to display as many as four, with or without title text.

How do I add captions?
Select the **Captions Below All Pictures** check box in the Photo Album dialog box. (If this option is grayed out, choose a different layout option from the Picture Layout drop-down list.) Alternatively, add a text slide after each photo slide by clicking the **New Text Box** button. Type your captions after closing the Photo Album dialog box.

Create a Presentation with a Template

You can use PowerPoint's templates to help you create a new presentation, regardless of its subject matter. PowerPoint installs with a wide variety of presentation templates featuring various types of designs and color schemes. In addition to using templates that come preinstalled with Office, you can download PowerPoint templates from Office.com for use with your presentations. (Note that in order to use the templates offered on Office.com, your computer must be connected to the Internet.)

Create a Presentation with a Template

1 Click the **File** tab.

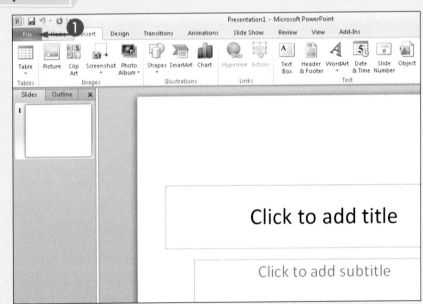

2 Click **New**.

3 Click **Sample templates**.

● You can click **New from existing** to create a new presentation based on the template of an existing one.

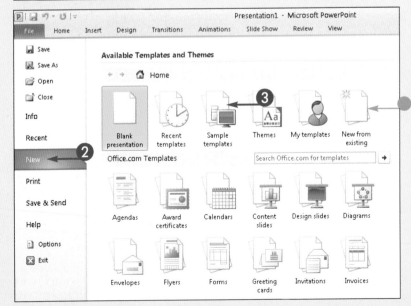

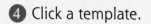
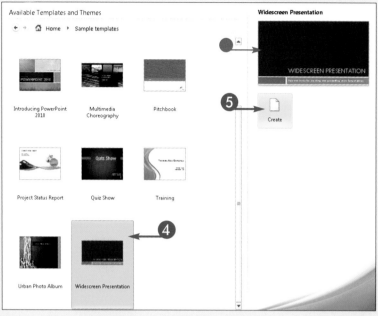

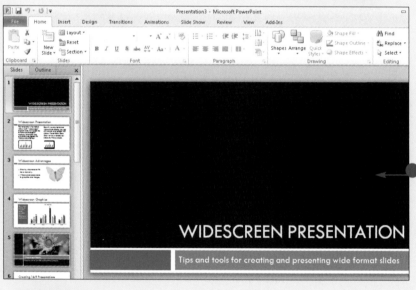

4️⃣ Click a template.

⬤ PowerPoint displays a preview of the template design.

5️⃣ Click **Create**.

⬤ PowerPoint creates the presentation using the template you chose and displays it in Normal view.

You can add your own text to each slide.

How do I download templates from Office.com?

To view available templates on Office.com, click the **File** tab in the PowerPoint program window, click **New**, and click the Office.com template category that you want to view, such as **Design Slides**. Click the template that you want, and then click the **Download** button to download it.

How do I navigate slides in a new presentation?

Click the **Outline** tab to view the new presentation in outline form. Click the **Slides** tab to view individual slides in the presentation. You can click a slide to view the larger slide in the work area and add your own presentation content.

Build a Blank Presentation

Whenever you start PowerPoint, it displays a blank slide. You can use this blank slide as the first slide in your presentation, adding more slides and formatting them as needed. Alternatively, if you are already working on a presentation, you can create a new blank presentation from scratch using the File menu.

Building a presentation in this manner rather than choosing from one of PowerPoint's existing templates allows you the freedom to create your own color schemes and apply your own design touches. If you build a presentation that you particularly like, you can save it as a template for future use.

Build a Blank Presentation

1 Click the **File** tab.

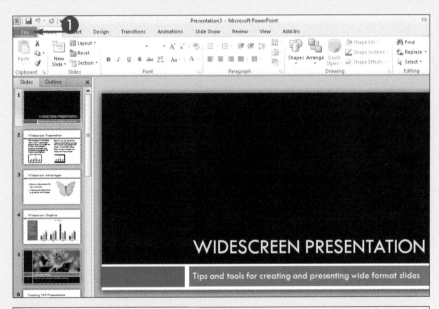

2 Click **New**.

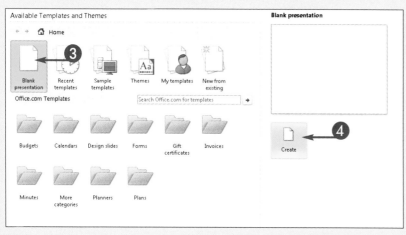

③ Click **Blank presentation**.

④ Click **Create**.

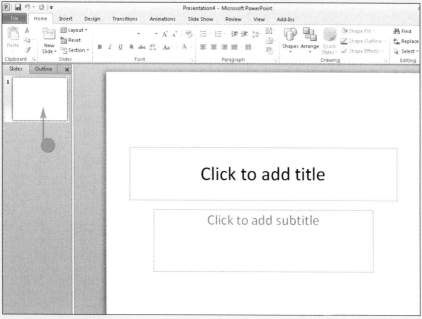

● PowerPoint creates a new presentation with one blank slide.

How do I save a presentation I create as a template?
If you create a presentation that you particularly like — for example, you have applied an eye-catching background and a pleasing font — you can turn that presentation into a template file that you can reuse to make new presentations. To do so, click the **File** tab and then click **Save As**. Then, in the Save As dialog box that appears, click the **Save as type** ⬒ and choose **PowerPoint Template**. Type a name for the template in the **File name** field and click **Save**. PowerPoint saves the presentation as a template, which you can access alongside other PowerPoint templates.

Change PowerPoint Views

You can use PowerPoint's views to change how your presentation appears on-screen. By default, PowerPoint displays your presentation in Normal view, with the Slides tab showing the order of slides in your presentation. You can view the Outline tab to see your presentation in an outline format, or switch to Slide Sorter view to see all the slides at the same time.

In addition to changing PowerPoint views, you can use the PowerPoint zoom settings to change the magnification of a slide. You can also change the size of the panes in the PowerPoint window, making them larger or smaller as needed.

Change PowerPoint Views

Use Outline View

1. While in Normal view, click the **Outline** tab.

   PowerPoint displays the presentation in an outline format.

● You can click the outline text to edit it.

● You can click a slide icon to view the slide.

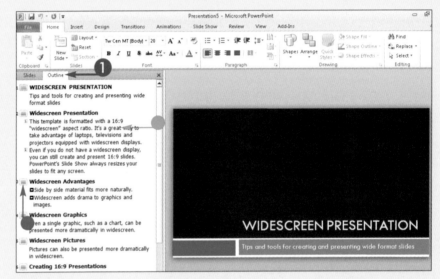

Use Slides View

1. Click the **Slides** tab.

● PowerPoint displays the current slide in the presentation.

● To view a particular slide, you can click the slide in the Slides tab.

● To close the tabs pane entirely and free up on-screen workspace, you can click the ⊠.

   Note: To redisplay the tabs pane, you can click the **View** tab on the Ribbon, and then click the **Normal** button.

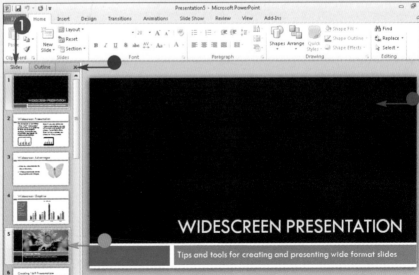

218

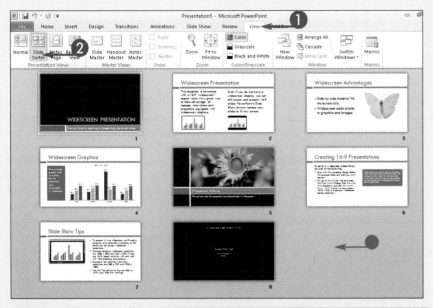

Use Slide Sorter View

1 Click the **View** tab.

2 Click the **Slide Sorter** button.

● PowerPoint displays all of the slides in the presentation.

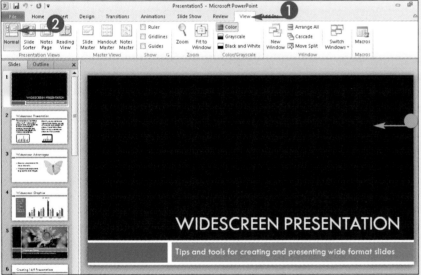

Use Normal View

1 Click the **View** tab.

2 Click the **Normal** button.

● PowerPoint returns to the default view, displaying the current slide in the presentation.

Simplify It

How do I zoom my view of a slide?
To change the magnification of a slide, you can drag the **Zoom** bar on the status bar at the bottom of the PowerPoint window. Alternatively, click the **View** tab, click the **Zoom** button, and choose the desired magnification in the Zoom dialog box that opens. Click the **Fit to Window** button to return to the default view.

Can I resize the PowerPoint panes?
Yes. Position the mouse pointer over the pane's border. When the ⬡ changes to ╫, click and drag inward or outward to resize the pane.

Insert Slides

PowerPoint makes it easy to add more slides to a presentation. To add a slide, you use the New Slide button on the Home tab.

Clicking the top half of the New Slide button adds a slide with the same layout as the one you selected in the Slides pane; alternatively, you can click the bottom half of the button and select a different layout.

You can add and remove slides on the Slides tab in Normal view, or you can switch to Slide Sorter view and manage your presentation's slides.

Insert Slides

1. In the Slides pane, click the slide after which you want to insert a new slide.

2. Click the **Home** tab.

3. Click the bottom half of the **New Slide** button.

4. Click a slide design.

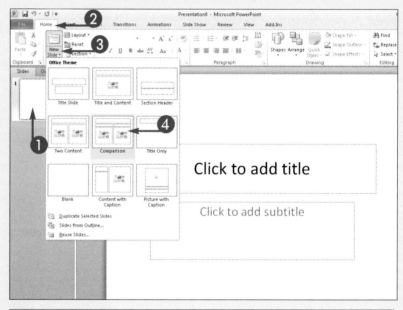

● PowerPoint adds a new slide.

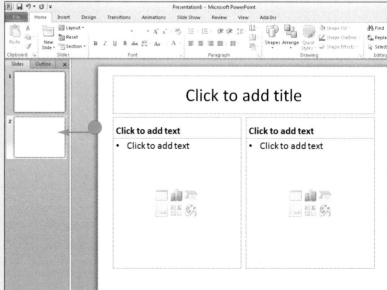

Change the Slide Layout

PowerPoint includes several predesigned slide layouts that you can apply to your slide. For example, you might apply a layout that includes a title with two content sections or a picture with a caption.

For best results, you should assign a new layout before adding content to your slides; otherwise, you may need to make a few adjustments to the content's position and size to fit the new layout.

In addition to using PowerPoint's predesigned slide layouts, you can also create your own custom layouts. To learn how to create a custom layout, see the next section, "Create a Custom Layout."

Change the Slide Layout

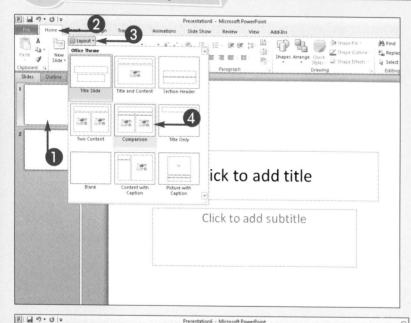

① Click the slide whose layout you want to change in the Slides tab.

② Click the **Home** tab on the Ribbon.

③ Click the **Layout** button.

④ Click a layout.

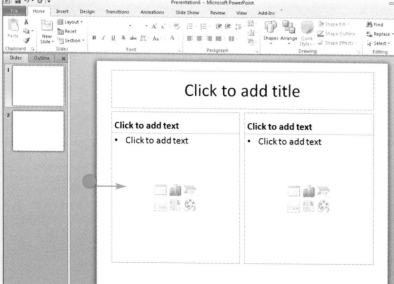

● PowerPoint assigns the layout to the slide.

Create a Custom Layout

In addition to choosing from a variety of preset layouts, as described in the preceding section, "Change the Slide Layout," you can create your own custom layouts.

When you create a custom layout, you control how many slide elements, also called objects, appear on the slide. These include text boxes, pictures, tables, charts, and more. You also control the placement of these items as well as their size.

You can reuse the custom layouts you create as needed; you apply these custom layouts the same way you do the predesigned layouts included in PowerPoint.

Create a Custom Layout

1 Click the **View** tab on the Ribbon.

2 Click the **Slide Master** button.

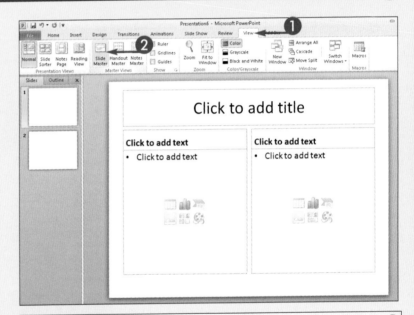

● PowerPoint displays the Slide Master view and opens the Slide Master pane.

3 Click the **Insert Layout** button on the Slide Master tab.

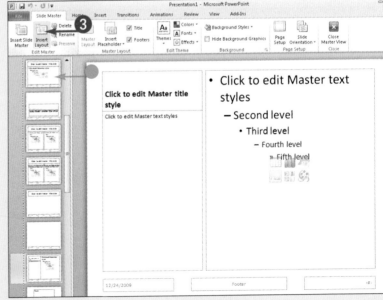

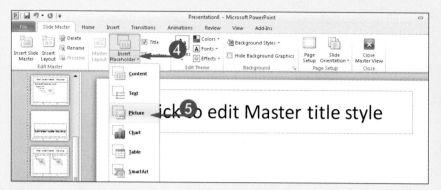

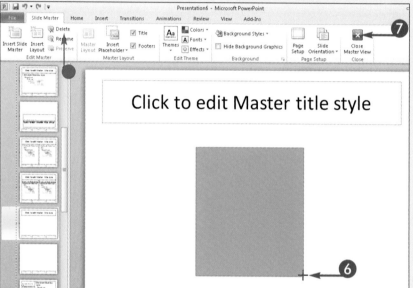

PowerPoint inserts a new layout that you can customize to suit your needs.

④ Click the bottom half of the **Insert Placeholder** button.

⑤ Click a slide object type.

⑥ Click and drag to set the object's size and placement.

You can add more elements.

● You can delete an object on the slide by selecting it and clicking the **Delete** button or pressing Delete.

***Note:** A quick way to delete the title and footer placeholders that appear in each new layout by default is to deselect the Title and Footers check boxes in the Slide Master tab's Master Layout group.*

⑦ Click the **Close Master View** button to close Slide Master view.

Simplify It

How do I apply my custom layout?
When you create a custom layout, you apply it to a slide the same way you do any predefined PowerPoint layout: by clicking the **Home** tab, clicking the **Layout** button, and choosing the layout from the list that appears (●). For more information, refer to the preceding section, "Change the Slide Layout."

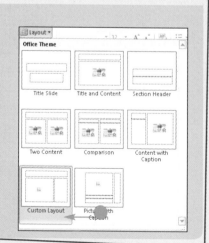

Add and Edit Slide Text

When you apply one of PowerPoint's text layouts to a slide, the text box appears with placeholder text. You can replace the placeholder text with your own text. You can do so either typing directly in the slide, as described in this section, or typing in the Outline tab that appears in the pane on the left side of the screen, as described in the tip on the next page. After you add your text, you can change its font, size, color, and more, as shown in the next section.

Add Slide Text

① Click the text box to which you want to add text.

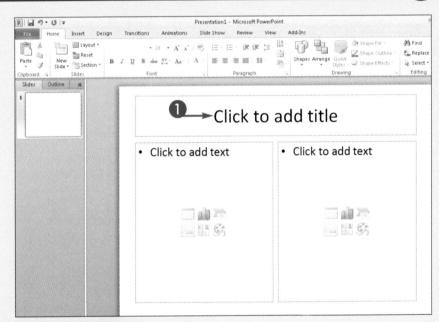

PowerPoint hides the placeholder text and displays a cursor.

② Type the text that you want to add.

224

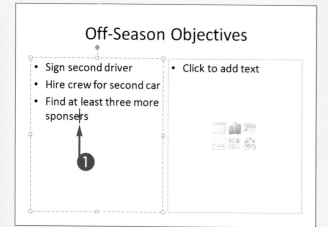

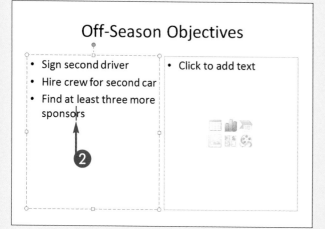

Edit Slide Text

① Click in the text box where you want to edit.

PowerPoint selects the text box and adds a cursor to the text box.

② Make any changes that you want to the slide text.

You can use the keyboard arrow keys to move the cursor in the text, or you can click where you want to make a change.

How do I add text using the Outline tab?

As mentioned, you can add text to a slide via the Outline tab in the pane on the left side of the screen. This tab enables you to view your entire presentation in outline format. You can also add text to slides in Outline view. To do so, follow these steps:

① Click the **Outline** tab.

② Click the slide that you want to edit.

③ Type the text that you want to add or change.

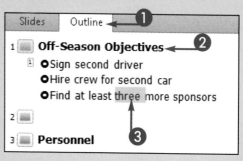

Change the Font, Size, and Color

After you add text to a slide (as described in the preceding section, "Add and Edit Slide Text"), you can change the slide text's font, size, color, and style to alter its appearance. For example, you might choose to increase the size of a slide's title text in order to draw attention to it, or change the font of the body text to match the font used in your company logo. Alternatively, you might change the text's color to make it stand out against the background color. You can also apply formatting to the text, such as bold, italics, underlining, shadow, or strikethrough.

Change the Font, Size, and Color

Change the Font

1 Select the text that you want to edit.

2 Click the **Home** tab on the Ribbon.

3 Click the **Font** ⏷.

4 Click a font.

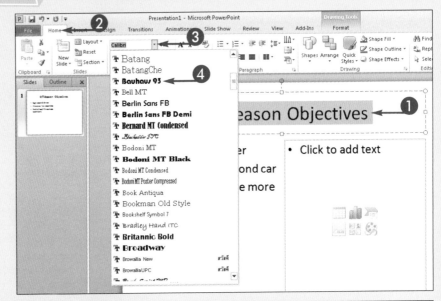

● PowerPoint applies the font you chose to the selected text.

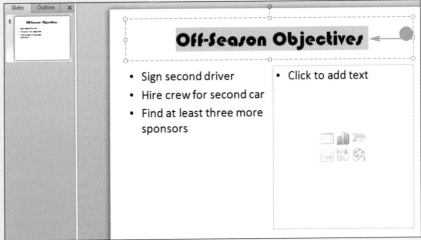

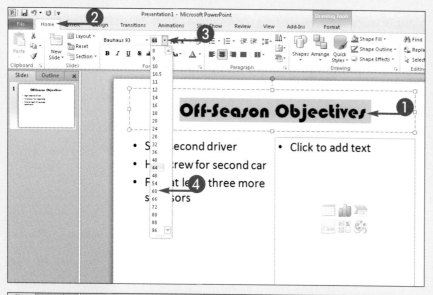

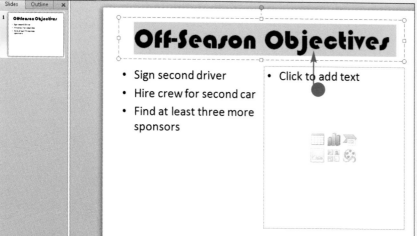

Change the Size

1. Select the text that you want to edit.

2. Click the **Home** tab on the Ribbon.

3. Click the **Font Size** ⊡.

4. Click a size.

● PowerPoint applies the font size you chose to the selected text.

Is there a quicker way to change the text size?
Yes. To quickly increase or decrease the font size, you can select the text you want to change and then click the **Increase Font Size** (A⏶) or **Decrease Font Size** (A⏷) button in the Home tab's Font group as many times as needed until the text is the desired size.

How do I apply text formatting?
Select the text whose format you want to change, and then click the **Bold** button (B), the **Italic** button (I), the **Underline** button (U), the **Shadow** button (S), or the **Strikethrough** button (abc).

continued

Change the Font, Size, and Color *(continued)*

In addition to changing the text's font and size, you can change its color. You might do so to make the text better stand out against the background, or to coordinate with colors used in other slide elements such as photographs.

You can change the text color using a number of methods. One is to select a color from the Font Color button on the Home tab; another is to launch the Colors dialog box and select a color from the palette that appears. In addition, you can apply your own custom color to text.

Change the Font, Size, and Color *(continued)*

Choose a Coordinating Color

1 Select the text that you want to edit.

2 Click the **Home** tab on the Ribbon.

3 Click the ▾ next to the **Font Color** button (△).

● PowerPoint displays coordinating theme colors designed to go with the current slide design.

4 Click a color.

● PowerPoint applies the color you chose to the selected text.

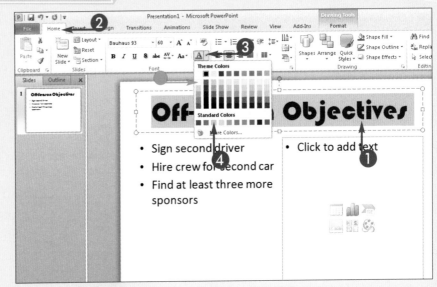

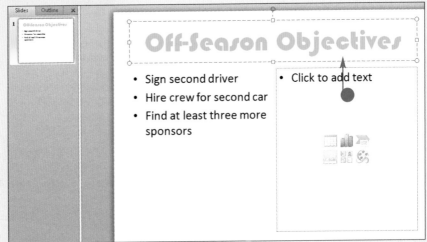

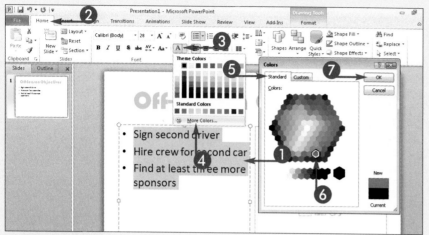

Open the Colors Dialog Box

1. Select the text that you want to edit.

2. Click the **Home** tab on the Ribbon.

3. Click the ⬝ next to the **Font Color** button (▣).

4. Click **More Colors**.

   The Colors dialog box appears.

5. Click the **Standard** tab.

6. Click a color.

7. Click **OK**.

● PowerPoint applies the color you chose to the selected text.

Simplify It

How do I set a custom color?

You set your own custom color for use with the slide text or other slide elements. Follow these steps:

1. Open the Colors dialog box, as shown in this section, and click the **Custom** tab.

2. Click the color that you want to customize.

3. Drag the intensity arrow to adjust the color intensity.

● You can also adjust the color channel settings.

4. Click **OK**.

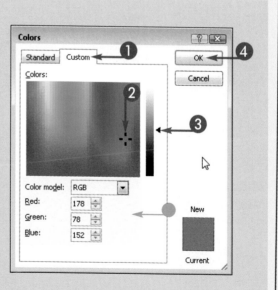

Apply a Theme

PowerPoint includes a variety of preset designs, called themes. A *theme* is a predesigned set of colors, fonts, backgrounds, and other visual attributes.

When you apply a theme to your presentation, you give every slide in your presentation the same look and feel. Alternatively, you can apply a theme to selected slides in your presentation. After you apply the theme, you can use controls in the Design tab to change various aspects of it.

Themes are shared among the Office programs; you can use the same theme in your PowerPoint presentations that you have applied to worksheets in Excel or documents in Word.

Apply a Theme

① Click the **Design** tab.

● You can scroll through the available themes; click the **More** button (▣) to view the full palette of themes.

② Right-click a theme from the Themes group.

③ Choose **Apply to All Slides** to apply the theme to the entire presentation.

Note: *To apply the theme to selected slides only, first select the slides to which you want to apply the theme in the Slides pane and then choose **Apply to Selected Slides** in Step 3.*

● PowerPoint applies the theme. Any slides you add will use the same theme.

● You can use these controls to customize various aspects of the theme, such as color and font.

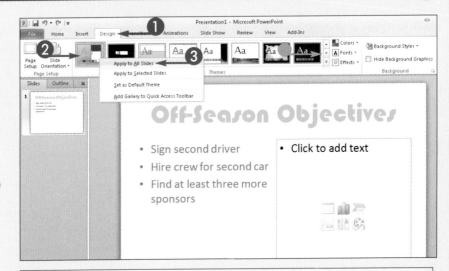

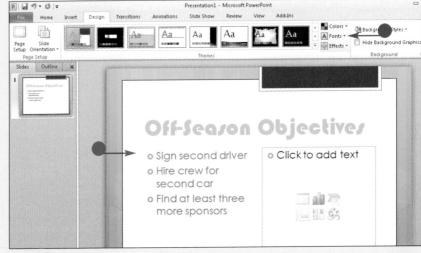

Set Line Spacing

You can change the line spacing in a PowerPoint slide to create more or less space between lines of text in the slide. For example, you might want to increase line spacing from the default 1.0 setting to a setting like 2.0 or even 3.0 so the text fills up more space in the text box, or to make the text easier to read. If, after increasing line spacing, you find that your text does not quite fit in its text box, you could reduce the line spacing to make room. You access PowerPoint line-spacing options from the Home tab.

Set Line Spacing

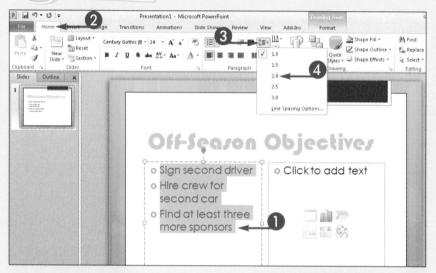

① Select the text that you want to edit.

② Click the **Home** tab on the Ribbon.

③ Click the ⬝ next to the **Line Spacing** button (⬛).

④ Click a line spacing amount.

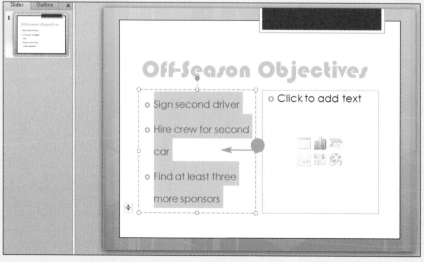

PowerPoint applies the line spacing.

● This example applies 2.0 spacing.

Align Text

By default, PowerPoint centers most text in text boxes (bulleted lists are left-aligned). If you want, you can use PowerPoint's alignment commands, located on the Home tab, to change how text is positioned horizontally in a text box. You can choose to center text in a text box (using the Center command), align text to the right side of the text box (using the Right Align command), or justify text and objects so they line up at both the left and right margins of the text box (using the Justify command).

Align Text

1 Select the text that you want to edit.

2 Click the **Home** tab on the Ribbon.

3 Click an alignment button.

Click the **Align Left** button (▤) to align the text to the left side of the text box.

Click the **Center** button (▤) to align the text in the center of the text box.

Click the **Align Right** button (▤) to align the text to the right side of the text box.

Click the **Justify** button (▤) to justify text between the left and right margins.

PowerPoint assigns the formatting.

● In this example, the text is right-aligned.

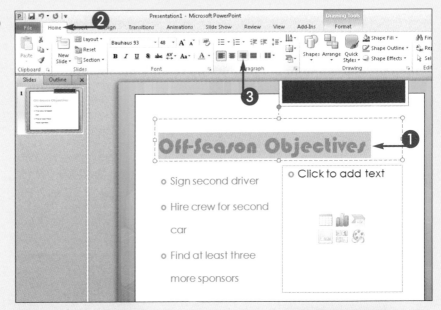

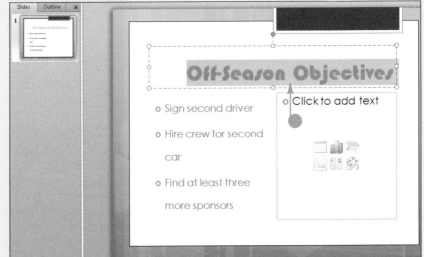

Add a Text
Box to a Slide

Often, you may choose to insert slides containing a predefined layout. You can customize the slide layout, however, by adding a new text box to it. A text box is simply a receptacle for text in a slide. (For help adding text to a text box, refer to the section "Add and Edit Slide Text" earlier in this chapter.)

When you add a new text box to a slide, you can control the placement and size of the box. (For help moving and resizing text boxes and other slide objects, see the sections "Move a Slide Object" and "Resize a Slide Object" later in this chapter.)

Add a Text Box to a Slide

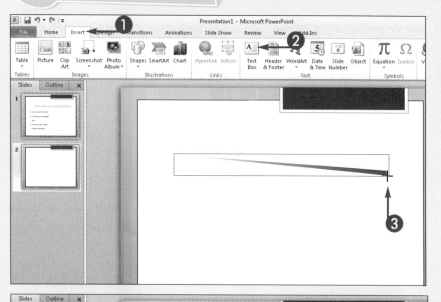

① Click the **Insert** tab on the Ribbon.

② Click the **Text Box** button.

③ Click and drag in the slide where you want to place a text box.

④ Click in the new text box and type your text.

You can click anywhere outside the text box to deselect it.

Add a Table to a Slide

You can customize the layout of a slide by adding a table to it. You might add tables to your slides to organize data in an orderly fashion. For example, you might use a table to display a list of products or classes. Tables use a column-and-row format to present information.

When you add a table to a slide, you can control the placement and size of the table. (For help moving and resizing tables and other slide objects, see the sections "Move a Slide Object" and "Resize a Slide Object" later in this chapter.)

Add a Table to a Slide

1 Click the **Insert Table** icon (▦) in your slide.

● If no Insert Table icon appears, click the **Table** button on the Insert tab and choose **Insert Table**.

The Insert Table dialog box appears.

2 Type the number of columns that you want to appear in the table.

3 Type the number of rows that you want to appear in the table.

4 Click **OK**.

● PowerPoint inserts the table into the slide.

● PowerPoint displays the Table Tools tabs on the Ribbon.

● Click an option in the Table Styles group to change the table style.

5 Click the first table cell and type your data.

Press Tab to move from cell to cell.

6 Type more table cell data to fill the table.

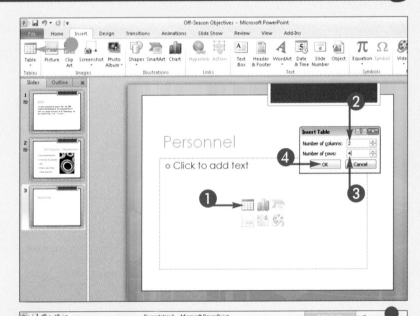

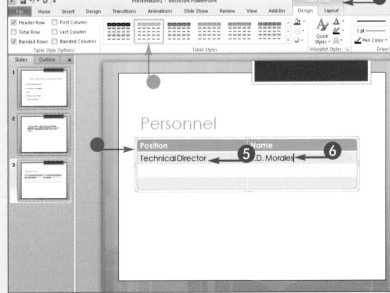

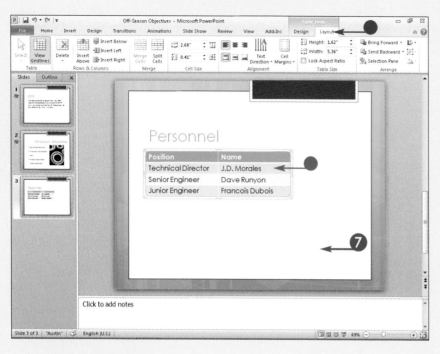

- You can use the tools in the Layout tab to merge table cells, split table cells, change alignment, add borders, and more.

- You can resize columns or rows by clicking and dragging the borders.

⑦ When you finish typing table data, click anywhere outside of the table area to deselect the table.

How do I add a column or a row to my table?
To add a column or a row to a table, follow these steps:

① Select a row or column adjacent to where you want to insert a new row or column.

② Click the **Layout** tab on the Ribbon.

③ Click an **Insert** button, such as **Insert Above** or **Insert Right**.

- PowerPoint inserts a new row or column.

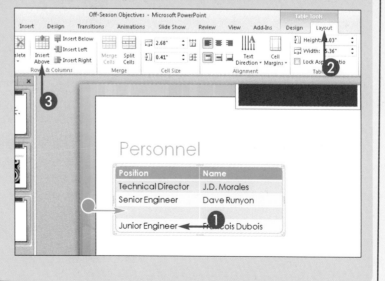

Add a Chart to a Slide

You can customize the layout of a slide by adding a chart to it. You might add a chart to a PowerPoint slide to turn numeric data into a visual element that your audience can quickly interpret and understand. When you add a chart, PowerPoint launches an Excel window, which you use to enter the chart data.

When you add a chart to a slide, you can control the placement and size of the chart. (For help moving and resizing charts and other slide objects, see the sections "Move a Slide Object" and "Resize a Slide Object" later in this chapter.)

Add a Chart to a Slide

1 If an **Insert Chart** icon (◨) appears in your slide, click it.

● If no Insert Chart icon appears in your slide, click the **Chart** button on the Insert tab.

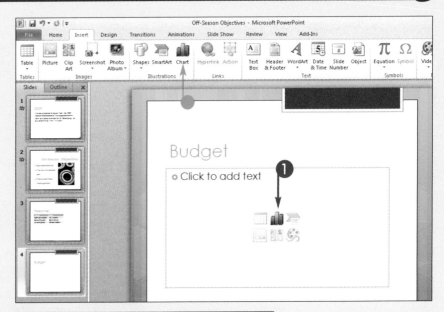

The Insert Chart dialog box appears.

2 Click a chart category.

3 Click a chart type.

4 Click **OK**.

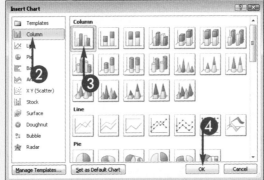

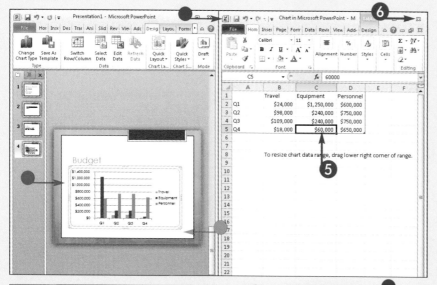

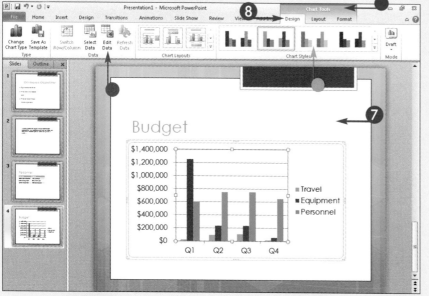

● PowerPoint displays a sample of the chart type on the slide.

● The Excel program window opens.

⑤ Replace the placeholder data with the chart data that you want to illustrate.

You can press **Tab** to move from cell to cell.

● The chart is updated to reflect the data you enter.

⑥ Click the **Close** button (❎) to close the Excel window.

⑦ Click in the chart.

● PowerPoint displays the Chart Tools tabs on the Ribbon.

⑧ Click the **Design** tab.

● To edit the chart data, click the **Edit Data** button.

● Click a Chart Styles button to change the chart style.

Can I insert an existing Excel chart into my PowerPoint slide?
Yes. You can use the Copy and Paste commands to copy an Excel chart and insert it into a PowerPoint slide. To learn more about copying and pasting data between Office programs, see Chapter 2.

How do I make changes to my chart formatting?
When you click a chart in a PowerPoint slide, the Ribbon displays three tabs: **Design**, with options for changing the chart layout and style; **Layout**, with tools for changing the axis, legend, and other chart elements; and **Format**, with tools for changing fill colors and shape styles.

Add a Picture to a Slide

One way to make your slides more visually appealing is to insert photographs or other pictures. When you add a picture to a slide, you can control the placement and size of the picture as well as perform other types of edits on the image. (For help moving and resizing charts and other slide objects, see the sections "Move a Slide Object" and "Resize a Slide Object" later in this chapter.)

In addition to inserting your own picture files into your PowerPoint slides, you can insert clip art, which is premade artwork supplied by Microsoft.

Add a Picture to a Slide

1 If an **Insert Picture** icon (⊡) appears in your slide, click it.

● If no Insert Picture icon appears in your slide, click the **Picture** button on the Insert tab.

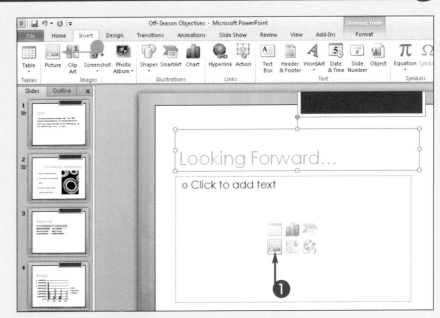

The Insert Picture dialog box opens.

2 Locate and select the picture you want to insert.

3 Click **Insert**.

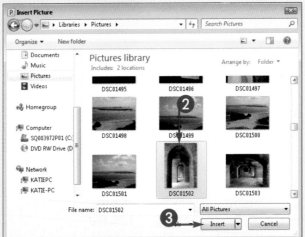

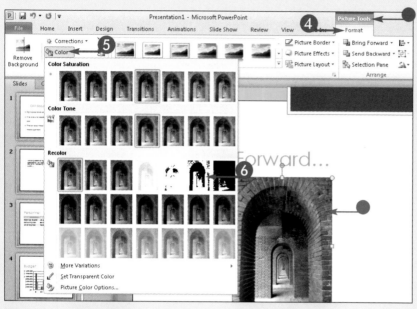

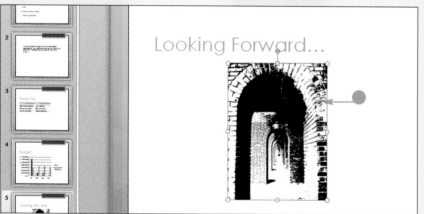

● PowerPoint inserts the picture into the slide.

● PowerPoint displays the Picture Tools Format tab on the Ribbon.

④ To edit the picture (in this example, to change its color), click the **Format** tab.

⑤ Click the **Color** button.

⑥ Choose a color option.

● PowerPoint updates the image to reflect your edits.

How do I add clip art to a slide?
To add clip art to a slide, follow these steps:

① Click the **Clip Art** icon (📧) in your slide or click the **Clip Art Pane** button on the Insert tab.

② In the Clip Art task pane, type a keyword or phrase for the type of clip art that you want to insert.

③ Click **Go**.

● The Clip Art task pane displays any matches for the keyword or phrase that you typed. To add a clip art image to your slide, click the image.

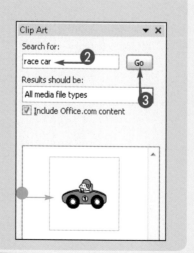

Add a Video Clip to a Slide

You can add video clips to your PowerPoint slides to play during a slide show presentation. For example, when creating a presentation showcasing the latest company product, you might place a video clip of the department head discussing the new item.

When you add a video to a slide, you can control the placement and size of the video.

(For help moving and resizing charts and other slide objects, see the sections "Move a Slide Object" and "Resize a Slide Object" later in this chapter.)

After you insert a video into a PowerPoint slide, you can make certain edits to that video from within PowerPoint.

Add a Video Clip to a Slide

1 If an **Insert Media Clip** icon (🎞) appears in your slide, click it.

● If no Insert Media Clip icon appears in your slide, click the **Video** button on the Insert tab.

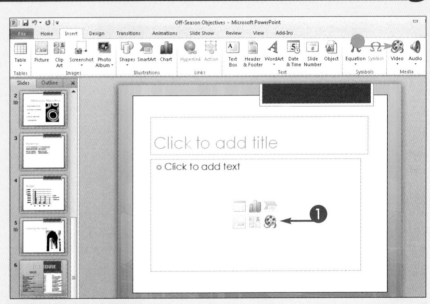

The Insert Video dialog box appears.

2 Locate and select the video you want to insert.

3 Click **Insert**.

● PowerPoint inserts the clip into the slide.

● PowerPoint displays the Video Tools tabs on the Ribbon.

④ Click the **Format** tab.

● You can click an option in the Video Styles group to change the appearance of the video.

● You can use the options in the Size group to adjust the size of the clip on the slide.

● Click the **Play** button (▶) to play back the clip.

Note: *You can click the **Playback** tab and use the settings in the Video Options group to specify when the clip should start playing, whether it should be looped, how loudly it should play, and so on.*

Simplify It

Can I edit my video clip in PowerPoint?
Yes. You can edit your video using the tools in the Playback tab's Editing group. Specifically, you can set up the clip to fade in and fade out using the **Fade In** and **Fade Out** fields. You can also click the **Trim Video** button to open the Trim Video dialog box, where you can change the duration of the video by trimming frames from the beginning or end of the clip.

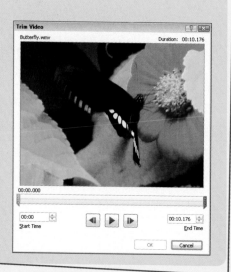

Move a Slide Object

You can move any slide element, such as a text box, table, chart, picture, video clip, or any other element, to reposition it in the slide. (These slide elements are often referred to as objects.) For example, you might move a text box to make room for a clip-art object or move a picture to improve the overall appearance of the slide.

One way to move a slide object is to use the standard Office Cut and Paste buttons, discussed in Chapter 2. Another is to drag and drop the object, as discussed in this section.

Move a Slide Object

① Click the slide object that you want to move to select it.

The ▷ changes to ✥.

② Drag the object to a new location on the slide.

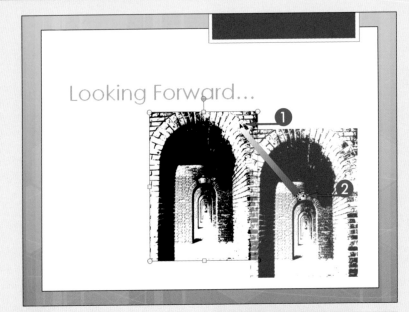

③ Release the mouse button.

● PowerPoint repositions the object.

④ Click outside the slide object to deselect it.

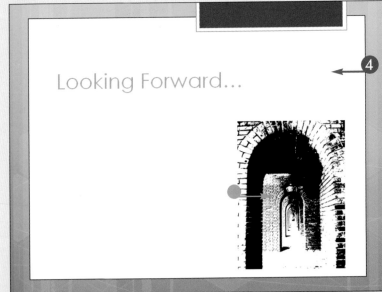

Resize a Slide Object

After you insert an object, such as a text box, table, chart, picture, video clip, or any other element, you may find that you need to make it larger or smaller in order to achieve the desired effect. For example, you might want to resize a text box to make room for more text or resize a picture object to enlarge the artwork. Fortunately, PowerPoint makes it easy to change the size of a slide object. When you select an object in a PowerPoint slide, handles appear around that object; you can use these handles to make the object larger or smaller.

Resize a Slide Object

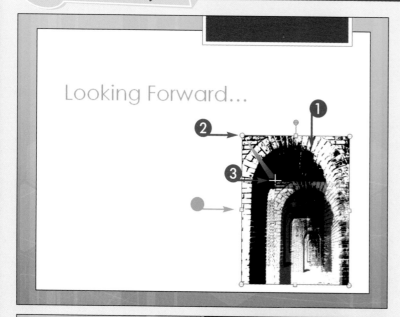

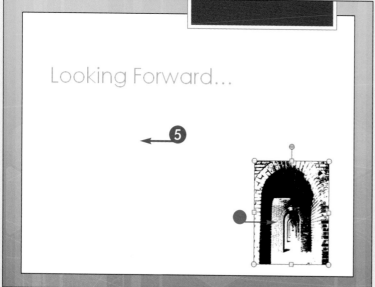

① Click the slide object that you want to resize to select it.

● PowerPoint surrounds the object box with handles.

② Position your mouse pointer over a handle.

The ▷ changes to ⤢.

③ Click and drag the handle inward or outward to resize the slide object.

Drag a corner handle to resize the object's height and width at the same time.

Drag a side handle to resize the object only along the one side.

④ Release the mouse button.

● PowerPoint resizes the object.

⑤ Click outside the slide object to deselect it.

Note: *To delete a slide object that you no longer need, select the object and press* `Delete`.

Reorganize Slides

You can change the order of your slides. For example, you may want to move a slide to appear later in the presentation, or swap the order of two side-by-side slides. PowerPoint makes it easy to change the slide order in Slide Sorter view or by using the Slides tab in Normal view. (To switch to Slide Sorter view, click the View tab and then click the Slide Sorter button. To switch back to Normal view, click the Normal button in the View tab.) You can move individual slides, or move multiple slides at once.

Move Slides in Normal View

1 In Normal view, click the slide that you want to move on the Slides tab.

Note: *You can move multiple slides at once. To do so, press and hold* **Ctrl** *as you click each slide, and then drag the slides to a new location.*

2 Drag the slide to a new location on the tab.

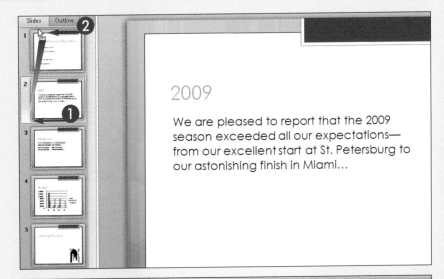

3 Release the mouse button.

● PowerPoint moves the slide.

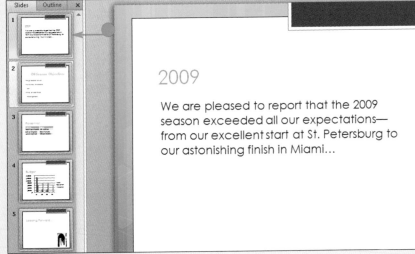

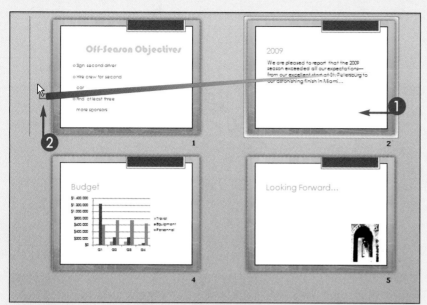

Move Slides in Slide Sorter View

① In Slide Sorter view, click the slide that you want to move.

Note: *You can move multiple slides at once. To do so, press and hold* **Ctrl** *as you click each slide, and then drag the slides to a new location.*

② Drag the slide to a new location in the presentation.

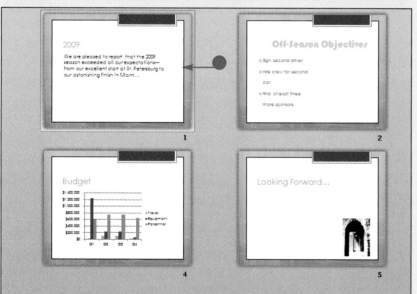

③ Release the mouse button.

● PowerPoint moves the slide.

How do I hide a slide?

Suppose you frequently give the same presentation, but your next audience does not require the information in one of the presentation slides. In that case, you can hide the slide. To do so, switch to Slide Sorter view, click the **Slide Show** tab, and then click the **Hide Slide** button. The Hide Slide icon (▨) appears next to the slide in Slide Sorter view. To unhide the slide, repeat these steps.

How do I delete a slide?

To delete a slide, right-click it in Slide Sorter view or in the Slides tab and choose **Delete Slide** from the menu that appears.

Reuse a Slide

Suppose you are creating a new PowerPoint presentation, but you want to reuse a slide from an old one. Assuming the presentation containing the slide you want to reuse has been saved on your hard drive or is accessible to you via a network connection, you can easily do so. To choose the slide you want to reuse, you use the Reuse Slides pane.

When you reuse a slide, PowerPoint updates the slide to match the formatting used in the new presentation.

You can reuse a single slide from a presentation, multiple slides from a presentation, or all the slides in a presentation.

Reuse a Slide

1 In Slide Sorter view, click where you want the new slide to appear.

2 Click the **Home** tab.

3 Click the bottom half of the **New Slide** button.

4 Click **Reuse Slides**.

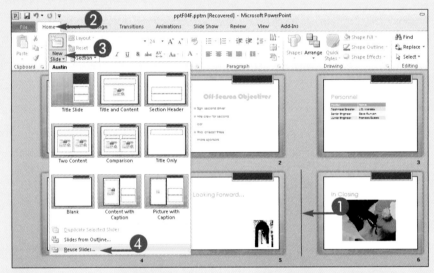

The Reuse Slides pane opens.

5 Click the **Browse** button.

6 Click **Browse File**.

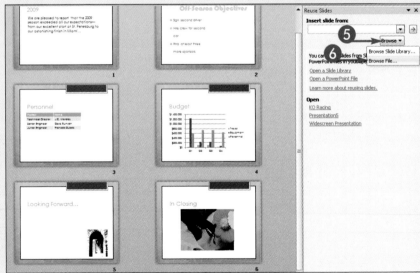

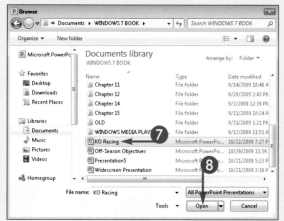

The Browse dialog box opens.

7 Locate and select the presentation containing the slide you want to reuse.

8 Click **Open**.

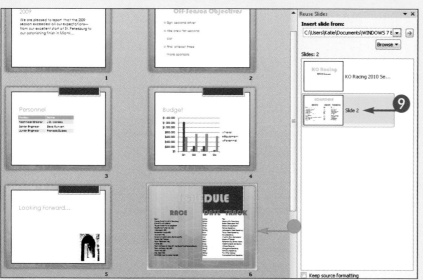

PowerPoint populates the Reuse Slides pane with slides in the presentation you selected.

9 Click the slide you want to reuse.

● PowerPoint adds the slide to your presentation.

Can I retain the reused slide's original formatting?
Yes. To retain the reused slide's original formatting, select the **Keep Source Formatting** check box in the Reuse Slides pane. To change all the slides in the new presentation to match the reused slide, right-click the reused slide in the Reuse Slides pane and choose **Apply Theme to All Slides**.

How do I reuse all the slides in a presentation?
To reuse all the slides in a presentation, right-click any one slide in the Reuse Slides pane and choose **Insert All Slides**. PowerPoint inserts all the slides from the existing presentation into the new presentation.

Define Slide Transitions

You can add transition effects, such as fades, dissolves, and wipes, to your slides to control how one slide segues to the next. You control the speed of the transition to appear fast or slow. You can also specify how PowerPoint advances the slides, either manually or automatically. In addition to adding transition

effects between your slides that are visual in nature, you can add sound effects to serve as transitions.

Take note: You must use good judgment when assigning transitions. Using too many different types of transitions may detract from your presentation.

Define Slide Transitions

1 In Slide Sorter view, click the slide to which you want to apply a transition.

2 Click the **Transitions** tab on the Ribbon.

● You can scroll through the available transition effects and click the **More** button (▾) to view all of the transition effects.

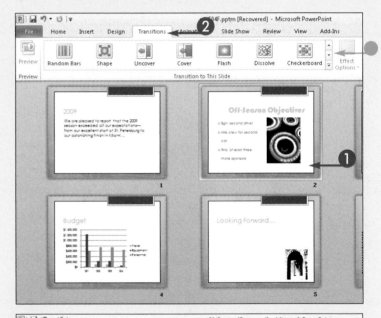

3 Click a transition.

● PowerPoint displays a preview of the transition effect.

● PowerPoint adds an animation icon (▢) below the slide.

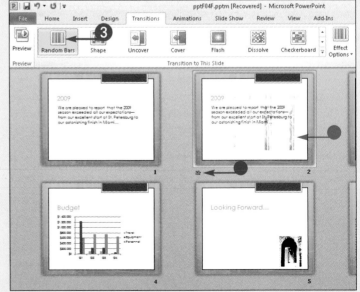

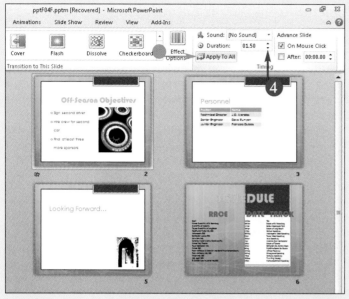

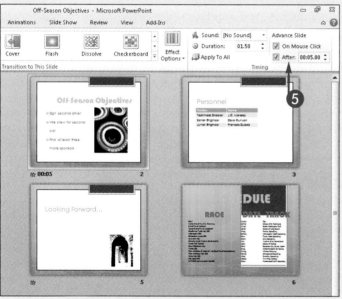

④ Click the **Duration** � to specify a speed setting for the transition.

● You can click **Apply To All** to apply the same transition to the entire slide show.

⑤ Under Advance Slide, click an advance option.

To use a mouse click to move to the next slide, select the **On Mouse Click** check box.

To move to the next slide automatically, select the **After** check box and use the 🔳 to specify a duration.

Simplify It

How do I remove a transition effect?
In Slide Sorter view, select the slide containing the transition that you want to remove; then click the **Transitions** tab and click the **None** option in the Transition to This Slide group. PowerPoint removes the transition that you assigned.

How do I assign a sound as a transition effect?
To assign a sound transition, click the **Sound** ▾ in the Transitions tab's Timing group and select a sound. You might assign the Applause sound effect for the first or last slide in a presentation, for example.

Add Animation Effects

You can use PowerPoint's animation effects to add visual interest to your presentation. For example, if you want your audience to notice a company logo on a slide, you might apply an animation effect to that logo.

There are four types of animation effects: entrance effects, emphasis effects, exit effects, and motion paths. You can add any of these

effects to any slide element, such as a text box or a picture. You can also edit your animations.

Take note: You must use good judgment when adding animation effects. To avoid overwhelming your audience, limit animations to slides in which the effects will make the most impact.

Add Animation Effects

Add a Simple Animation Effect

1. In Normal view, click the slide object to which you want to apply an animation.

2. Click the **Animations** tab.

● You can scroll through the available animation effects and click the **More** button (⊡) to view all of the animation effects.

● You can also click the **Add Animation** button and choose **More Entrance Effects**, **More Emphasis Effects**, **More Exit Effects**, or **More Motion Paths** from the menu that appears.

3. Click an animation effect.

● PowerPoint applies the effect and previews the effect on the slide.

● You can click the **Preview** button to preview the effect again.

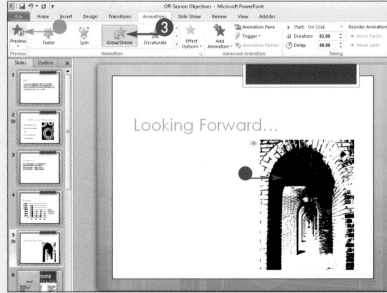

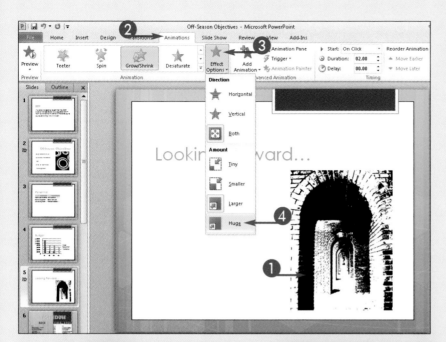

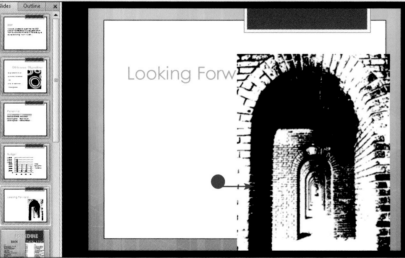

Edit an Animation

1 In Normal view, click the slide element containing the animation you want to edit.

2 Click the **Animations** tab on the Ribbon.

3 Click the **Effect Options** button.

A list of editing options for the animation appears.

4 Select an option from the list.

● PowerPoint applies the change and previews the effect on the slide.

Can I copy an animation effect to another slide object?
Yes. PowerPoint's Animation Painter feature enables you to copy an animation effect applied to one slide object to another slide object. To copy an animation effect, select the slide object whose effect you want to copy; then, in the Animations tab's Advanced Animation group, click the **Animation Painter** button. Next, in the Slides tab, click the slide containing the object to which you want to apply the effect to display it; then click the object. PowerPoint copies the animation effect to the slide object.

Create a Custom Animation

In addition to applying one of PowerPoint's predesigned animation effects to a slide object, such as a text box, picture, chart, or table, you can use these effects as building blocks to create your own custom effects. That is, you build a custom animation by applying two or more of these predesigned "building block"

animations to a PowerPoint object. (Note that when you apply multiple animation effects to a slide object, you must use the Add Animation button instead of choosing an effect from the Animation group. Otherwise, the new effect overwrites the existing one.)

Create a Custom Animation

① In Normal view, click the slide element to which you want to apply an animation.

② Click the **Animations** tab.

③ Apply an animation effect. (This effect is the first "building block" of your custom animation.)

PowerPoint applies the animation effect.

④ Click the **Animation Pane** button in the Advanced Animation group.

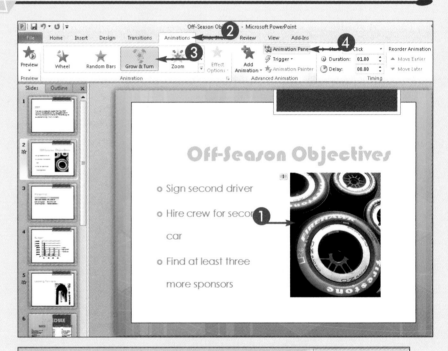

PowerPoint displays the Animation pane.

● The animation you applied appears in the pane.

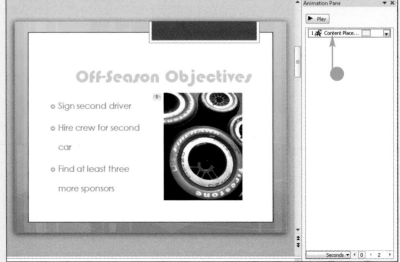

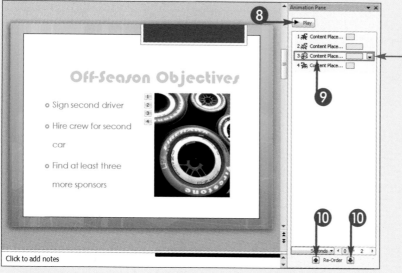

⑤ To add your next building block, click the **Add Animation** button in the Advanced Animation group.

⑥ Click an effect.

PowerPoint adds the effect to the Animation pane.

⑦ Repeat Steps **5** and **6** to add more building blocks.

● PowerPoint places each effect in the Animation pane, in the order you added them.

⑧ To preview your custom effect, click **Play**.

PowerPoint plays back your custom animation.

⑨ To change the order in which effects are played back, click an effect.

⑩ Click the **Re-Order** buttons (⬆ or ⬇) to move the selected effect up or down in the list.

Simplify It

How do I remove an animation?
Select the slide element containing the effect, click the **Animations** tab, and click **No Animation**. If the animation is a custom animation, click the **Animation Pane** button. Then, in the Animation pane, click the effect that you want to remove, click the ⬛ that appears, and click **Remove**.

Can I change the duration of an effect?
Yes. Select the slide element containing the effect, click the **Animation Pane** button, click the effect whose duration you want to change, click the ⬛ that appears, choose **Timing**, and use the settings in the dialog box that opens to achieve the desired effect.

Record Narration

Many presentations benefit from narration. One way to provide narration is to simply speak during your presentation. Alternatively, you can use PowerPoint's Record Narration feature to record a narration track to go along with the show (assuming, of course, that your computer has a microphone). That way, you need not be present for your audience to receive the full impact of your presentation. PowerPoint saves the recorded narration along with the presentation file. When you finish recording, an audio icon appears at the bottom of each slide for which you have recorded narration.

Record Narration

1. Click the **Slide Show** tab on the Ribbon.

2. Click **Record Slide Show**.

   The Record Slide Show dialog box appears.

   ● Make sure the **Narrations and laser pointer** check box is selected.

3. Click **Start Recording**.

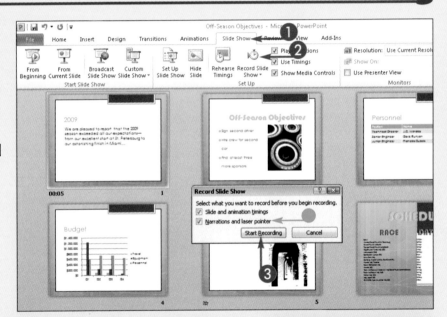

PowerPoint starts the show, and you can begin talking into the computer's microphone to record your narration.

● Click 🔁 to move to the next slide in the show.

● Click � to pause the recording.

● Click 🔄 to start over on the current slide.

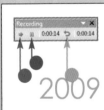

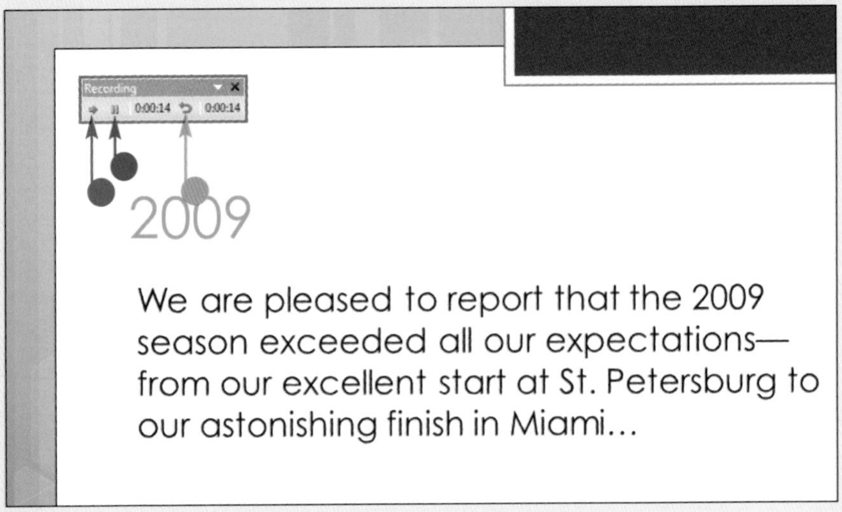

Set Up a Slide Show

You can set up how you want your presentation to run. For example, you can specify whether it should loop continuously, be played back in full, be shown without narration or animations, and more. If the presentation will be presented by a speaker (rather than, for example, run at

a kiosk), you can choose a pen color and a laser pointer color; the speaker can then use his or her mouse pointer to draw on or point to slides. To set up your slide show, you use the Set Up Show dialog box.

Set Up a Slide Show

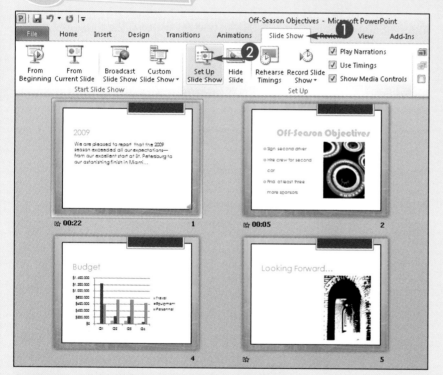

① Click the **Slide Show** tab on the Ribbon.

② Click **Set Up Slide Show**.

The Set Up Show dialog box appears.

③ Set any options that you want to assign to the show.

● The Show Type settings specify how the slide show is presented.

● The Show Options settings control looping, narration, and animation.

● The Show Slides settings specify what slides appear in the show.

● The Advance Slides settings specify how each slide advances.

● If your system has multiple monitors, you can use the Multiple Monitors settings to specify what monitor to use for your presentation.

④ Click **OK**.

PowerPoint assigns the new settings.

Create Speaker Notes

You can create speaker notes for your presentation. Speaker notes, also called notes pages, are notations that you add to a slide and that you can print out and use to help you give a presentation. (Be aware that in order to print out your notes, you must change the PowerPoint print settings. For guidance, see the tip at the end of this section.) You can also use speaker notes as handouts for your presentation. When creating notes pages, PowerPoint includes any note text that you add, as well as a small picture of the actual slide.

Create Speaker Notes

1. In Normal view, click a slide in the Slides tab to which you want to add notes.

2. Click in the Notes pane.

3. Type any notes about the current slide that you want to include.

   You can repeat Steps 1 to 3 for other slides to which you want to add notes.

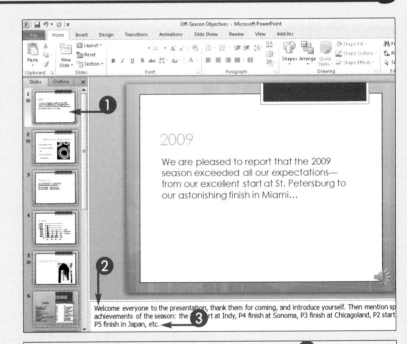

4. Click the **View** tab.

5. Click **Notes Page**.

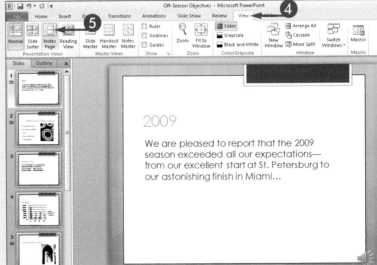

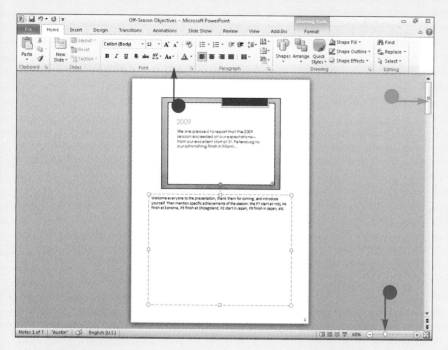

The Notes Page view opens and displays the first page in your slide show.

● You can use the scroll bars to scroll through the notes.

● You can drag the Zoom slider to magnify your view of the notes.

● You can edit and format your notes text.

Note: *To return to Normal view, click the* **View** *tab and click the* **Normal** *button.*

Simplify It

How do I print my notes?
Before you can print your notes, you must configure PowerPoint to do so. Follow these steps:

❶ Click the **File** tab and then click **Options**.

The PowerPoint Options dialog box appears.

❷ Click **Advanced**.

❸ Under When Printing This Document, click the **Use the following print settings** radio button.

❹ Click the **Print what** ⊡ and choose **Notes**.

❺ Click **OK**.

❻ Click the **File** tab, choose **Print**, and choose the desired settings.

When printing this document: 🄿 Off-Season Objectives ▼

○ Use the most recently used print settings ⓘ

● Use the following print settings: ⓘ

    Print what: Full Page Slides ▼

    Color/grayscale: Full Page Slides

    ☐ Print hidden s   Handouts (2 slides per page)

    ☐ Scale to fit pa   Handouts (3 slides per page)

                  Handouts (6 slides per page)

    ☐ Fra_me slides   Notes

General   Outline

Rehearse a Slide Show

You can time exactly how long each slide displays during a presentation using PowerPoint's Rehearse Timings feature. When you use Rehearse Timings, PowerPoint switches to Slide Show mode, displaying your slides in order; you control when PowerPoint advances to the next slide in the show.

When recording how long each slide is shown, you should rehearse what you want to say during each slide as well as allow the audience time to read the entire content of each slide.

After you record the timings, PowerPoint saves them for use when you present the slide show to your audience.

Rehearse a Slide Show

① Click the **Slide Show** tab.

② Click the **Rehearse Timings** button.

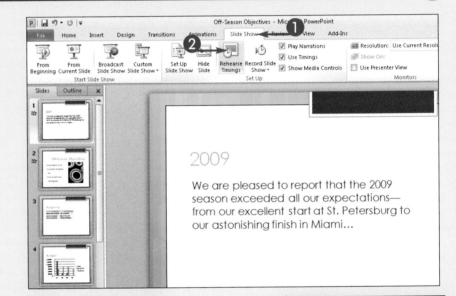

● PowerPoint switches to Slide Show mode and displays the first slide.

● PowerPoint displays the Record Slide Show toolbar and starts a timer.

③ Rehearse what you want to say while the slide plays.

● Click the **Pause** button (⏸) to pause the timer. To restart the timer, you can click ⏸ again.

④ When you finish with the first slide, click the **Next** button (➡).

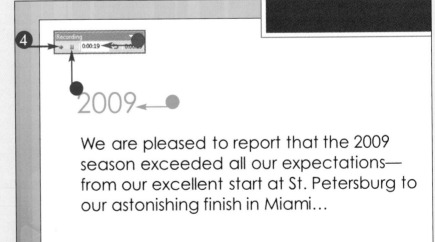

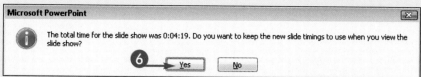

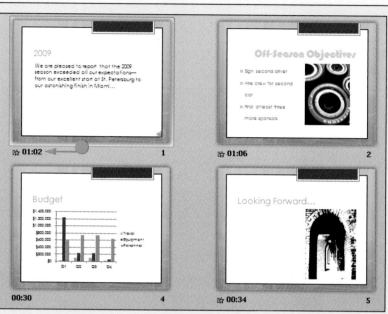

PowerPoint displays the next slide.

⑤ Repeat Steps **3** and **4** for each slide in your presentation.

When the slide show is complete, a dialog box appears, displaying the total time for the slide show.

⑥ Click **Yes**.

● PowerPoint saves the timings and displays them below each slide.

How do I create handouts for my audience?
One way to create handouts is to send your presentation to Microsoft Word. Follow these steps:

① Click the **File** tab and then click **Share**.

② Click **Create Handouts**.

③ Click **Create Handouts**.

The Send To Microsoft Word dialog box appears.

④ Choose a page layout.

⑤ Click **OK**.

Office launches Microsoft Word, with your presentation pasted in.

⑥ Click the **File** tab, choose **Print**, and choose the desired settings.

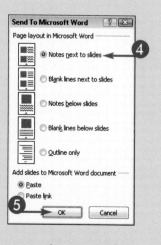

Run a Slide Show

You can run a slide show presentation using PowerPoint's Slide Show view. Slide Show view displays full-screen images of your slides. You can advance each slide manually by clicking buttons that appear on-screen; alternatively, you can instruct PowerPoint to advance the slides for you.

To enrich the experience for your audience, you can use PowerPoint's pointer options to draw directly on the screen using the mouse pointer. (You can choose from several pen tools and colors.) For example, you might circle an important sales figure or underline a critical point on a slide. You can end a slide show at any time by pressing Esc.

Run a Slide Show

1 Click the **Slide Show** tab.

2 Click the **From Beginning** button.

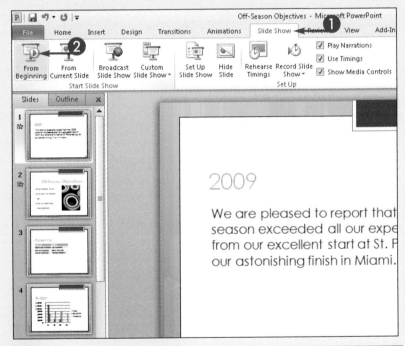

PowerPoint switches to Slide Show mode and displays the first slide.

● When you move the mouse pointer to the bottom left corner, faint slide show control buttons appear.

3 Click anywhere in the slide to advance to the next slide or click the **Next** button (⬛).

● To return to a previous slide, you can click the **Previous** button (⬛).

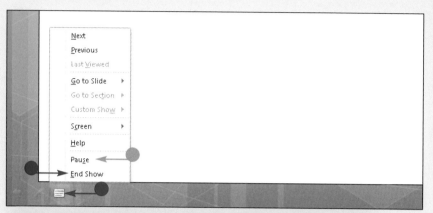

● To view a menu of slide show commands, click ▤.

● You can pause the show by clicking the **Pause** command.

● You can end the show early by clicking the **End Show** command.

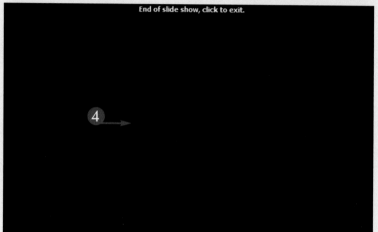

④ When the slide show is complete, click anywhere on the screen.

PowerPoint closes the presentation.

Simplify It

How do I draw on my slides as I present the show?
As mentioned, you can use PowerPoint's pointer options to draw directly on the screen using the mouse pointer. You can choose from several pen tools and colors. Follow these steps:

① During the slide show, click the **Pen** button (✎).

② Click a pen style.

● You can click here to choose a pen color.

③ Click and drag to draw on the slide.

To erase your markings, press Ⓔ.

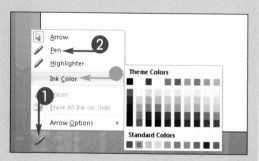

Package Your Presentation on a CD

You can save your PowerPoint presentation to a CD to enable you to share your presentation with others. With the Package for CD feature, PowerPoint bundles the presentation along with all of the necessary clip art, multimedia elements, and other items needed to run your show, including any linked files contained in your presentation. The CD even includes a PowerPoint Viewer with the file in case the recipient does not have PowerPoint installed on his or her computer.

If you prefer, you can save your presentation as a WMV movie file that includes any narration and timings you record.

Package Your Presentation on a CD

① Click the **File** tab.

② Click **Save & Send**.

③ Click **Package Presentation for CD**.

④ Click **Package for CD**.

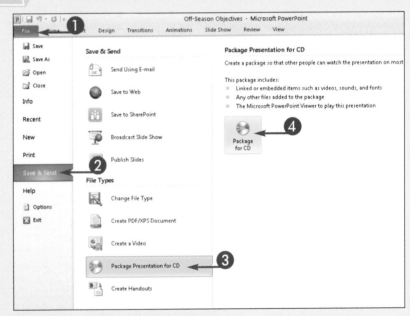

The Package for CD dialog box appears.

⑤ Type a name for the CD.

⑥ Click **Copy to CD**.

Note: *If your presentation contains linked files, PowerPoint asks you if you want to include those files on the CD. If you trust the source of each linked file, click* ***Yes***.

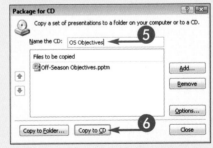

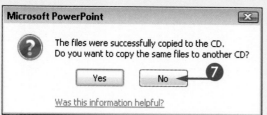

● PowerPoint copies the presentation files.

Depending on the size of the presentation, the copying process can take a few minutes.

When the copying process is complete, a dialog box appears.

7 Click **No**.

If you want to continue packing additional copies of the presentation, you can click **Yes**.

8 Click **Close**.

The Package for CD dialog box closes.

How do I save my presentation as a video?
To save your presentation as a WMV movie file, follow these steps:

1 Click the **File** tab and then click **Save & Send**.

2 Click **Create a Video**.

3 Choose a quality level.

4 Specify whether recorded narration and timings should be used.

5 Click **Create Video**.

6 In the Save As dialog box, specify the folder in which the video should be saved.

7 Click the **Save** button.

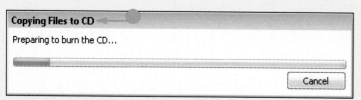

PowerPoint saves the presentation as a movie file in the folder you specified.

Part V

Access

Access is a robust database program you can use to store and manage large quantities of data. You can use Access to manage anything from a home inventory to a database of clients to a giant warehouse of products. Access can help you organize your information into tables, speed up data entry with forms, and perform powerful analysis using filters and queries. In this part, you

learn how to build and maintain a database file, add tables, create forms, enter data into your database, and analyze your data using filters, sorting, and queries. You also learn how to run reports on your data.

Understanding Database Basics

Access is a popular database program that you can use to catalog and manage large amounts of data. You can use Access to manage anything from a simple table of data to large, multifaceted lists of information. For example, you might use Access to maintain a list of your clients or a catalog of products you sell.

If you are new to Access, you should take a moment and familiarize yourself with the basic terms associated with the program, such as *database*, *table*, *record*, *field*, *form*, *report*, and *query*. This section contains definitions of all these key terms.

Defining Databases

Simply defined, a *database* is a collection of information. Whether you are aware of it or not, you use databases every day. Common databases include telephone directories or television program schedules. Your own database examples might include a list of contacts that contains addresses and phone numbers. Other examples of real-world databases include product inventories, client invoices, and employee payroll lists.

Tables

The heart of any Access database is a table. A *table* is a list of information organized into columns and rows. In the example of a client contact database, the table might list the names, addresses, phone numbers, company names, titles, and e-mail addresses of your clients. You can have numerous tables in your Access database. For example, you might have one table listing client information and another table listing your company's products.

Records and Fields

Every entry that you make in an Access table is called a *record*. Records always appear as rows in a database table. You can organize the information for each record in a separate column, called a *field*. For example, in a client contact list, you might include fields for first name, last name, company name, title, address, city, ZIP code, phone number, and e-mail address. Field names appear at the top of the table.

Forms

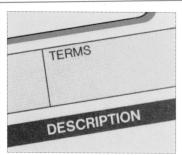

You can enter your database records directly into an Access table or you can simplify the process by using a *form*. Access forms present your table fields in an easy-to-read, fill-in-the-blank format. Forms allow you to enter records one at a time. Forms are a great way to speed up data entry, particularly if other users are adding information to your database list.

Reports and Queries

You can use the report feature to summarize data in your tables and generate printouts of pertinent information, such as your top ten salespeople and your top selling products. You can use queries to sort and filter your data. For example, you can choose to view only a few of your table fields and filter them to match certain criteria.

Planning a Database

Planning your database in advance can save you time. The first step to building an Access database is deciding what sort of data you want it to contain and what sorts of actions you want to perform on your data. Ask yourself, how do you want to organize it? How many tables of data do you need? What types of fields do you need for your records? What sort of reports and queries do you hope to create?

Create a Database Based on a Template

You can build a new database based on any of the predefined Access templates. For example, the Business category includes templates for creating contact lists, assets, marketing projects, and events. You can also log onto the Office Web site to find new featured templates you can download.

When you create a new database using a template, the database includes pre-built tables and forms, which you can populate with your own data. You control the structure of your database by determining what preset tables and fields are included in the file.

Create a Database Based on a Template

① Click the **File** tab.

② Click **New**.

③ Click **Sample templates**.

● You can also download templates from the Office Web site by clicking a template category under Office.com Templates.

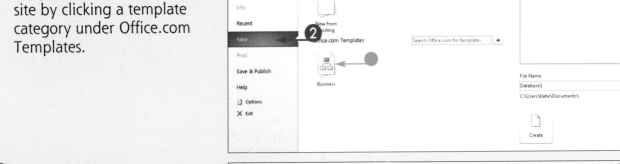

④ Click a template.

⑤ To change the name of the database, type a new name in the **File Name** field.

⑥ To change the folder in which the database file will be stored, click the **Browse** button (📋).

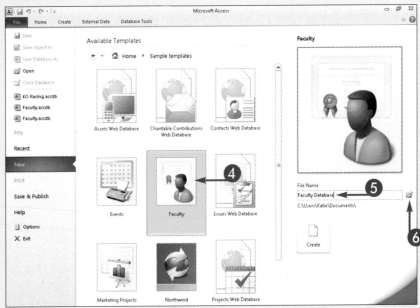

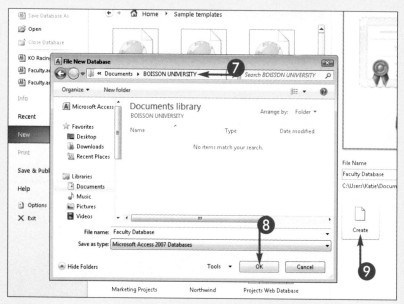

Access launches the File New Database dialog box.

⑦ Locate and select the folder in which you want to store the database file.

⑧ Click **OK**.

⑨ Click **Create**.

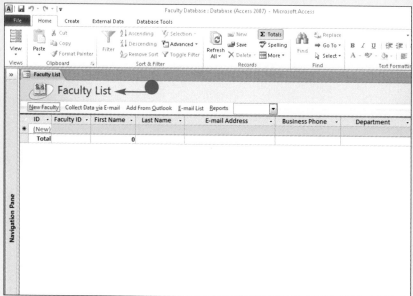

● Access creates a new, blank database based on the template you chose and opens a new table, ready for data.

How do I know what fields to keep in or remove from my table?
To determine what fields you need in your database, do a little preplanning. Decide what kinds of information you want to track in your database and what sorts of reports and queries you want to generate to view your data. For best results, use the suggested fields; you can always remove fields that you do not use at a later time. (For help removing fields from a table, see the section "Delete a Field from a Table" later in this chapter.)

Create a Blank Database

As mentioned, Access includes many predefined database templates, including templates for creating contact lists, assets, marketing projects, events, and more. You can also log onto the Office Web site to find additional downloadable templates.

If you determine that none of these predesigned Access templates suits your purposes, you can create a new, blank database. You can then decide what tables, fields, forms, and other database objects your database will include.

When you create a new database file, Access launches the File New Database dialog box and prompts you to assign a name to the file. You also specify the folder and drive in which the database file will be stored.

Create a Blank Database

1 Click the **File** tab.

2 Click **New**.

3 Click **Blank database**.

4 Type a name for the database in the **File Name** field.

5 To change the folder in which the database file will be stored, click the **Browse** button (⬚).

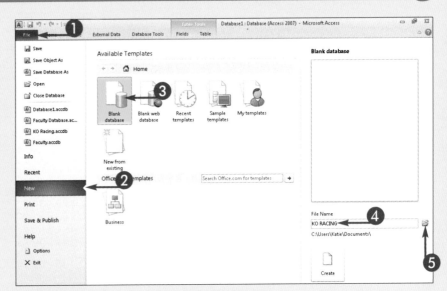

Access launches the File New Database dialog box.

6 Locate and select the folder in which you want to store the database file.

7 Click **OK**.

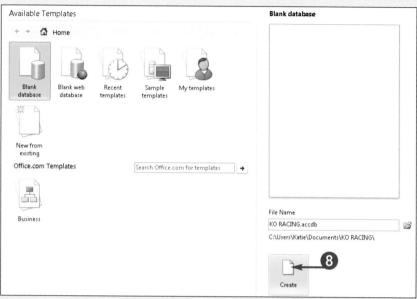

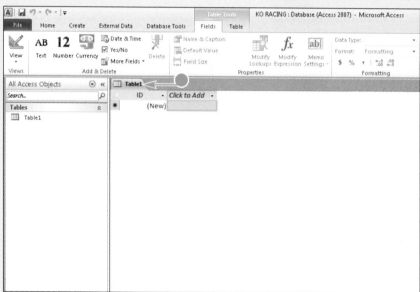

8 Click **Create**.

● Access creates a new, blank database and opens a new table, ready for data.

What is the pane on the left?
The pane on the left is the Navigation pane, which you can use to open various database objects. You can collapse the pane to increase the on-screen workspace; simply click the **Shutter Bar Open/Close** button (◁). Click the button again to expand the pane.

How do I open an existing database?
Click the **File** tab and click **Recent**, and click the database in the Recent Databases list that appears. If the database is not listed in the Recent Databases list, click the **File** tab, choose **Open** to launch an Open dialog box, locate and select the database file, and click **Open**.

Create a New Table

Access databases store all data in tables. A *table* is a list of information organized into columns and rows that intersect to form *cells* for holding data. A table might list the names, addresses, phone numbers, company names, titles, and e-mail addresses of your clients. Each row in a table is considered a *record*. You can use columns to hold *fields*, which are the individual units of information contained within a record.

If you need to add a table to a database, you can easily do so. All table objects that you create appear listed in the Navigation pane; simply double-click a table object to open it.

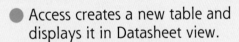

Create a New Table

1 With your database open in Access, click the **Create** tab.

2 Click the **Table** button.

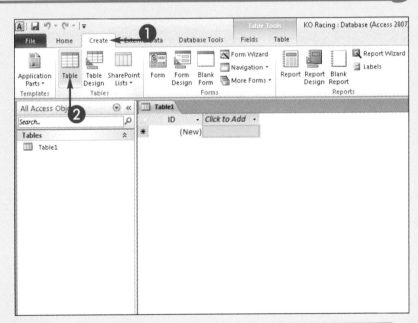

● Access creates a new table and displays it in Datasheet view.

Note: *See the upcoming "Change Table Views" section to learn more about Datasheet view.*

3 To name a field, click the **Click to Add** link at the top of the field column.

4 Click the type of field you want to add (here, **Text**).

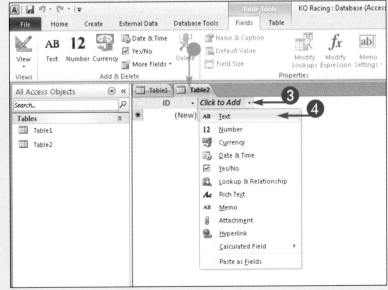

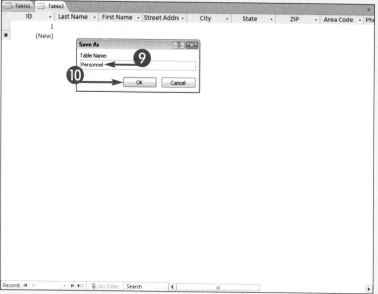

5 Type a name for the field and press Enter.

6 Repeat Steps **3** to **5** to create more fields for the table.

7 When you are finished adding fields, close the table by clicking the **Close** button (⊠).

Access prompts you to save the table changes.

8 Click **Yes**.

The Save As dialog box appears.

9 Type a name for the table.

10 Click **OK**.

Access lists the table among the database objects in the Navigation pane.

Can I rename table fields?
Yes. You can rename fields in any table. To do so, double-click the field label and type a new name. When you finish, press Enter.

How do I remove a table that I no longer want?
To delete the table, select it in the Navigation pane and press Delete. Access asks you to confirm the deletion before permanently removing the table, along with any data that it contains. Before attempting to remove a table, ensure that it does not contain any important data that you need.

Change Table Views

You can view your table data using two different view modes: Datasheet view and Design view. In Datasheet view, the table appears as an ordinary grid of intersecting columns and rows where you can enter data. In Design view, you can view the skeletal structure of your fields and their properties and modify the design of the table. For example, you can add fields by typing new field names in the Field Name column. You can also change the field names or change the type of data that is allowed within a field, such as text or number data.

Change Table Views

Switch to Design View

1. Click the **Home** tab on the Ribbon.

2. Click the bottom half of the **View** button.

3. Click **Design View**.

   Note: *An even quicker way to switch from Datasheet view to Design view is to click the top half of the **View** button.*

● Access displays the table in Design view, showing the table's field properties.

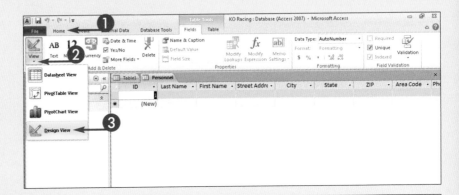

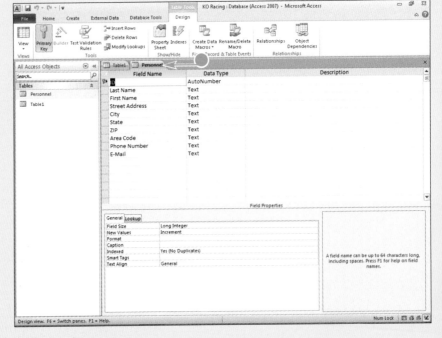

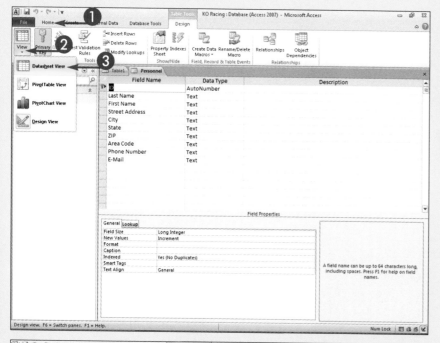

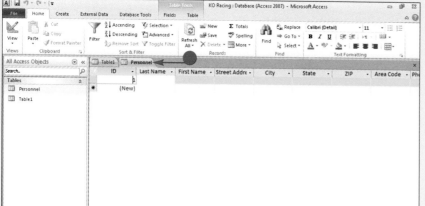

Switch to Datasheet View

1 Click the **Home** tab on the Ribbon.

2 Click the bottom half of the **View** button.

3 Click **Datasheet View**.

*Note: An even quicker way to switch from Design view to Datasheet view is to click the top half of the **View** button.*

● Access displays the default Datasheet view of the table.

What is the purpose of the Field Properties area in Design view?

The Field Properties area enables you to change the design of the field itself, specifying how many characters the field can contain, whether fields can be left blank, and other properties.

What do the PivotTable and PivotChart views do?

If you create a PivotTable, you can use PivotTable view to summarize and analyze data by viewing different fields. You can use the PivotChart feature to create a graphical version of a PivotTable and to see various graphical representations of the data. See the Access help files to learn more about the PivotTable and PivotChart features.

Add a Field to a Table

You can add fields to your table to include more information in your records. For example, you may need to add a separate field to a Contacts table for mobile phone numbers. Alternatively, you may need to add a field to a table that contains a catalog of products to track each product's availability.

After you add a field, you can name it whatever you want. To name a field, double-click the field label in Datasheet view, type a new name, and press Enter. Alternatively, change the field name in Design view.

Add a Field to a Table

1 Open the table to which you want to add a field in Datasheet view.

2 Click the column header where you want to insert a new field. Access will add the new field to the right of the column you select.

3 Click the **Fields** tab.

4 In the Add & Delete group, click the button for the type of field you want to add (here, **Text**).

● Access adds the new field.

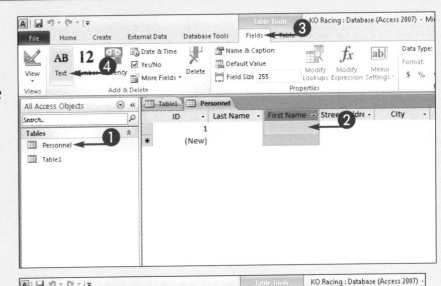

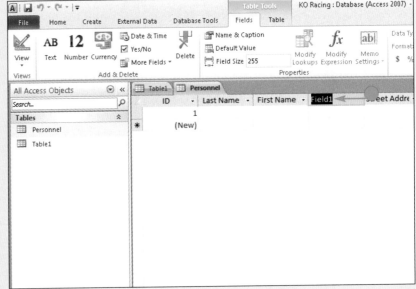

Delete a Field from a Table

You can delete a field that you no longer need in a table. For example, if you are working on a database of employee contact information that contains a Pager field, but your company no longer supports the use of pagers, you might opt to delete that field.

When you remove a field, Access permanently removes any data contained within the field for every record in the table. If you do not want to delete the information in the field, you might choose to hide, rather than delete, the field. For information about hiding fields, see the next section, "Hide a Field in a Table."

Delete a Field from a Table

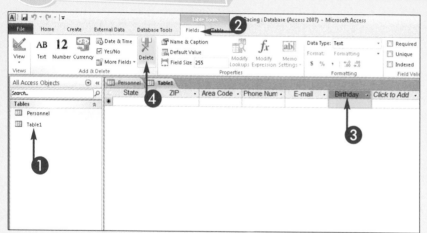

① Open the table that you want to edit in Datasheet view.

② Click the **Fields** tab.

③ Click the column header for the field you want to remove.

④ Click the **Delete** button.

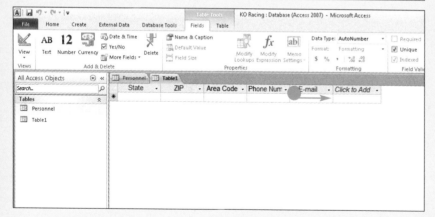

● Access removes the field and any record content for the field from the table.

Hide a Field in a Table

Suppose your table contains fields that you do not want to view on a regular basis, but that you do not want to delete from the table. For example, a table containing a catalog of products might include a field indicating the country in which the product was manufactured — information that you may not need to view on a regular basis. In that case, you can hide the fields. You might hide a field to focus on other fields for a printout or to prevent another user on your computer from seeing the field. When you are ready to view the field again, you can easily unhide it.

Hide a Field in a Table

1. Click the column header for the field you want to hide.

2. Right-click the selection.

3. Click **Hide Fields**.

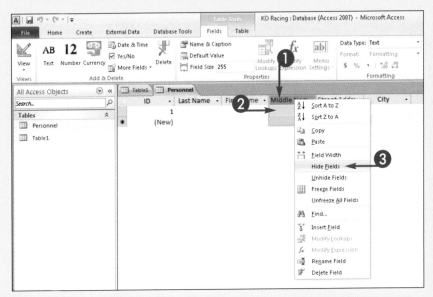

● Access hides the field.

Note: To view the field again, right-click the field next to the hidden field, click **Unhide Fields**, select the column that you want to display again, and click **OK**.

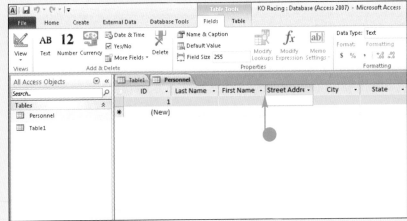

Move a Field in a Table

Especially if you built your database from a predesigned template, you may find that the order in which fields appear in the table does not suit your needs. If so, you may want to move a field so that it appears before another field to suit the way you type your record data. Fortunately, Access makes it easy to move a field in your table to change how you view and enter record data.

Move a Field in a Table

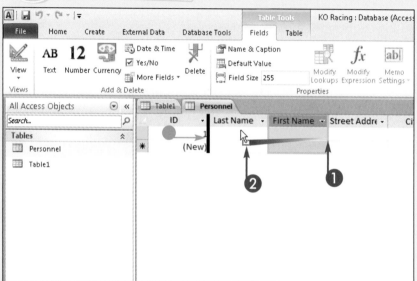

① In Datasheet view, click the column header for the field you want to move.

② Drag the column to a new position in the table.

The ⌖ changes to ⌖.

● A bold vertical line marks the new location of the column as you drag.

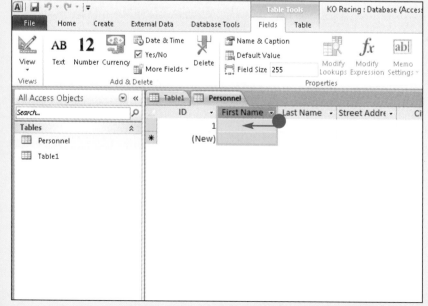

③ Release the mouse button.

● Access moves the field to the new location.

Create a Form

One way to enter data into your database is to type it directly into an Access table. Alternatively, you can create a form based on your table to simplify data entry.

Forms present your table fields in an easy-to-read, fill-in-the-blank format. When you create a form based on a table, Access inserts fields into the form for each field in the table.

Forms, which enable you to enter records one at a time, are a great way to speed up data entry, particularly if other users are adding information to your database list.

Create a Form

① With the table on which you want to base a form open in Access, click the **Create** tab.

② Click the **Form** button.

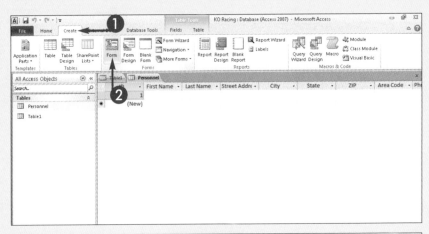

● Access creates the form.

③ Click the **Close** button (☒) to close the form.

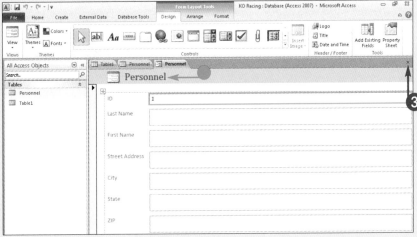

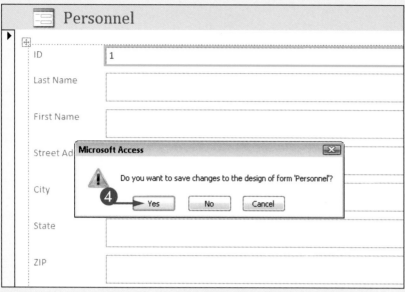

Access prompts you to save your changes.

④ Click **Yes**.

The Save As dialog box appears.

⑤ Type a name for the form.

⑥ Click **OK**.

Access lists the form among the database objects in the Navigation pane.

Note: After you save a form, you can reopen it by double-clicking it in the Navigation pane.

How do I delete a form that I no longer need?
To delete a form, click it in the Navigation pane. Then press `Delete` or click the **Delete** button on the Home tab. Access asks you to confirm the deletion; click **Yes**.

Can I create a blank form?
Yes. Click the **Blank Form** button on the **Create** tab to open a blank form and a field list containing all the fields from all of the tables in the database. To add a field to the form, drag it from the list onto the form. You can populate the form with as many fields as you need.

Change Form Views

You can view your form using various form views: Form view, Design view, and Layout view. Form view is the default; in this view, you can simply enter data. In Design view, each form object appears as a separate, editable element. For example, in this view, you can edit both the box that contains the data as well as the label that identifies the data. In Layout view, you can rearrange the form controls and adjust their sizes directly on the form. Access makes it easy to switch from Form view to Design view to Layout view and back.

Change Form Views

Switch to Design View

1 Click the **Home** tab on the Ribbon.

2 Click the bottom half of the **View** button.

3 Click **Design View**.

● Access displays the form in Design view.

Switch to Layout View

1 Click the **Home** tab on the Ribbon.

2 Click the bottom half of the **View** button.

3 Click **Layout View**.

● Access displays the form in Layout view.

To return to Form view, you can click the bottom half of the **View** button and then click **Form View**.

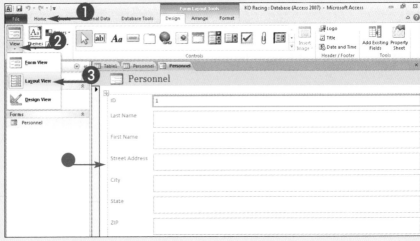

Move a Field in a Form

You can move a field to another location on your form. You might move a field to change the order in which data is entered in a form or simply to change the appearance of the form.

When you select a field for editing, the field label is also selected, making it easy to move both the field and the label at the same time. Although you can move a field in Design view or in Layout view, you might find it easier to make changes to your form in Layout view.

Move a Field in a Form

① Open the form that you want to edit in Layout view.

② Click the field that you want to move.

③ Click and drag the field to the new location on the form.

The ⌖ changes to ⌖.

● Access repositions the field.

Delete a Field in a Form

You can delete a field that you no longer need in a form. When you remove a field, you need to remove both the data box and the field label. Although you can delete a field in Design view or in Layout view, you might find it easier to make changes to your form in Layout view.

Note that removing a form field does not remove the field from the table upon which the form is originally based or any of the data within that field; it simply removes the field from the form.

Delete a Field in a Form

① Open the form that you want to edit in Layout view.

② Click the field that you want to delete.

③ Press Delete or click the **Delete** button on the Home tab.

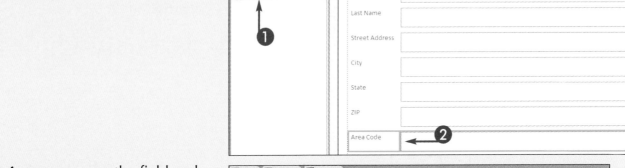

● Access removes the field and label from the form.

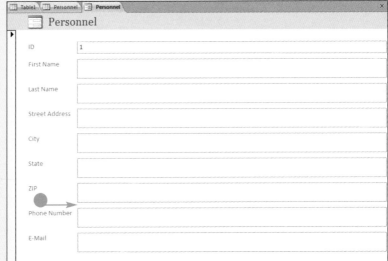

284

Apply a Database Theme

A *theme* is a predesigned set of color schemes, fonts, and other visual attributes. Applying a theme to an Access database is a quick way to add polish to it and make it more visually appealing. When you apply a theme to an Access database, that same theme is applied to all forms and tables in your database.

Themes are shared among the Office programs; you can use the same theme in your Access database that you have applied to worksheets in Excel, documents in Word, or slides in PowerPoint.

Apply a Database Theme

① Open a database form in Layout view.

② Click the **Design** tab on the Ribbon.

③ Click the **Themes** button.

④ Click the theme you want to apply.

● Access applies the theme to all forms in the database.

Add a Record to a Table

You build a database by adding records to a table in the database. Any new records that you add appear at the end of the table. You add records to a table in Datasheet view.

As your table grows longer, you can use the navigation buttons on your keyboard to navigate it. You can press `Tab` to move from cell to cell, or you can press the keyboard arrow keys. To move backward to a previous cell, press `Shift` + `Tab`.

After you enter a record in a database table, you can edit it if necessary. You edit records in a table in Datasheet view.

Add a Record to a Table

1 In the Navigation pane, double-click the table to which you want to add a record.

● Access opens the table, placing the cursor in the first cell of the first blank row.

● By default, the first field in each table is an ID field, containing a unique ID number for the record. This value is set automatically.

2 Press `Tab`.

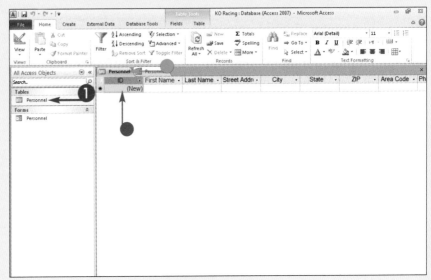

Access moves your cursor to the next cell in the row.

3 Type the desired data in the selected cell.

4 Press `Tab`.

5 Repeat Steps **3** and **4** until you have filled the entire row.

6 Press `Enter` or press `Tab` to move to the next row, or record.

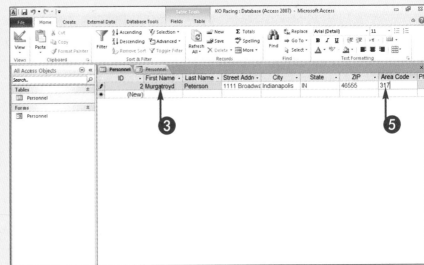

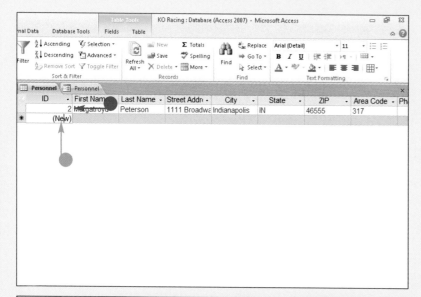

● Access adds the new record.

● Access moves your cursor to the first cell in the next row.

⑦ Repeat Steps **2** to **6** to add more records to the table.

Access adds your records.

● You can resize a column by dragging the column border left or right.

● You can use the scroll bars to view different portions of the table.

Note: *To edit a record in a table, open the table in Datasheet view, click in the cell whose data you want to change, double-click the data to select it, and type over the data to replace it.*

What is a primary key?
A *primary key* uniquely identifies each record in a table. For many tables, the primary key is the ID field by default. The ID field, which is created automatically, stores a unique number for each record as it is entered into the database. If you want, however, you can designate another field (or even multiple fields) as a primary key. To do so, switch the table to Design view, select the field that you want to set as the primary key, and click the **Primary key** button on the Design tab.

Add a Record to a Form

You can use forms to quickly add records to your Access databases. Forms present your record fields in an easy-to-read format. You add records to a form in Form view; this view presents each field in your table as a box that you can use to enter data.

After you enter a record in a form, you can edit it if necessary. (See the tip at the end of this section for more information.) For help locating a particular record in the form window in order to edit it, see the next section, "Navigate Records in a Form."

Add a Record to a Form

① In the Navigation pane, double-click the form to which you want to add a record.

Note: *If the form is not visible in the Navigation pane, click the* ⊙ *along the top of the pane, choose* **Object Type***, and locate the desired form under the Forms heading.*

● Access opens the form.

② Click the **Home** tab.

③ Click the **New** button in the Records group.

● Access opens a blank form, placing the cursor in the first cell of the first field.

● By default, the first field in the table associated with this form is an ID field, containing a unique ID number for the record. This value is set automatically.

④ Press `Tab`.

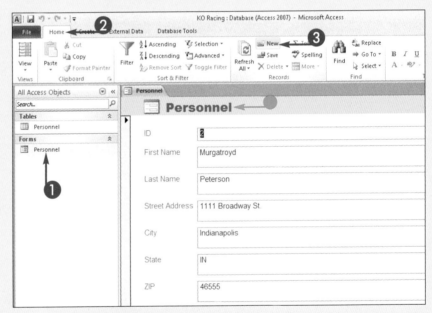

Personnel

ID	32
First Name	Petal ◄ — ⑤
Last Name	
Street Address	
City	
State	
ZIP	
Area Code	

Access moves your cursor to the next field in the form.

⑤ Type the desired data in the selected field.

⑥ Press Tab.

Personnel

ID	32
First Name	Petal
Last Name	Hauptman
Street Address	40 W. 14th St.
City	Indianapolis
State	IN
ZIP	46432
Area Code	317
Phone Number	5551001
E-Mail	frauleinhaup@hotmail.com ◄ — ⑦

Access moves to the next field in the form.

⑦ Repeat Steps **5** and **6** until you have filled the entire form.

⑧ Press Enter or Tab.

Access displays another blank record, ready for data.

● To close the form window, you can click the **Close** button (⊠).

Simplify It

Are there other ways to insert a new record?
Yes. You can click the **New (Blank) Record** button (▶※) on the form window's navigation bar (located along the bottom of the form) to create a new, blank record.

How do I edit a record in a form?
You can reopen the form, navigate to the record that you want to change, and make your edits directly to the form data. When you save your changes, Access automatically updates the data in your table. To learn how to display a particular record in a form, see the next section, "Navigate Records in a Form."

Navigate Records in a Form

You may find it easier to read a record using a form instead of reading it from a large table containing other records. Similarly, editing a record in a form may be easier than editing a record in a table. You can locate records you want to view or edit using the navigation bar that appears along the bottom of the form window. This navigation bar contains buttons for locating and viewing different records in your database. The navigation bar also contains a Search field for locating a specific record. (You learn how to search for a record in a form in the next section.)

Navigate Records in a Form

① In the Navigation pane, double-click the form whose records you want to navigate.

Note: If the form is not visible in the Navigation pane, click the ⊙ along the top of the pane, choose **Object Type**, and locate the desired form under the Forms heading.

● Access displays the form.

● The Current Record box indicates what record you are viewing.

② Click **Previous Record** (◁) or **Next Record** (▷) to move back or forward by one record.

● Access displays the previous or next record in the database.

● Click **First Record** (◁◁) or **Last Record** (▷▷) to navigate to the first or last record in the table.

● Click **New (Blank) Record** (▷*) to start a new, blank record.

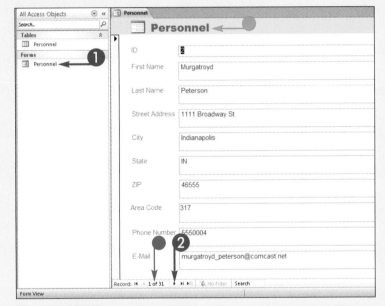

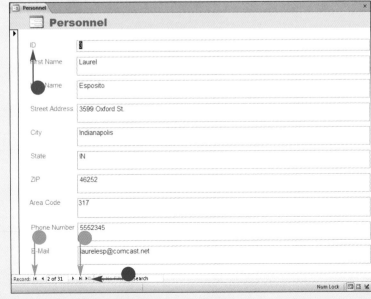

Search for a Record in a Form

As mentioned, you may find it easier to read and edit records in a form than in a large table containing other records.

One way to locate records you want to view or edit is to use the various buttons in the navigation bar, such as the Previous Record button, the Next Record button, and so on.

(Refer to the preceding section for help using these buttons.) This method can become time-consuming, however, if the form contains numerous records. An easier approach is to search for the record using Access's search functionality, also accessible from the navigation bar.

Search for a Record in a Form

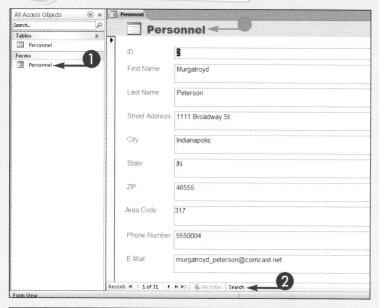

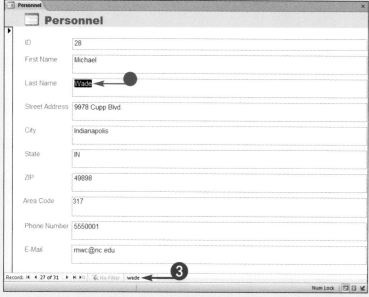

1 In the Navigation pane, double-click the form containing the record you want to find.

   Note: *If the form is not visible in the Navigation pane, click the* ⊡ *along the top of the pane, choose* **Object Type**, *and locate the desired form under the Forms heading.*

● Access displays the form.

2 Click in the **Search** field.

3 Type a keyword that relates to the record you want to find (here, a person's last name).

● As you type, Access displays matching records.

Delete a Record from a Table

You can remove a record from your database if it holds data that you no longer need. Removing old records can reduce the overall file size of your database and make it easier to manage. When you delete a record, all of the data within its fields is permanently removed.

You can remove a record from a database by deleting it from a table or by deleting it from a form. This section shows you how to delete a record from a table. (For help deleting a record from a form, see the next section, "Delete a Record from a Form.")

Delete a Record from a Table

① In the Navigation pane, double-click the table that contains the record you want to delete.

● Access opens the table.

② Position your mouse pointer over the gray box to the left of the record that you want to delete (the mouse pointer changes to ➡) and click.

● The record is selected.

③ Click the **Home** tab.

④ Click the **Delete** button in the Records group.

Note: *You can also right-click the record and then click **Delete Record**.*

Access displays a warning box about the deletion.

⑤ Click **Yes**.

● Access permanently removes the record from the table.

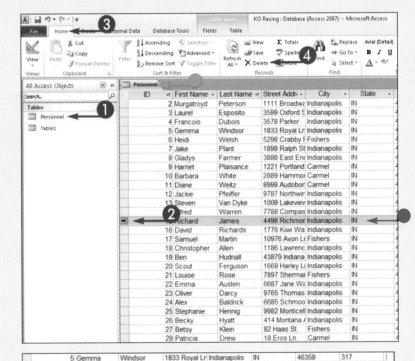

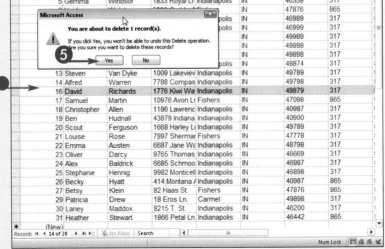

Delete a Record from a Form

In addition to removing records directly from a table, as described in the preceding section, "Delete a Record from a Table," you can remove records that you no longer need by using a form.

The first step is to locate the record you want to delete; refer to the sections "Navigate Records in a Form" and "Search for a Record in a Form" for help locating the record.

Removing old records can reduce the overall file size of your database and make it easier to manage. When you delete a record, whether from a table or a form, all the data within its fields is permanently removed.

Delete a Record from a Form

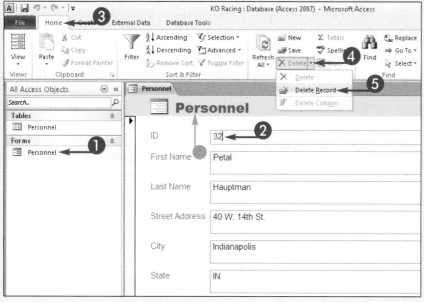

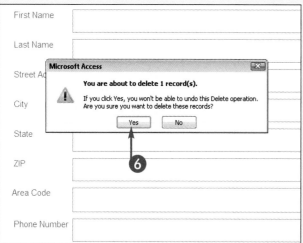

① In the Navigation pane, double-click the form containing the record you want to delete.

Note: *If the form is not visible in the Navigation pane, click the* ⊙ *along the top of the pane, choose* **Object Type***, and locate the desired form under the Forms heading.*

● Access displays the form.

② Navigate to the record you want to delete.

③ Click the **Home** tab on the Ribbon.

④ Click the **Delete** button's ⊡.

⑤ Click **Delete Record**.

Access displays a warning box about the deletion.

⑥ Click **Yes**.

Access permanently removes the record.

Sort Records

Sorting enables you to arrange your database records in a logical order to match any criteria that you specify. For example, with a contacts database, you might sort the records alphabetically or based on the ZIP code. You can sort in ascending order or descending order. For example, if you are sorting alphabetically, you can sort from A to Z (ascending) or from Z to A (descending).

You can sort records in a table, or you can use a form to sort records. In this section, you learn how to do both.

Sort Records

Sort a Table

1. Open the table you want to sort.

2. Position your mouse pointer over the column header for the field by which you want to sort (the mouse pointer changes to ↓) and click.

3. Click the **Home** tab on the Ribbon.

4. Click a sort button.

Click **Ascending** to sort the records in ascending order.

Click **Descending** to sort the records in descending order.

Access sorts the table records based on the field you choose.

● This example sorts the records alphabetically by last name in ascending order.

● In the prompt box that appears when you close the table, you can click **Yes** to make the sort permanent, or **No** to leave the original order intact.

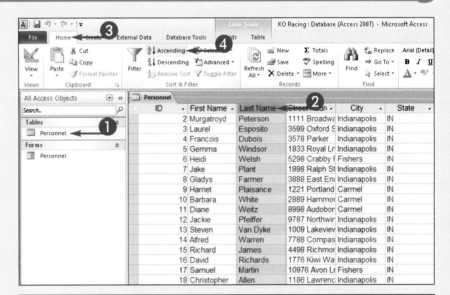

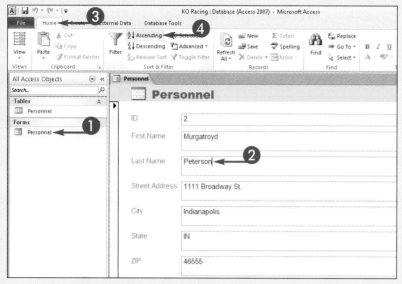

Sort Using a Form

① Open the form you want to sort.

② Click in the field by which you want to sort.

③ Click the **Home** tab on the Ribbon.

④ Click a sort button.

Click **Ascending** to sort the records in ascending order.

Click **Descending** to sort the records in descending order.

Access sorts the table records based on the field you choose.

● This example sorts the records alphabetically by last name in ascending order.

● You can use the navigation buttons to view the sorted records.

How are empty records sorted?
If you perform a sort on a field for which some records are missing data, those records are included in the sort. Records with empty fields are sorted first when you perform an ascending sort, or last with a descending sort.

How do I remove a sort order?
With the sorted table or form open, click the **Remove Sort** button in the Sort & Filter group on the Home tab. This returns the table to its original sort order. You can also use this technique to remove a sort from a query or report. (Queries and reports are covered later in this chapter.)

Filter Records

You can use an Access filter to view only specific records that meet criteria you set. For example, you may want to view all clients buying a particular product, anyone in a contacts database who has a birthday in June, or all products within a particular category. You can also filter by exclusion — that is, filter out records that do not contain the search criteria that you specify.

You can apply a simple filter on one field in your database using the Selection tool, or you can filter several fields using the Filter by Form command.

Filter Records

Apply a Simple Filter

1 Open the form you want to filter.

2 Click in the field by which you want to filter.

3 Click the **Home** tab on the Ribbon.

4 Click the **Selection** button.

5 Click a criterion.

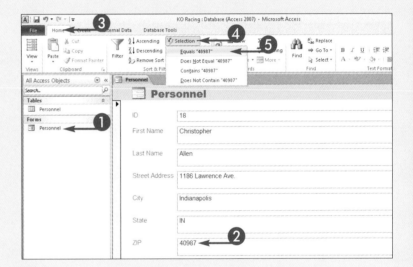

Access filters the records.

● In this example, Access finds two records matching the filter criterion.

● You can use the navigation buttons to view the filtered records.

● To undo a filter, click the **Toggle Filter** button.

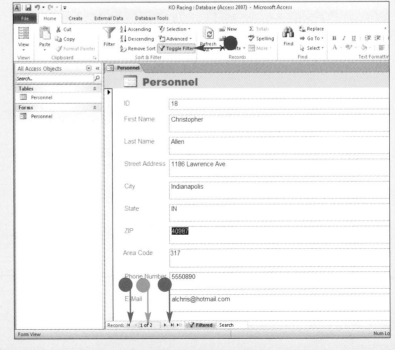

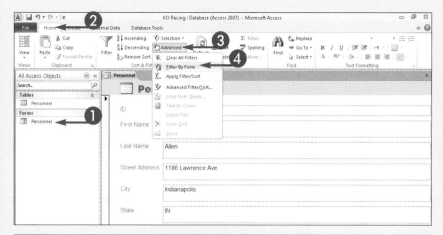

Filter by Form

1 Open the form you want to filter.

2 Click the **Home** tab on the Ribbon.

3 Click the **Advanced** button.

4 Click **Filter By Form**.

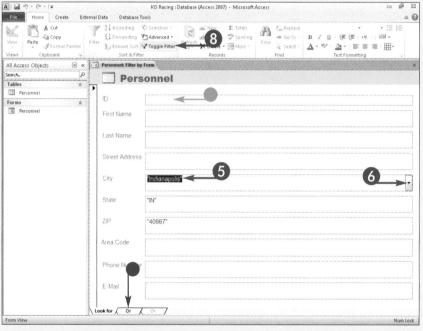

● A blank form appears.

5 Click in the field by which you want to filter.

6 Click the ▼ that appears and choose a criterion.

7 Repeat Steps **5** and **6** to add more criteria to the filter.

● You can set OR criteria using the tabs at the bottom of the form.

8 Click the **Toggle Filter** button.

Access filters the records.

To remove the filter, you can click the **Toggle Filter** button again.

How do I filter by exclusion?
First click in the field that you want to filter in the form, click the **Selection** button on the Home tab, and then click an exclusion option. Access filters out any records that do not contain the data found in the field that you selected.

What are OR criteria?
Setting OR criteria enables you to display records that match one set of criteria or another. For example, you might set up your filter to display only those records with the value 46989 in the ZIP field OR the value 46555 in the ZIP field.

Apply Conditional Formatting

You can use Access's Conditional Formatting tool to apply certain formatting attributes, such as bold text or a fill color, to data in a form when the data meets a specified condition.

For example, if your database tracks weekly sales, you might set up Access's Conditional Formatting feature to alert you if sales figures fall below what is required for you to break even.

You apply conditional formatting by creating a rule, which specifies the criteria that the value in a field must meet. Values that meet the criteria are formatted using settings you specify.

Apply Conditional Formatting

1 Open the form to which you want to apply conditional formatting in Layout view.

2 Click the field to which you want to apply conditional formatting.

3 Click the **Format** tab.

4 Click the **Conditional Formatting** button.

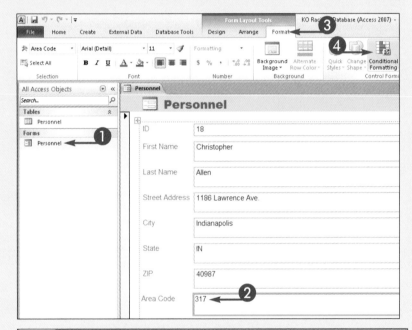

The Conditional Formatting Rules Manager dialog box opens.

5 Click the **New Rule** button.

The New Formatting Rule dialog box opens.

6 Set the criteria you want to use to apply conditional formatting.

7 Specify how values that meet your criteria should be formatted.

8 Click **OK**.

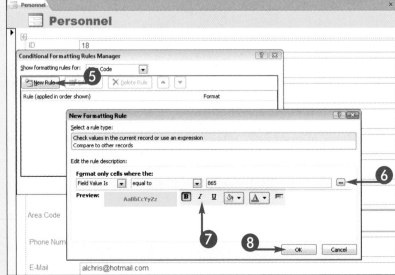

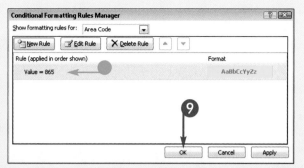

● Access creates a rule based on the criteria you set.

9 Click **OK**.

● Access applies the conditional formatting.

Personnel

ID	26
First Name	Becky
Last Name	Hyatt
Street Address	414 Montana Ave.
City	Indianapolis
State	IN
ZIP	40987
Area Code	865

How do I remove conditional formatting?
To remove conditional formatting, follow these steps:

1 Open the Conditional Formatting Rules Manager dialog box. (To open this dialog box, follow Steps **1** to **4** in this section.)

2 Click the conditional formatting rule you want to remove.

3 Click the **Delete Rule** button.

4 Click **OK**.

Access removes the conditional formatting.

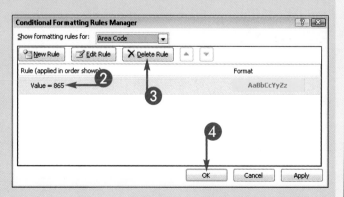

Perform a Simple Query

You can use a query to extract information that you want to view in a database. Queries are especially useful when you want to glean data from multiple tables.

Queries are similar to filters, but offer you greater control when it comes to viewing records. You can use the Query Wizard to help you select what fields you want to include in

the analysis. There are several types of Query Wizards. These include Simple, covered here; Crosstab, to display information in a spreadsheet-like format; Find Duplicates, to find records with duplicate field values; and Find Unmatched, to find records in one table with no related records in another table.

Perform a Simple Query

Create a Query

① Open the table or form for which you want to perform a simple query.

② Click the **Create** tab on the Ribbon.

③ Click the **Query Wizard** button.

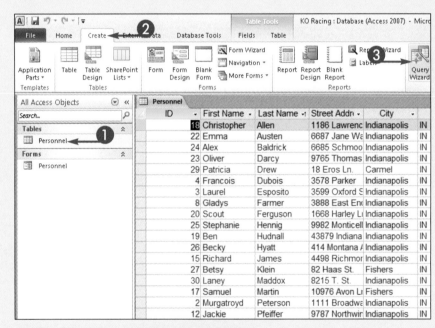

The New Query dialog box appears.

④ Click **Simple Query Wizard**.

⑤ Click **OK**.

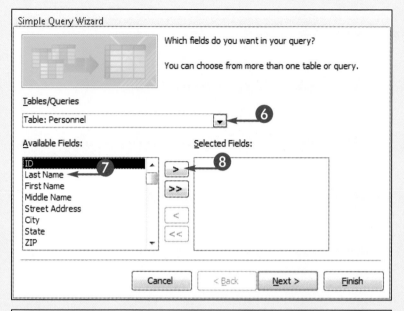

The Simple Query Wizard opens.

6 Click the **Tables/Queries** ☑ and choose the table containing the fields on which you want to base the query.

7 In the Available Fields list, click a field that you want to include in the query.

8 Click the **Add** button (☐).

● The field is added to the Selected Fields list.

9 Repeat Steps **7** and **8** to add more fields to your query.

You can repeat Step **6** to choose another table from which to add fields.

Note: *When using fields from two or more tables, the tables must have a prior relationship.*

10 Click **Next**.

What is a table relationship?
Table relationships enable you to combine related information for analysis. For example, you might define a relationship between one table containing customer contact information and another table containing customer orders. With that table relationship defined, you could then perform a query to, for example, locate all customers who have ordered the same product. To access tools for defining table relationships, click the **Database Tools** tab in the Ribbon and then click **Relationships**. (If you created your database from a template, then certain table relationships are predefined.)

continued

Perform a Simple Query *(continued)*

During the process of creating a new query, the Query Wizard asks you to give the query a unique name. This is so that you can refer to the query later. All queries that you create are saved in the Navigation pane; you can double-click a query in the Navigation pane to perform it again.

If, after performing a query, you determine that you need to add more criteria to it, you can easily do so. For example, you may realize that the query needs to include an additional table in your database. You can also sort and filter your query results.

Perform a Simple Query *(continued)*

⑪ Type a name for the query.

⑫ Click the **Open the query to view information** radio button.

⑬ Click **Finish**.

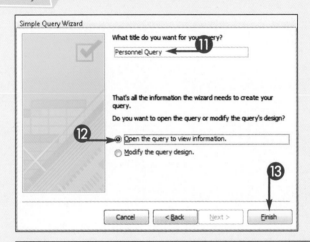

● A query datasheet appears, listing the fields.

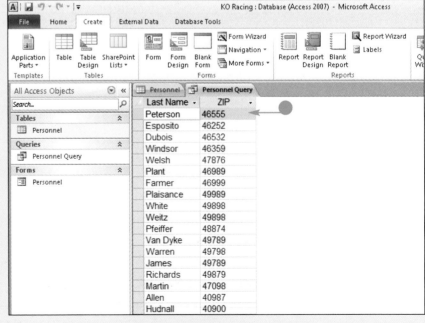

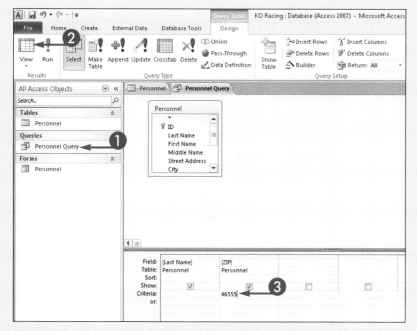

Add Criteria to the Query

1. Double-click the query in the Navigation pane to open it.

   *Note: If the query is not visible in the Navigation pane, click the ☉ along the top of the pane, choose **Object Type**, and locate the desired query under the Queries heading.*

2. Click the **View** button to switch to Design view.

3. Click in the **Criteria** field and type the data that you want to view.

   This example lists a ZIP code as the criterion.

4. Click the **View** button again to switch back to Datasheet view to see the results.

● The table now shows only the records matching the criteria.

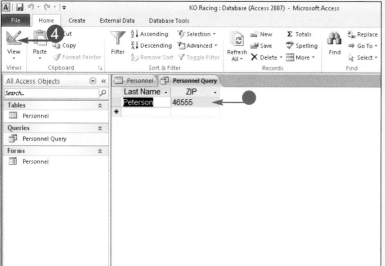

Simplify It

How do I add another table to my query?
Switch to Design view, click the **Design** tab on the Ribbon, and then click the **Show Table** button. This opens the Show Table dialog box, where you can add another table to the query and choose from among the available fields to customize the query.

Can I sort or filter my query?
Yes. You can use the sorting and filtering features to further define your query results. To learn how to sort data, see the "Sort Records" section, earlier in this chapter. To learn how to apply a filter, see the "Filter Records" section, also earlier in this chapter.

Create a Report

You can use Access to create a report based on one or more database tables. This can be a simple report, which contains all the fields in a single table, or a custom report, which can contain data from multiple tables in a database. (Note that to use fields from two or more tables, the tables must have a prior relationship; refer to the tip "What Is a Table Relationship?" in the preceding section for more information.)

To create a custom report, you can use the Report Wizard; it guides you through all the steps necessary to turn complex database data into an easy-to-read report.

Create a Report

Create a Simple Report

1. Open the table for which you want to create a simple report.

2. Click the **Create** tab on the Ribbon.

3. Click the **Report** button.

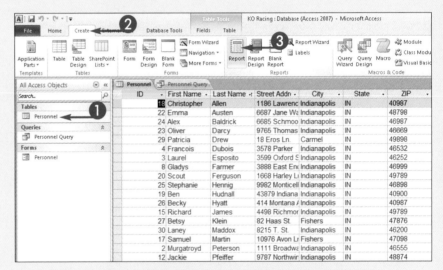

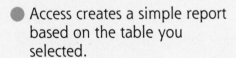

● Access creates a simple report based on the table you selected.

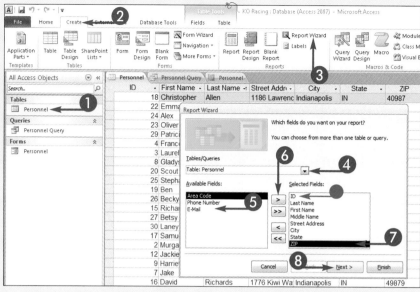

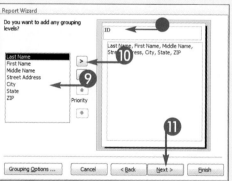

Create a Custom Report

1 Open a table you want to include in a custom report.

2 Click the **Create** tab.

3 Click the **Report Wizard** button.

The Report Wizard opens.

4 Click the **Tables/Queries** ⦾ and choose a table you want to include in the report.

5 Under Available Fields, click a field that you want to include in the report.

6 Click the **Add** button (▸).

● The field is added to the Selected Fields list.

7 Repeat Steps **5** and **6** to add more fields.

8 Click **Next**.

9 Click the field you want to use to group the data.

10 Click the **Add** button (▸).

● A preview of the grouping appears here.

11 Click **Next**.

Simplify It

How do I choose fields from different tables in a custom report?
Repeat Step **3** under "Create a Custom Report" to select additional tables that contain the fields you want to include.

How do I remove a field from a custom report?
If you have not yet completed the wizard, you can remove a field from the report by clicking the **Back** button until you reach the wizard's first screen. Then click the field you want to remove in the **Selected Fields** list and click the **Remove** button (◂) to remove the field. To remove all the fields, click the **Remove All** button (◂◂).

continued

Create a Report

(continued)

As the Report Wizard guides you through the steps for building a report, you are asked to decide upon a sort order. You can sort records by up to four fields, in ascending or descending order. The wizard also prompts you to select a layout for the report. Options include Stepped, Block, and Outline, in either portrait or landscape mode. (Note that you can change other design aspects of the report by opening it in Design view; for more information, see the tip at the end of this section.) After you create the report, you can print it.

Create a Report *(continued)*

⑫ To sort your data, click the first ⊡ and click the field by which you want to sort.

You can add more sort fields as needed.

Note: *Fields are sorted in ascending order by default. Click the **Ascending** button to toggle to descending order.*

⑬ Click **Next**.

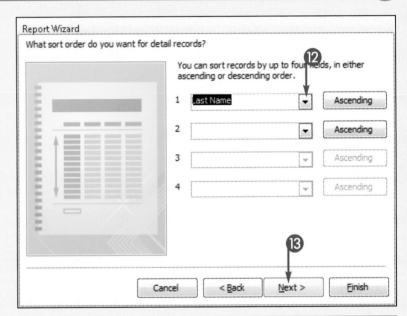

⑭ Click a layout option.

● You can set the page orientation for a report using these options.

⑮ Click **Next**.

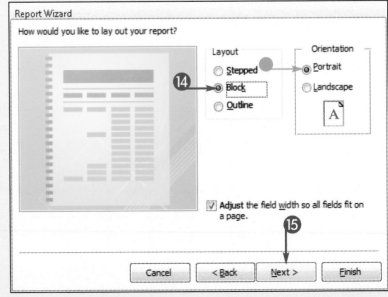

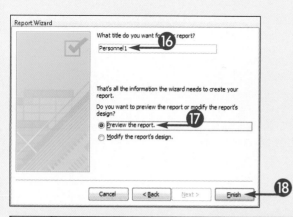

⓰ Type a name for the report.

⓱ Click the **Preview the report** radio button.

⓲ Click **Finish**.

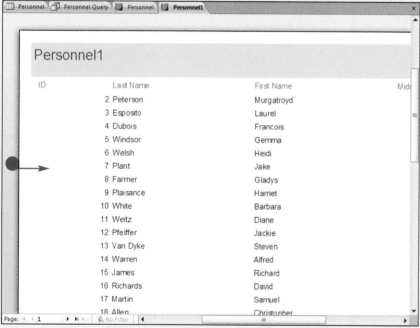

● Access creates the report and displays the report in Print Preview mode.

How do I print a report?
To print a report from Print Preview view, click the **Print Preview** tab and click the **Print** button. Alternatively, click the **File** button and click **Print** to open the Print dialog box, where you can select various printing options.

How can I customize a report in Access?
You can further customize a report using Design view. You can change the formatting of fields, move fields around, and more. You can even apply conditional formatting to the report by clicking the **Conditional Formatting** button in the Format tab. (For more about conditional formatting, refer to the section "Apply Conditional Formatting" earlier in this chapter.)

Part VI

Outlook

Outlook is a personal information manager for the computer desktop. You can use Outlook's Calendar component to manage appointments in your calendar; its Contacts component to keep track of contacts; its Tasks component to organize lists of tasks you need to complete; its Mail component to send and receive e-mail messages; and more. You can perform a wide variety of everyday tasks from the Outlook window. In this part, you learn how to put Outlook to work for you using each of the major components to manage everyday tasks.

View Outlook Components

You can use Outlook to manage everyday tasks. Outlook works much like a personal organizer, with components for performing certain tasks: Mail, Calendar, Contacts, and Tasks.

The Outlook Mail component enables you to send and receive e-mail messages. The Outlook Calendar component enables you to keep track of appointments. The Outlook Contacts

component enables you to maintain a database of your contacts. The Outlook Tasks component enables you to keep a to-do list. In addition, Outlook features a To-Do Bar to help you stay organized at a glance.

You can easily switch between components, depending on the task that you want to perform.

View Outlook Components

① Click the **Calendar** button in the Navigation pane.

● You can use the To-Do Bar to see your daily items at a glance.

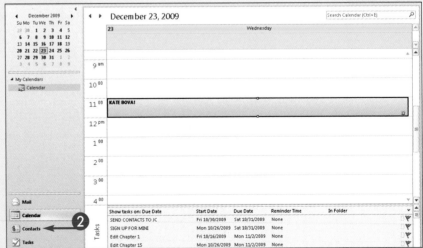

Outlook displays the Calendar component.

② Click the **Contacts** button in the Navigation pane.

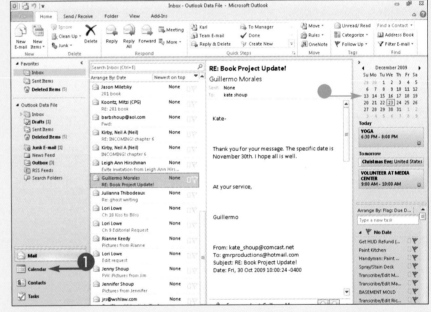

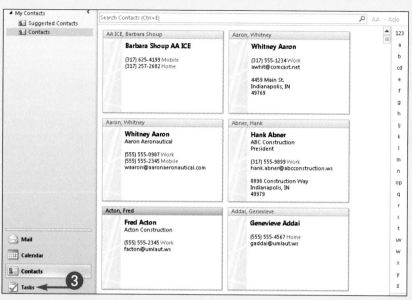

Outlook displays the Contacts component.

3 Click the **Tasks** button in the Navigation pane.

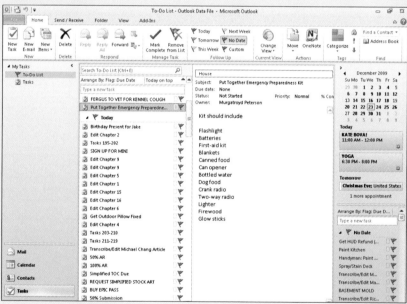

Outlook displays the Tasks component.

How I change what component opens by default when I start Outlook?
By default, Outlook opens the Mail component's Inbox folder when you start the program. To start with a different Mail folder or another component, such as Calendar, click the **File** tab, click **Options**, and click **Advanced** in the Outlook Options dialog box that opens. Under Outlook Start and Exit, click the **Browse** button. Then click the component or Mail folder that you want to set as the default component in the Select Folder dialog box, and click **OK** in both dialog boxes to close them.

Schedule an Appointment

You can use Outlook's Calendar component to keep track of your schedule. When you add a new appointment to the Calendar, you fill out appointment details such as the name of the person with whom you are meeting, the location of the appointment, the date of the appointment, and the start and end times of the appointment. You can also enter notes about the appointment, as well as set up Outlook to remind you of the appointment in advance. When you set a reminder, Outlook displays a prompt box at the designated time to remind you about the appointment (assuming, of course, that Outlook is running).

Schedule an Appointment

① Click the **Calendar** button in the Navigation pane to open the Calendar component.

② Click the date for which you want to set an appointment.

● Click the Date Navigator's arrow buttons to choose a different month.

③ Double-click the time slot for the appointment that you want to set.

Outlook opens the Appointment window, displaying the Appointment tab.

④ Type a name for the appointment.

● Outlook adds the name to the window's title.

⑤ Type a location for the appointment.

⑥ Click the **End time** ▾ and set an end time for the appointment.

● If you did not select the correct time slot in Step **3**, you can click the **Start time** ▾ and click a start time.

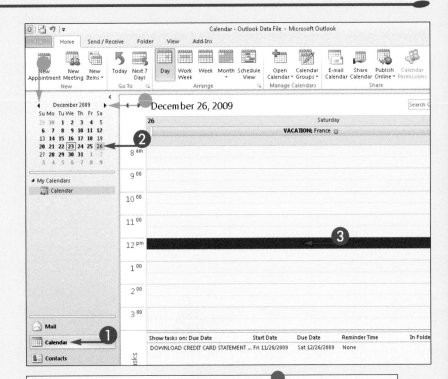

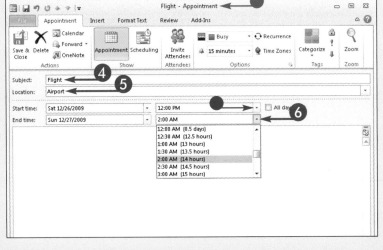

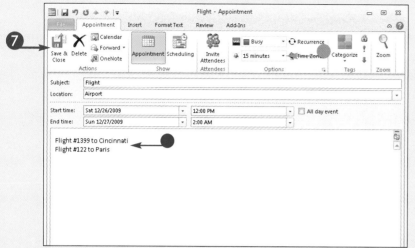

Outlook automatically sets a reminder for the appointment.

● You can click the ⊡ to change the reminder setting.

● You can type any notes about the appointment here.

7 Click the **Save & Close** button.

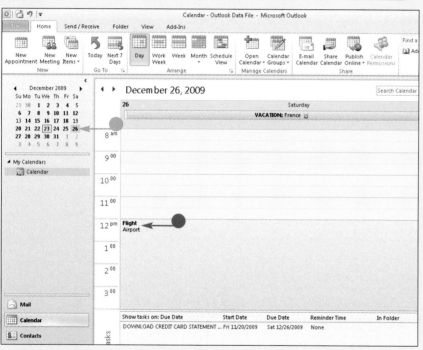

● Outlook displays the appointment in the Calendar.

To view the appointment details or make changes, you can double-click the appointment to reopen the Appointment window.

● The days on which you have any appointments scheduled appear bold in the Date Navigator.

Simplify It

How do I categorize an appointment?
Click the **Categorize** button to assign color categories to your appointments; this helps you keep them organized in your calendar. For example, you might categorize all work appointments as blue and all non-work appointments as red.

How do I delete an appointment from the Calendar?
To remove an appointment, right-click the appointment in the Calendar and click **Delete**. You can also click the appointment to select it and press Delete on your keyboard, or open the appointment window and click the **Delete** button. Outlook immediately deletes the appointment from your schedule.

Schedule a Recurring Appointment

If your schedule includes a weekly department meeting or a lunch date with a friend on the second Friday of every month, you can set the appointment as a recurring appointment. When you set up a recurring appointment, Outlook adds the appointment to each week or month as you require. (Note that you can use this same technique to set recurring tasks in your Outlook Tasks.)

Before you can indicate that an appointment should be recurring, you must first create the appointment. For help creating appointments, see the preceding section, "Schedule an Appointment."

Schedule a Recurring Appointment

① With the Appointment window for the recurring appointment open in Outlook, click the **Recurrence** button on the Appointment tab.

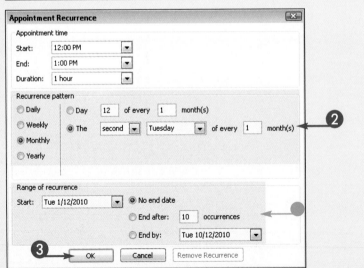

The Appointment Recurrence dialog box opens.

② Select the recurrence pattern.

● You can also set a range of the recurrence if the appointments will continue for only a set number of weeks or months.

③ Click **OK**.

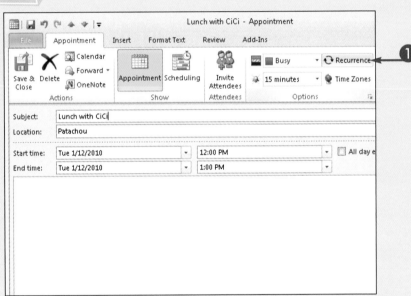

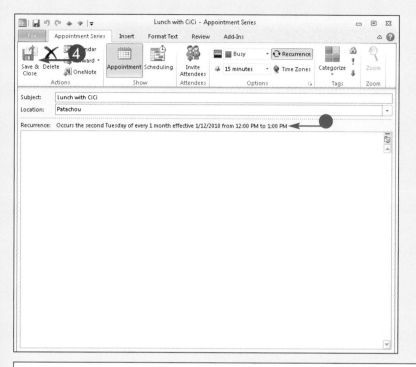

● Outlook marks the appointment as a recurring appointment.

④ Click the **Save & Close** button.

Outlook displays the appointment in the Calendar.

● Recurring appointments are indicated by a recurrence icon (⟳) in the lower right corner of the appointment on the Calendar.

Is there an easy way to set an appointment with one of my contacts?
Yes. Open the Contacts component and right-click the contact with whom you want to schedule an appointment. Next, click **Create**; then click **Meeting**. A Meeting window opens; here, you can enter appointment details and e-mail a meeting request to the contact.

How do I add holidays to my calendar?
Click the **File** tab, click **Options**, click **Calendar** in the Outlook Options dialog box, and click the **Add Holidays** button under Calendar Options. The Add Holidays to Calendar dialog box opens; click the country or religion whose holidays you want to add to the calendar, and click **OK**.

Schedule an Event

If you need to track an activity that lasts the entire day or spans several days, such as an anniversary or a conference, you can schedule the activity as an event. Events appear as banners at the top of the scheduled date.

Scheduling an event is similar to scheduling a regular appointment. As with scheduling a

regular appointment, you enter a name for the event, specify a location, and enter notes about the event as needed. In addition to scheduling events, you can schedule meetings. (For more information, see the tip at the end of this section.)

Schedule an Event

1. Click the **Home** tab.
2. Click the **New Items** button.
3. Click **All Day Event**.

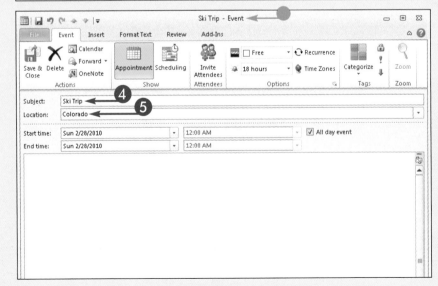

Outlook displays the Event window, which looks the same as the Appointment window.

4. Type a subject for the event.

● Outlook adds the subject to the window's title.

5. Type a location for the event, if applicable.

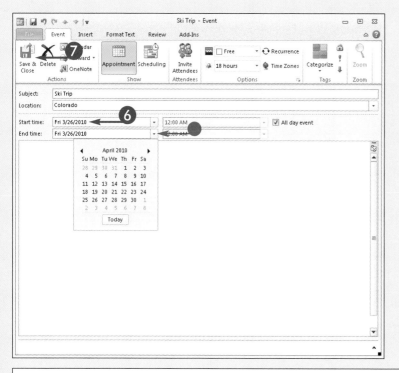

6 Enter the event's date in the **Start time** and **End time** fields.

● You can click each field's ⊡ to choose the date from a pop-up calendar.

7 Click the **Save & Close** button.

● Outlook displays the event as a banner in the Calendar for the date of the event.

To edit an event, you can double-click the event banner and make your changes in the appointment window that opens.

How do I plan a meeting?
To schedule meetings with other users, click the **Home** tab and click the **New Meeting** button to open a Meeting window; then enter the requested information.

Can I publish my calendar online?
Yes. Click the **Home** tab, click **Publish Online**, and then click **Publish to Office.com**. Outlook prompts you to register with Office Online before launching a wizard to step you through the publication process. After your calendar is published, Outlook prompts you to invite others to view it; follow the on-screen instructions.

Create a New Contact

You can use Outlook's Contacts component to maintain contact information for people with whom you want to remain in touch, such as family members, co-workers, and clients. Using Outlook Contacts, you can keep track of information about your contacts such as their home address, their business address, their e-mail address, their home phone number, their work phone number, their mobile number, and their fax number. You can also enter notes about a contact.

If you use a different program to keep track of your contacts, you may be able to import that information into Outlook. For more information, see the tip at the end of this section.

Create a New Contact

1. Click the **Contacts** button in the Navigation pane to open the Contacts component.

2. Click the **New Contact** button.

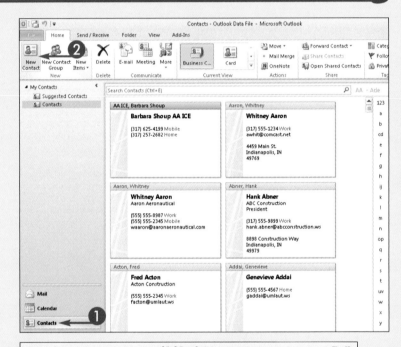

Outlook opens a Contact window.

3. Fill in the contact's information.

   You can press Tab to move from field to field.

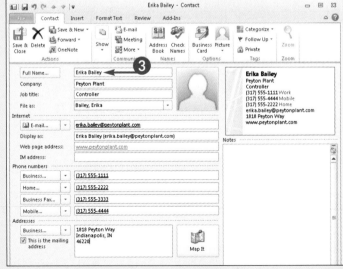

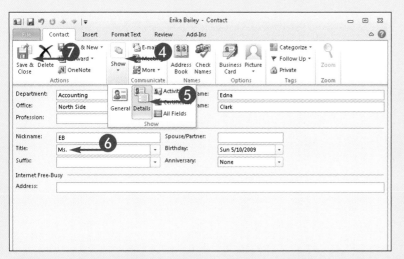

4 Click the **Show** button.

5 Click the **Details** button.

6 Fill in additional information about the contact, as needed.

7 Click the **Save & Close** button.

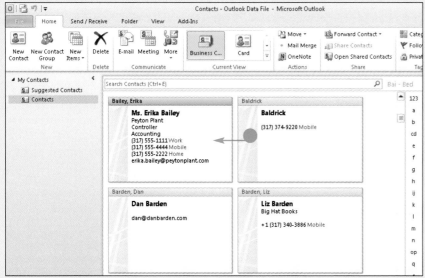

● Outlook saves the information and displays the contact in the Contacts list.

To edit contact details, you can double-click the contact to reopen the Contact window.

How do I import a list of contacts from another program?
Click the **File** tab, click **Open**, and click **Import** to open the Import and Export Wizard, which steps you through the import process. (To import contacts from another program, you must first export the contacts from that program to a special file.)

How do I send an e-mail to a contact?
One way to send an e-mail to a contact is to right-click the contact, click **Create**, and then click **E-mail**. Outlook opens a Message window with the contact's e-mail address in the To field; add a subject, type your message text, and click **Send**.

Create a New Task

You can use Outlook's Tasks component to keep track of things that you need to do, such as a daily list of activities or project steps that you need to complete. You can assign a due date to each task, as well as prioritize and categorize tasks. You can even use Outlook Tasks to assign tasks to other people.

When you are finished with a task, you can mark it as complete. Depending on the current view, completed tasks may appear with a strikethrough on the Tasks list or may be hidden.

Create a New Task

① Click the **Tasks** button in the Navigation pane to open the Tasks component.

② Click the **New Task** button.

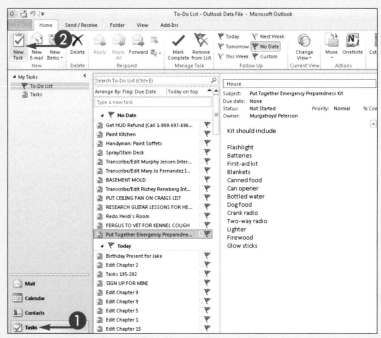

Outlook displays a Task window.

③ Type a subject for the task.

● Outlook adds the subject to the window's title.

④ Enter a due date for the task.

⑤ Click the **Status** ⊡ and click a progress option.

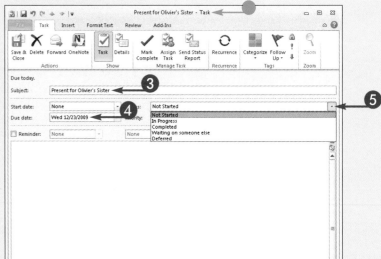

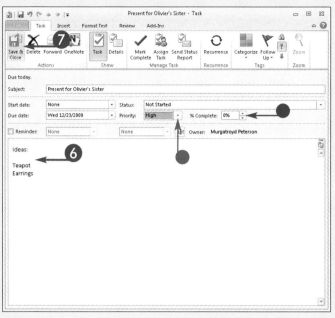

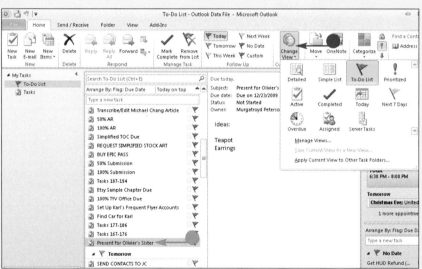

6 Type a note or details about the task here.

● You can set a priority level for the task using the **Priority** ▼.

● To set a completion amount, you can click the **% Complete** ⬍.

7 Click the **Save & Close** button.

● Outlook displays the task in the Tasks list.

To view the task details again or make changes, you can double-click the task to reopen the Task window.

● To change your view of tasks in the Tasks list, you can click the **Change View** button and choose a view option from the menu that appears.

How do I mark a task as complete?
Click a task in the Tasks list, click the **Home** tab, and click **Mark Complete**. To remove a task from the list, click it to select it and then click the **Remove from List** button in the Home tab.

How do I assign a task to someone else?
You assign a task to someone else by e-mailing it to him or her. To do so, open the task, click the **Home** tab, and click **Assign Task**. In the Task window, add an e-mail address and a message concerning the task, and then send the message.

Add a Note

In addition to the Mail, Calendar, Contacts, and Tasks components, Outlook includes a Notes component. You can use this component to create notes for yourself. Much like an electronic version of yellow sticky notes, Outlook's Notes component enables you to quickly and easily jot down your ideas and thoughts. You can attach Outlook Notes to other items in Outlook, such as appointments or e-mail messages, as well as drag them from the Outlook window onto the Windows desktop for easy viewing. When you no longer need a note, you can delete it.

Add a Note

1 Click the **Notes** button (▣) in the Navigation pane to open the Notes component.

2 Click the **New Note** button.

● Outlook displays a yellow note.

3 Type your note text.

4 When you finish, click the note's **Close** button (▣).

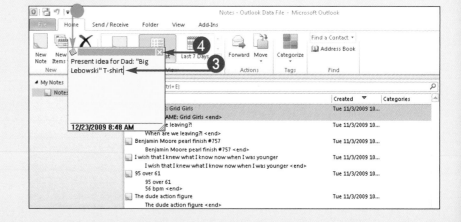

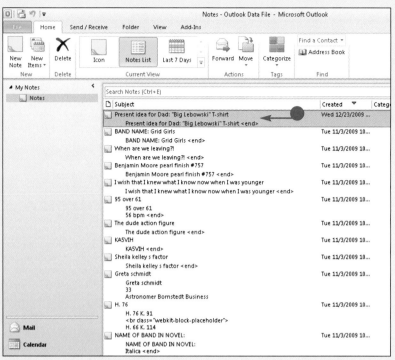

● Outlook adds the note to the Notes list.

To view the note again or to make changes, you can double-click the note to reopen it.

● To change your view of notes in the Notes list, you can click an option in the **Current View** group.

This example displays the Icon view.

Can I forward the note to another user?
Yes. To turn a note into an e-mail attachment, right-click the note in the Notes list and click **Forward**. An e-mail Message window opens with the note attached and the contents of the note in the Subject line. Simply enter the recipient's e-mail address and add any message text; then click the **Send** button.

How do I delete a note?
Click the note in the Notes list and then click the **Delete** button in the Home tab or press Delete. Alternatively, right-click the note in the Notes list and click **Delete**.

Organize Outlook Items

You can store your Outlook items, whether they are messages, tasks, or notes, in folders. By default, Outlook creates a set of folders for you to use when you install the program, including e-mail folders for managing incoming, outgoing, and deleted messages.

You can use the Folders list to move items from one folder to another and create new folders in

which to store Outlook items. You can even create subfolders within these folders. For example, you might create a subfolder in your Inbox folder to place all the corporate correspondence that you send and receive, or create a folder in the Tasks folder for a special project.

Organize Outlook Items

View the Folder List

① Click the **Folder List** button (▢) in the Navigation pane.

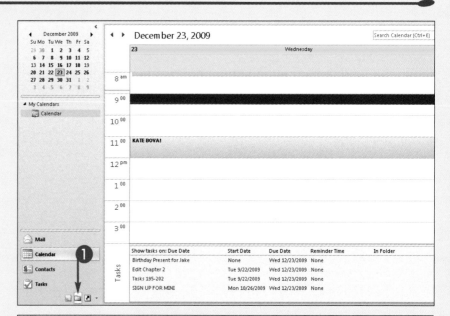

● Outlook displays the Folder List pane.

To move an item to another folder, you can click and drag the item and drop it on the folder's name.

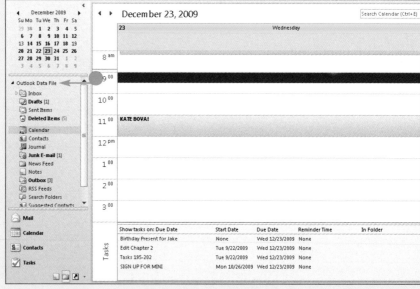

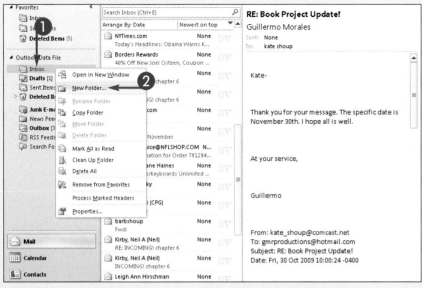

Create a New Folder

1. In the Folder list, right-click the folder in which you want to create a new folder.

2. Click **New Folder**.

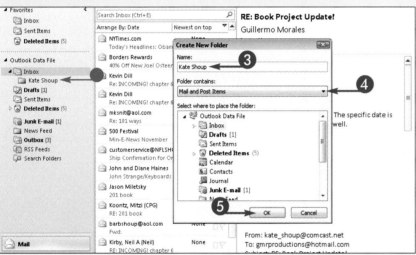

The Create New Folder dialog box appears.

3. Type a name for the new folder.

4. Click the **Folder contains** ▾ and choose an item type.

5. Click **OK**.

● Outlook creates the new folder.

How do I delete an item from a folder?
To delete an item from a folder, click the folder in the Folders list containing the item, click the item you want to delete, click the **Home** tab, and click the **Delete** button. To delete an entire folder and all of its items, click the folder in the Folders list and then press Delete . Outlook places items you delete in the Deleted Items folder; to empty the Deleted Items folder (and thereby remove any items it contains from your system), right-click it and choose **Empty "Deleted Items" Folder**.

Perform an Instant Search

Suppose you need to locate an Outlook item — for example, an e-mail message about a project you are working on, an item on your to-do list that you need to review, or the contact record for a co-worker that you need to call. Instead of sifting through your Outlook folders to locate it, you can use Outlook's Search tool to quickly find it. Each component includes an Instant Search box; simply enter a keyword or phrase, and Outlook searches for a match, even displaying items that match your criteria as you type.

Perform an Instant Search

① Click the Outlook component that you want to search.

② Click in the **Search Component** box.

● Outlook displays a Search tab, with several search-specific tools.

③ Type your keyword or phrase.

● Double-click an item to view it in its own window.

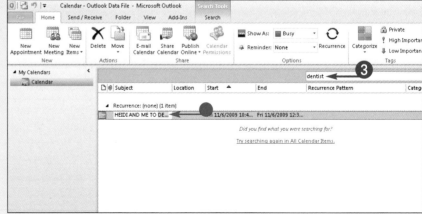

Customize the To-Do Bar

You can use Outlook's To-Do Bar to quickly view the Date Navigator and the current day's appointments and tasks, as well as to enter new tasks.

You can customize the To-Do Bar to change what items appear in the list. For example, you might opt to display Date Navigators for this month and the next or change how many appointments appear in the To-Do Bar.

If the To-Do Bar is not visible, click the Expand the To-Do Bar button (⊡) on the right side of the Outlook screen to display it.

Customize the To-Do Bar

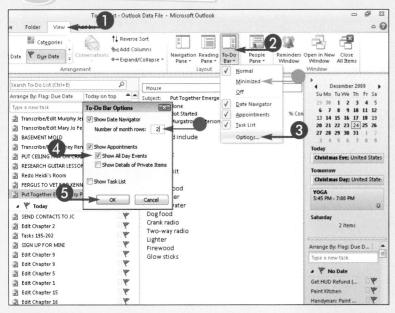

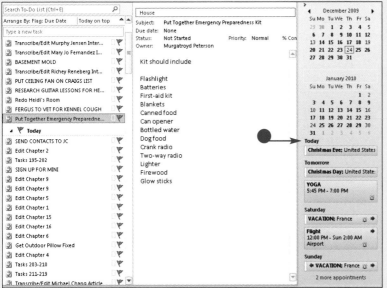

1 Click the **View** tab.

2 Click **To-Do Bar**.

3 Click **Options**.

● You can click **Minimized** to minimize the bar.

The To-Do Bar Options dialog box appears.

4 Click a check box to deselect a feature on the To-Do Bar view.

● You can control the number of months or appointments that appear on the bar.

5 Click **OK**.

● Outlook applies the changes.

Compose and Send a Message

You can use Outlook to compose and send e-mail messages. When you compose a message in Outlook, you designate the e-mail address of the message recipient (or recipients) and type your message text. You can also give the message a subject title to indicate to recipients what the message is about. Although you can compose a message offline, you must log on to your Internet connection to send a message. If you do not have time to finish composing your message during your current work session, you can save the message as a draft for access at a later time instead of sending it.

Compose and Send a Message

① Click the **Mail** button in the Navigation pane to open the Mail component.

② Click the **Home** tab.

③ Click the **New E-mail** button.

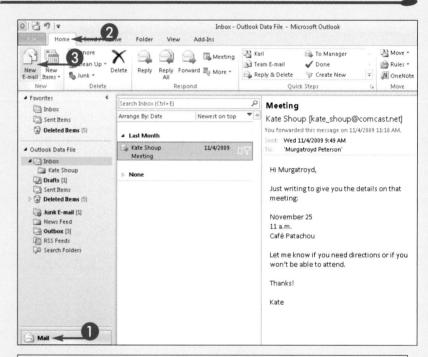

Outlook opens an untitled message window.

④ Type the recipient's e-mail address.

● If the e-mail address is already in your Address Book, you can click the **To** button and select the recipient's name.

If you enter more than one e-mail address, you must separate each address with a semicolon (;) and a space.

⑤ Type a subject title for the message.

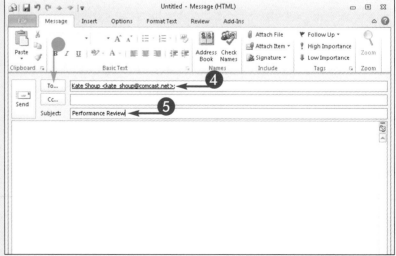

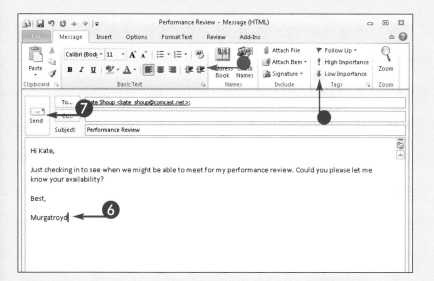

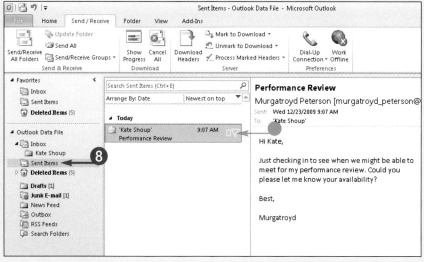

6 Type the message text.

● You can use Outlook's formatting buttons to change the appearance of your message text.

● To set a priority level for the message, you can click **High Importance** or **Low Importance**.

Note: By default, the message priority level is Normal.

7 Click **Send**.

Outlook sends the e-mail message.

Note: You must be connected to the Internet to send the message.

Messages you have sent are stored in the Sent Items folder.

8 Click the **Sent Items** folder in the Navigation pane.

● The message you sent appears in the Item list.

Simplify It

How do I save a message as a draft?
Click the message window's [×] button and click **Yes** when prompted to save the message. Outlook saves the message in the Drafts folder. When you are ready to recommence composing your message, click the **Drafts** folder in the Folders list and double-click the saved message to open it.

How do I carbon-copy my message to someone?
You can use the Cc or Bcc field to copy or blind carbon copy the message to another recipient. Either type his or her e-mail address directly in the field or click the **Cc** or **Bcc** button to select it from your contacts.

Send a File Attachment

You can send files stored on your computer to other e-mail recipients. For example, you might send an Excel worksheet or Word document to a work colleague, or send a digital photo of your child's birthday to a relative. Assuming that the recipient's computer has the necessary software installed, that person can open and view the file on his or her own system.

Note that some e-mail systems are not set up to handle large file attachments. If you are sending a large attachment, check with the recipient to see if his or her system can handle it.

Send a File Attachment

① Create a new e-mail message, entering the recipient's e-mail address, a subject title, and the message text.

Note: *Refer to the preceding section for help creating a new e-mail message.*

② Click the **Message** tab.

③ Click the **Attach File** button.

The Insert File dialog box appears.

④ Locate and select the file you want to send.

⑤ Click **Insert**.

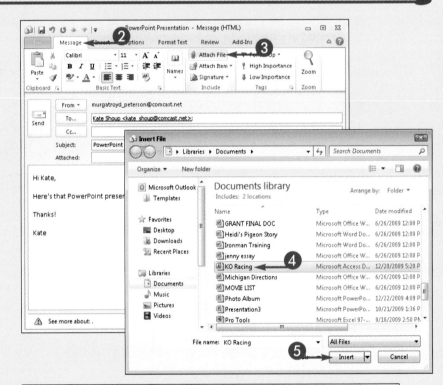

● Outlook adds the file attachment to the message and displays the filename and the file size.

⑥ Click **Send**.

Outlook sends the e-mail message and attachment.

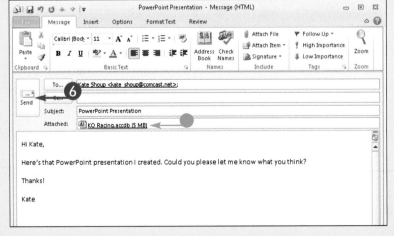

Read an Incoming Message

You can use Outlook's Mail feature to access your e-mail account, download new e-mail messages that others have sent you, and view them on-screen. You can view a message in a separate message window or in the Reading pane. If the Reading pane is not visible, click the View tab, click Reading Pane, and choose a display option from the list that appears.

You can also view any files attached to the messages you receive (although you should never open a file unless you trust the person who sent it). Note that in order to receive e-mail messages, you must be connected to the Internet.

Read an Incoming Message

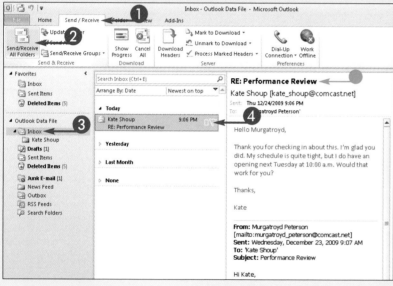

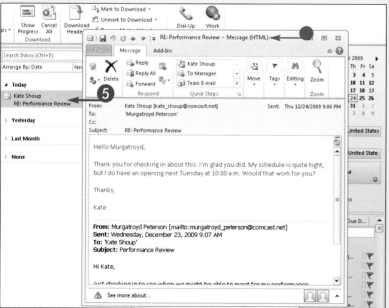

① Click the **Send/Receive** tab.

② Click **Send/Receive All Folders**.

Outlook accesses your e-mail account and downloads any new messages.

③ If the Inbox is not shown, you can click the **Inbox** folder.

④ Click a message in the Item list.

● The contents of the message are shown in the Reading pane.

⑤ Double-click a message in the Item list.

● The message opens in a message window.

Note: *If the message contains a file attachment, double-click it to open it. A warning dialog box appears; click **Open** to open and display the file in the appropriate program, or click **Save** to save the attachment.*

Reply To or Forward a Message

You can reply to an e-mail message by sending a return message to the original sender. For example, if you receive an e-mail message containing a question, you can reply to that e-mail with your answer. When you reply to an e-mail, the original sender's name is added to the message's To field.

You can also forward the message to another recipient. For example, you might forward a message that you receive from one co-worker to another co-worker who will find its contents useful.

Note that you must be connected to the Internet in order to send replies or forward e-mail messages.

Reply To or Forward a Message

Reply To a Message

① Open the message to which you want to reply.

Note: *Refer to the preceding section to learn how to open an e-mail message.*

② Click the **Reply** button to reply to the original sender.

● To reply to the sender as well as to everyone else who received the original message, you can click the **Reply All** button.

● The original sender's address appears in the To field.

③ Type your reply.

④ Click **Send**.

Outlook sends the e-mail message.

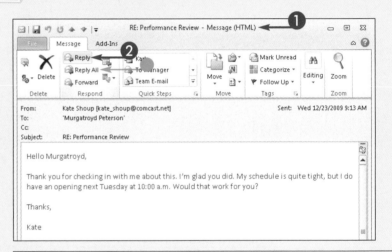

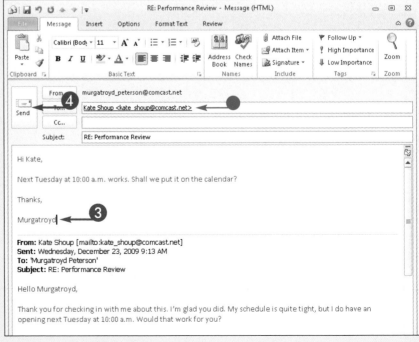

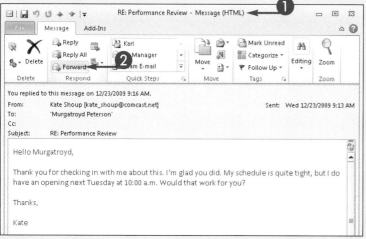

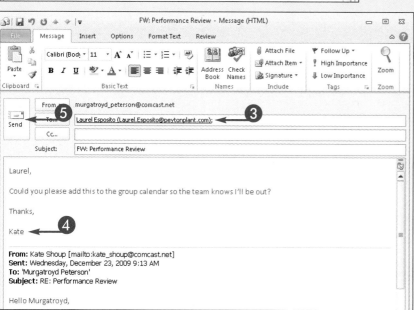

Forward a Message

1 Open the message that you want to forward.

Note: *Refer to the preceding section to learn how to open an e-mail message.*

2 Click the **Forward** button on the Message tab.

3 Enter the recipient's e-mail address in the **To** field.

4 Type any message that you want to add to the forwarded e-mail.

5 Click **Send**.

Outlook forwards the e-mail message.

Simplify It

How do I get rid of the original message in my reply?

By default, Outlook retains the original message when you click the **Reply** or **Reply All** button. To turn off this feature, click the **File** tab and then click **Options**. In the Outlook Options dialog box, click **Mail**. Under Replies and Forwards, click the **When replying to a message** ▾ and click **Do not include original message** (●). Click **OK**.

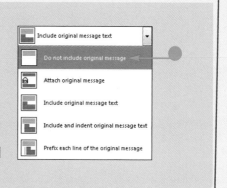

Add a Sender to Your Outlook Contacts

Suppose you receive an e-mail message from someone, and you do not have a record for that individual in Outlook Contacts. Fortunately, Outlook makes it easy to add the contact information of the sender of any message you receive to your Outlook Contacts, directly from

the message itself. Once the person has been added to Outlook Contacts, if you want to send a new message to that person at a later time, you can click the To button in the message window and choose his or her name from the Select Names: Contacts dialog box that appears.

Add a Sender to Your Outlook Contacts

① Open the message whose sender you want to add to your Outlook Contacts.

Note: Refer to the section "Read an Incoming Message" earlier in this chapter to learn how to open an e-mail message.

② Right-click the sender's name.

③ Click **Add to Outlook Contacts**.

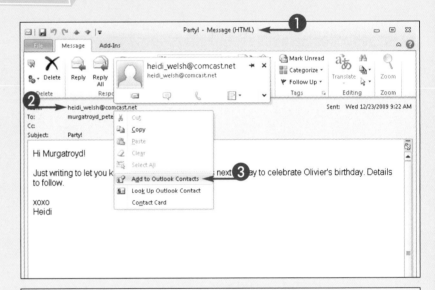

● The Contact window opens with the sender's name and e-mail address already filled in.

● You can add additional information as needed.

④ Click **Save & Close**.

Outlook saves the contact information.

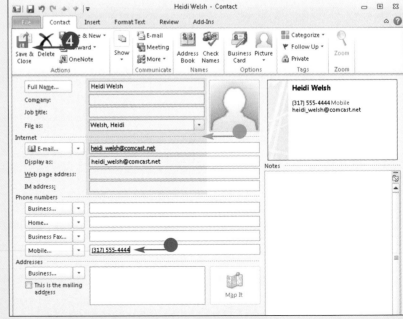

Delete a Message

As you receive more and more e-mail messages, you may find it difficult to keep your Inbox and other Outlook folders organized. One way to eliminate clutter and keep things manageable is to delete messages you no longer need from your Inbox and other Outlook folders.

Note that when you delete a message from your Inbox or any other Outlook folder,

Outlook does not remove it from your system. Rather, it moves it to the Deleted Items folder. To permanently remove deleted messages from your system, thereby maximizing your computer's storage capacity, you should purge the Deleted Items folder on a regular basis.

Delete a Message

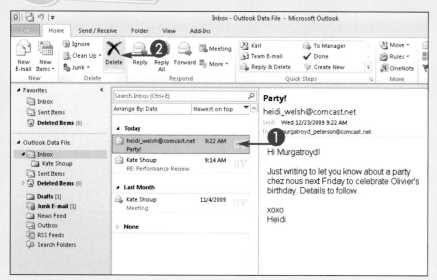

① Locate and select the message that you want to delete.

② Press **Delete** or click the **Delete** button on the Home tab.

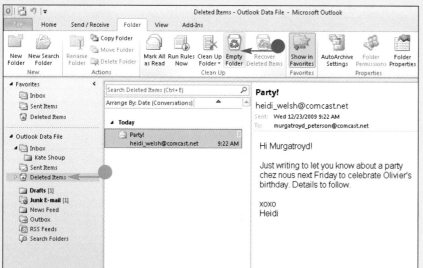

Outlook deletes the message from the Inbox and adds it to the Deleted Items folder.

● You can click the **Deleted Items** folder to view the message that you deleted.

● To empty the Deleted Items folder, click the **Deleted Items** folder, click the **Folder** tab, and click **Empty Folder**.

View Conversations

Outlook 2010 supports a new feature called Conversation view. With Conversation view, you can group messages that are within the same thread, or conversation, in the Item list. This makes your Item list easier to navigate by compressing all related messages, including messages that you have sent as replies or forwarded to others, under a single heading. You can expand this heading to view these related messages. By default, Outlook displays all messages from all folders in Conversation view. You can, however, view only those messages in the current folder if you prefer.

View Conversations

1 Click the **View** tab.

2 Click the **Conversations** button in the Arrangement group.

3 Click **Show Messages in Conversations**.

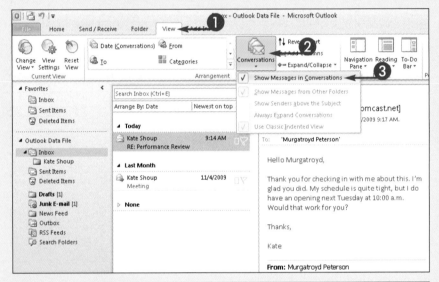

● Outlook organizes your message by conversation.

4 Click the conversation heading.

5 Click the ▷ to expand the conversation.

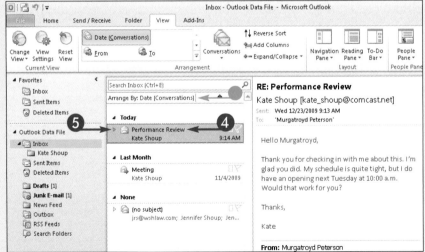

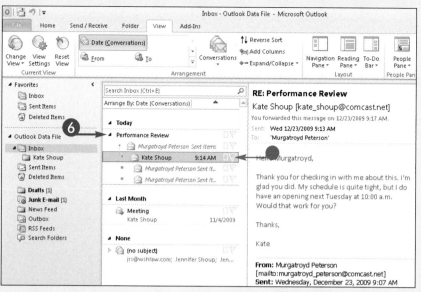

● Outlook expands the conversation, displaying all the related messages.

⑥ Click the ◪ to compress the conversation.

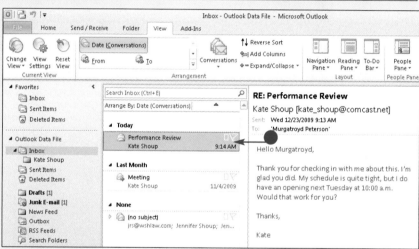

● Outlook compresses the conversation, displaying only the conversation heading.

Simplify It

What other view options does Outlook offer?
You can organize your messages using any one of several Outlook views, including Date view, in which messages are organized by date; From view, in which messages are organized by sender; To view, in which messages are organized by recipient; Categories view, in which messages are organized by category; and Importance view, in which high-priority messages are listed first.

How do I limit what messages are included in the conversation?
To view only those messages in the current folder, click the **View** tab, click the **Conversations** button, and deselect **Show Messages from Other Folders** in the menu that appears.

Clean Up a Conversation

You may find that as various people contribute to an e-mail conversation, redundant messages begin to appear in your Inbox. For example, your Inbox may suddenly contain replies to replies to replies, meaning that several of the messages contain redundant text. To clean up a conversation — that is, to move these redundant messages to the Deleted Items folder — you can use Outlook's Clean Up feature. (To permanently remove deleted messages from your system, thereby maximizing your computer's storage capacity, you should purge the Deleted Items folder on a regular basis.)

Clean Up a Conversation

① With your Outlook messages shown in Conversation view, click a message in the conversation you want to clean up.

② Click the **Home** tab.

③ Click the **Clean Up** button in the Delete group.

④ Click **Clean Up Conversation**.

The Clean Up Conversation dialog box opens.

⑤ Click **Clean Up**.

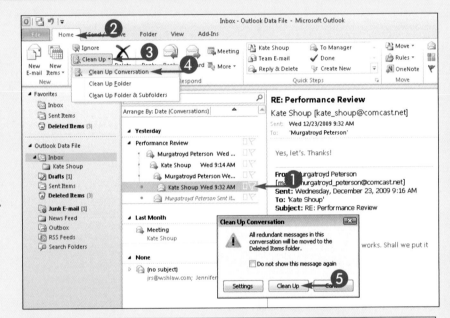

● Outlook removes redundant messages from the conversation.

● Messages are placed in the Deleted Items folder.

Note: To permanently remove the messages, click the **Deleted Items** folder, click the **Folder** tab, and click **Empty Folder**.

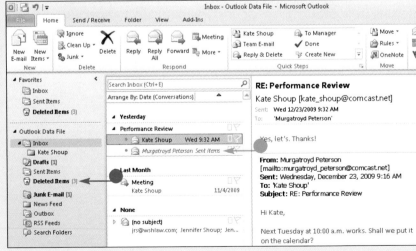

Ignore a Conversation

If you have been included in a conversation that is of no relevance to you, you can instruct Outlook to ignore the conversation. When you ignore a conversation, Outlook moves all messages in that conversation that you have received thus far to the Deleted Items folder. It also automatically moves any subsequent messages you receive during the course of the conversation to the Deleted Items folder. (To permanently remove deleted messages from your system, you should purge the Deleted Items folder on a regular basis.) If you realize you have ignored a conversation in error, you can instruct Outlook to stop ignoring it.

Ignore a Conversation

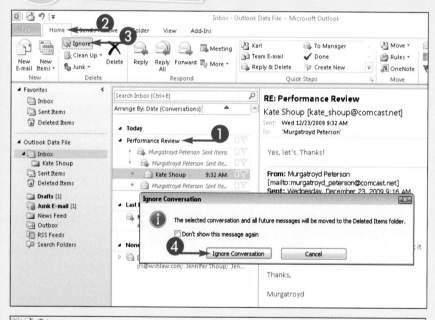

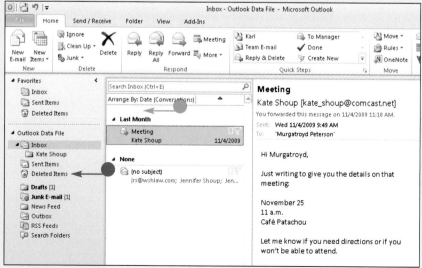

① With your Outlook messages shown in Conversation view, click the conversation you want to ignore.

② Click the **Home** tab.

③ Click the **Ignore** button in the Delete group.

The Ignore Conversation dialog box opens.

④ Click **Ignore Conversation**.

● Outlook removes the conversation.

● The conversation is placed in the Deleted Items folder.

Note: If you realize you have ignored a conversation in error, you can stop ignoring it. To do so, click the **Deleted Items** folder, click the conversation, click the **Home** tab, click the **Ignore** button, and click **Stop Ignoring Conversation**.

Screen Junk E-mail

Junk e-mail, also called *spam*, is overabundant on the Internet and likely finds its way onto your computer often. You can safeguard against wasting time viewing unsolicited messages by setting up Outlook's Junk E-mail feature. This feature enables you to make sure that e-mail from specific Web domains bypasses

your Inbox and is instead deposited into the Outlook Junk E-mail folder.

Note that sometimes e-mail that is *not* spam may be placed in the Junk E-mail folder in error. For this reason, you should periodically scan the contents of this folder to ensure that it does not contain any messages you want to read.

Screen Junk E-mail

View Junk E-mail Options

1 Click the **Home** tab.

2 Click the **Junk** ▾.

3 Click **Junk E-mail Options**.

The Junk E-mail Options dialog box appears.

● You can use the various tabs to view junk e-mail settings, blocked domains, and safe senders.

● You can click one of these options to control the level of junk e-mail filtering that Outlook applies.

4 Click **OK**.

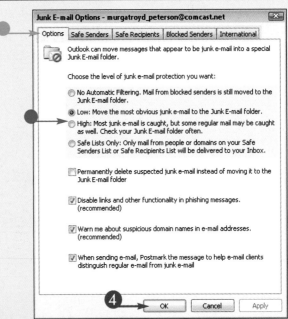

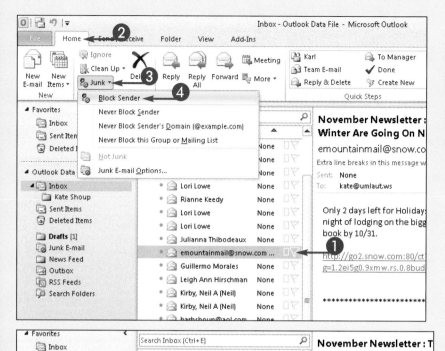

Designate a Message as Junk

1 Click the message.

2 Click the **Home** tab.

3 Click the **Junk** ⏷.

4 Click **Block Sender**.

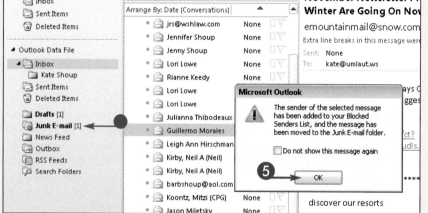

A prompt box appears.

5 Click **OK**.

● Outlook adds the sender's e-mail address to the list of filtered addresses and moves the message to the Junk E-mail folder.

Simplify It

How do I remove a message from the Junk E-mail folder?
If a message is sent to the Junk E-mail folder in error, open the **Junk E-mail** folder, click the message, click the **Home** tab, and click **Not Junk**, and click **OK**.

Does Outlook empty the Junk E-mail folder?
No. To empty the folder, click it in the Folders list, click the **Folder** tab, and click the **Empty Folder** button. Outlook moves all the items to the Deleted Items folder; to permanently remove the items from your system, click the **Deleted Items** folder in the Folders list, click the **Folder** tab, and click the **Empty Folder** button.

Create a Message Rule

You can use rules to determine what Outlook does when you receive a message that meets a specific set of conditions. For example, you might create a rule that ensures that messages from a certain sender are placed directly into a folder of your choosing as soon as Outlook downloads the message. Alternatively, you might set up Outlook to play a certain sound when you receive a message that meets criteria you set.

You can set rules that are quite simple, as outlined in this section, or rules that are very complex — involving various criteria, exceptions to the rule, and so on.

Create a Message Rule

1 Click the message on which you want to base a rule.

2 Click the **Home** tab.

3 Click **Rules**.

4 Click **Create Rule**.

The Create Rule dialog box appears.

5 Click to select the conditions that you want to apply.

6 Specify what you want the rule to do when the conditions are met. In this example, select the **Move the item to folder** check box.

7 Click the **Select Folder** button.

The Rules and Alerts dialog box appears.

8 Click the folder where you want Outlook to move the messages.

9 Click **OK**.

10 Click **OK**.

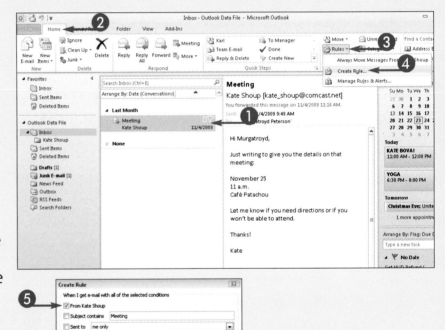

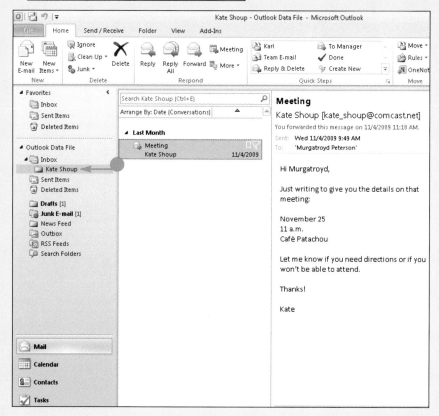

Outlook prompts you to run the rule now.

⓫ Click the check box to select it.

⓬ Click **OK**.

● Outlook moves any existing messages to the folder you specified.

The next time you receive a message matching the criteria you set, Outlook places it directly in the folder you selected.

How do I add more criteria to a message rule?
Click **Advanced Options** in the Create Rule dialog box to display the Rules Wizard. The Rules Wizard includes several sets of criteria that you can specify, such as exceptions to the rule, actions, and even a dialog box for naming the rule.

How do I remove a rule?
Click the **Home** tab, click **Rules**, and click **Manage Rules & Alerts** to open the Rules and Alerts dialog box. Next, click the rule you want to delete and click the **Delete** button.

Part VII

Publisher

Publisher is a desktop publishing program that you can use to design and produce a variety of publications — anything from a simple business card to a postcard to a newsletter to a complex brochure. Publisher installs with a large selection of predesigned publications that you can use as templates to build your own desktop publishing projects; additional templates are available on Office.com. In this part, you learn how to build and fine-tune all kinds of publications and tap into Publisher's formatting features to make each publication suit your own design and needs.

Create a Publication

You can use Publisher to create all kinds of publications, such as brochures, flyers, newsletters, and letterhead stationery.

Publisher installs with a wide variety of publication types, including preset designs, or *templates*, that control the layout and formatting of the publication. In addition, you can download templates from Office.com.

Two of the most important design options that you can change to customize a publication are the color scheme and font scheme. The color scheme controls the colors used throughout the design. The font scheme controls the font sets used for all of the various text elements in a publication.

Create a Publication

1 Click the **File** tab.

2 Click **New**.

3 Click a publication category from the list of available templates.

● You can use the scroll bar to scroll through the available publications in the category you chose.

4 Click a publication design.

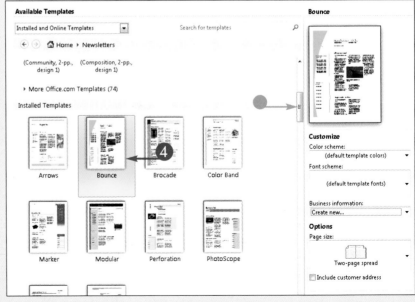

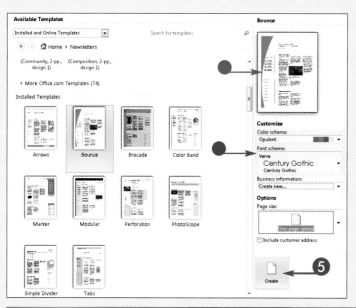

● Publisher displays a preview of the selected design here.

● You can customize a design's color scheme or fonts using these options.

⑤ Click **Create**.

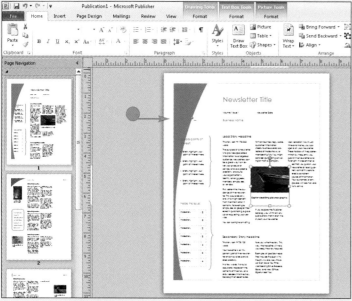

● Publisher creates the publication.

How do I change the design of my publication?
You can click the **Page Design** tab on the Ribbon to access other templates that you can apply to the publication. To change the color scheme, choose from a wide variety of preset color schemes in the **Schemes** group to create just the look you want. Click the **Fonts** button and select the desired font scheme; this affects the font sets used for all the various text elements in the publication. Finally, click the **Background** button to view and select from available backgrounds.

Create a Blank Publication

In the event none of Publisher's predesigned publication templates suits your needs, you can create a blank publication, populate it with your own text boxes, and design a layout to suit your project. For example, you might want to create your own brochure or invitation and

customize it by adding your own text boxes and art objects.

If you particularly like a publication you create on your own, you can turn it into a Publisher template, which you can then reuse in Publisher. For help, see the tip at the end of this section.

Create a Blank Publication

① Click the **File** tab.

② Click **New**.

● If you want to create an 8.5 by 11 publication, click the vertical or horizontal 8.5 by 11 option.

③ Click **More Blank Page Sizes**.

● You can use the scroll bar to scroll through the available page sizes.

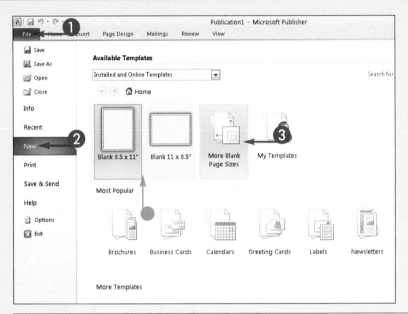

④ Click a page size.

● Publisher displays the selected size here.

● You can customize the color scheme or fonts using these options.

● You can click the **Business information** ⊡ and choose **Create new** to create a *business set*, which contains your business's name, address, and other information. After you create a business set, you can select it from the Business Information list to apply it to a publication.

⑤ Click **Create**.

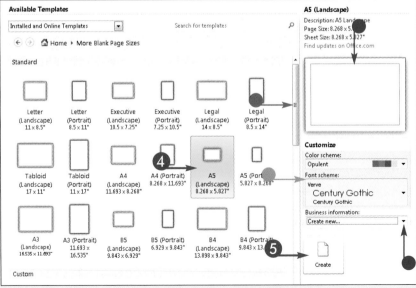

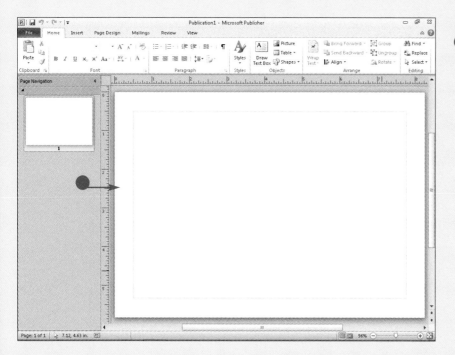

● Publisher creates and opens the blank publication.

You can now add your own text boxes and pictures to the publication.

How do I create my own Publisher templates?
Click the **File** tab and then click **Save As**. In the Save As dialog box, click the **Save as type** ▾ and then click **Publisher Template**. When you select Publisher Templates, Windows automatically opens the Templates folder (●) in the Save As dialog box; type a name for the file in the **File name** field and click **Save**. To create a new publication based on the template you saved, click the **File** tab, click **New**, click **My Templates**, and click the template in the window that appears.

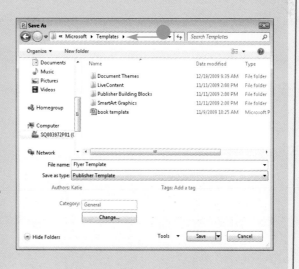

Zoom In and Out

You can use Publisher's Zoom feature to control the magnification of your publication. By default, Publisher displays your document in a zoomed-out view so that you can see all the elements on a page. When you begin working with the publication, adding text and formatting, you can zoom in to better see what you are doing.

There are a few ways to zoom in and out of your publication. One is to use the Zoom settings on the View tab. Another is to use the Zoom buttons. A third is to use your keyboard. You learn how to use all three of these techniques in this section.

Zoom In and Out

Specify a Magnification

1. Click the area of the publication where you want to change the zoom magnification.

- When you click an object on the page, Publisher surrounds it with selection handles.

2. Click the **View** tab.

3. Click the **Zoom** ☐.

4. Click a percentage.

- You can also type a value in the **Zoom** field.

   Note: *To quickly zoom to 100 percent, you can click the* **100%** *button in the* **View** *tab's Zoom group. To quickly view the whole page, click the* **Whole Page** *button.*

- Publisher changes the magnification setting for your publication.

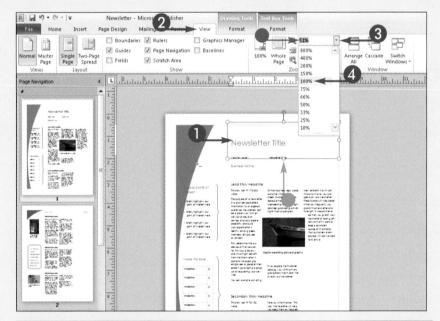

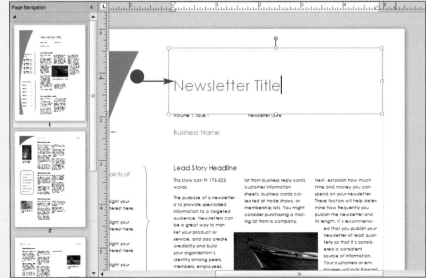

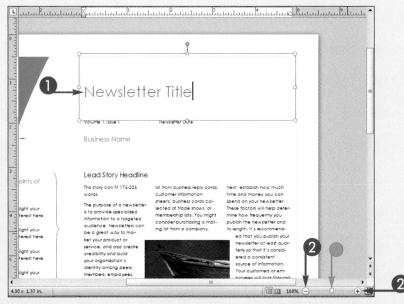

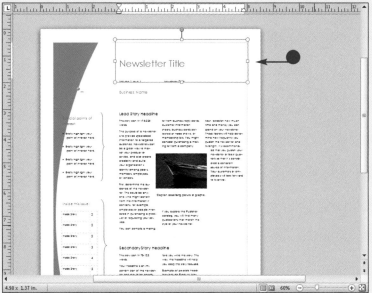

Use Zoom Buttons

① Click the area of the publication where you want to change the zoom.

② Click the **Zoom Out** (⊟) or **Zoom In** (⊞) button.

You can click the Zoom buttons multiple times to change the level of magnification.

● You can also click and drag the slider to change the zoom.

Publisher changes the magnification setting for your publication.

● In this example, the publication is zoomed out.

Simplify It

How can I free up more workspace on-screen?
You can minimize the Pages pane to quickly free up on-screen workspace. To do so, click the pane's ≪ button. Alternatively, click the **View** tab and then deselect the **Page Navigation** check box in the **Show** group. To view the pane again, click the **View** tab and reselect the **Page Navigation** check box or click the ≫ button.

How do I use my keyboard to zoom in and out?
Press F9 on the keyboard to quickly zoom in and out of a publication.

Add
Text

When you create a new publication based on a design, Publisher inserts a layout for the text and displays placeholder text in the text boxes, also called *objects* or *frames*. The placeholder text gives you an idea of the text formatting that the design applies and what sort of text you might place in the text box.

As you build your publication, you will almost certainly want to replace the placeholder text with your own text. After you add your text, you can apply formatting to it as well as move and resize it. (For help formatting, moving, and resizing text in Publisher, see the next chapter.)

Add Text

1 Click the text object that you want to edit.

You may need to zoom in first to see the text object.

● Publisher surrounds the selected object with handles.

● Publisher highlights the placeholder text within.

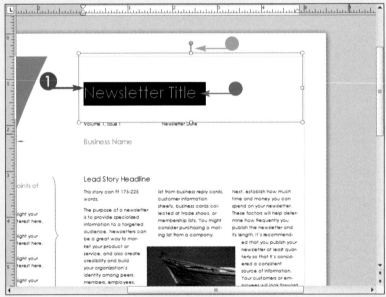

2 Type your own text.

Publisher replaces any placeholder text with the new text that you type.

● You can click anywhere outside of the text object to deselect the text box.

You can continue entering text to build your publication.

To edit the text at any time, you can click the text box and make your changes.

Add a New Text Box

You can add new text boxes to a publication and type your own text. For example, you may need to add a new text box to an empty area in your layout to include additional information, or you may need to add new text boxes to a blank publication.

After you add a text box, you can fill it with your own text. After you do so, you can apply formatting to your text as well as move and resize it. (For help formatting, moving, and resizing text in Publisher, see the next chapter.)

Add a New Text Box

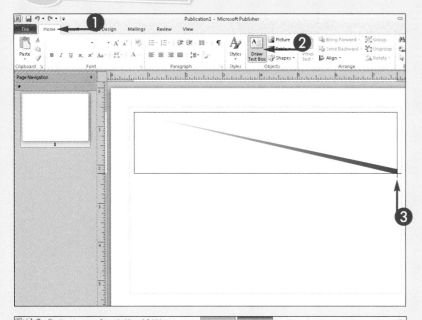

1 Click the **Home** tab.

2 Click the **Draw Text Box** button in the Objects group.

3 Click and drag the text box to the size that you want to insert.

4 Type the text that you want to insert into the text box.

● You can apply formatting to the text.

5 Click anywhere outside the text object to deselect the text box.

Add a Picture to a Publication

You can add digital photographs or other picture files to your Publisher creations. For example, you might add a photo of your company's latest product to a new brochure or include a snapshot of your baby on a family newsletter.

If you are working on a publication created with a template that includes a placeholder

picture object in the layout, adding a picture is simple. (See the tip at the end of this section for help.) However, even if your publication layout does not include a placeholder picture object, you can easily add a picture, as described in this section.

Add a Picture to a Publication

① Click the **Insert** tab.

② Click the **Picture** button in the Illustrations group.

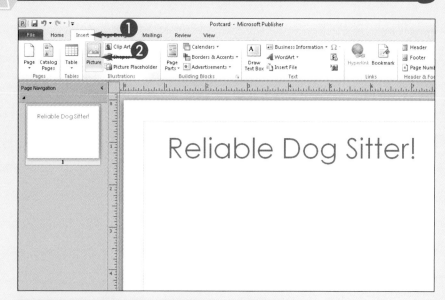

The Insert Picture dialog box appears.

③ Locate and select the picture file you want to use.

④ Click **Insert**.

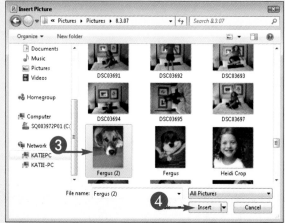

● Publisher inserts the picture file.

● The Format tab appears.

● You can move and resize the picture.

Note: *To learn how to move and resize objects in Publisher, see the next chapter.*

How do I fill in an existing picture object?
Click the picture object and then click the **Insert Picture** button (▢). The Insert Picture dialog box opens; locate and select the photo you want to use and click **Insert**.

Can I add clip art images?
Yes. Click the **Insert** tab and click the **Clip Art Pane** button. The Clip Art pane opens; type a keyword describing the type of clip art you want to insert and click **Go**. The Clip Art task pane displays possible matches; click the clip art that you want to insert. Publisher inserts the clip art and displays the Format tab.

Change the Font, Size, and Color

You can control the font, size, and color of the text in your publication. By default, when you assign a publication design, Publisher uses a predefined set of formatting for the text, including a specific font and size. You may need to change the font or increase the size to suit your own publication's needs. For example,

you might change the font, size, and color of the publication's title text to emphasize it. In addition, you can use Publisher's basic formatting commands — Bold, Italic, Underline, Subscript, and Superscript — to quickly add formatting to your text.

Change the Font, Size, and Color

Change the Font

① Click the text object or select the text that you want to format.

② Click the **Home** tab on the Ribbon.

③ Click the **Font** ⊡.

④ Click a font.

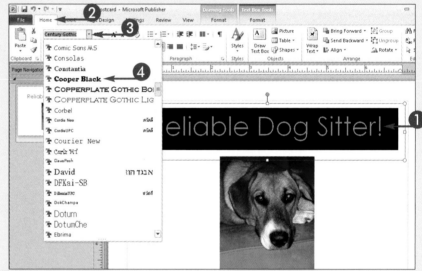

● Publisher applies the font to the text.

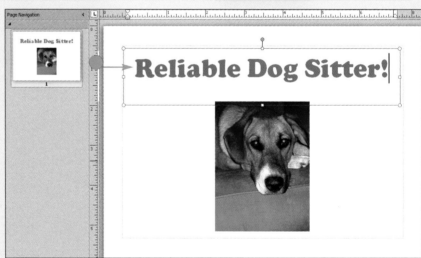

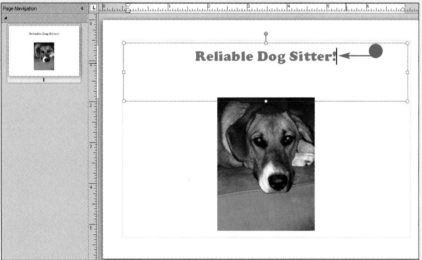

Change the Size

1 Select the text that you want to format.

2 Click the **Home** tab on the Ribbon.

3 Click the **Font Size** ⊡.

4 Click a size.

● Publisher applies the font size to the text.

This example applies a 26-point font size to the text.

Note: *Another way to change the font size is to click the* ***Grow Font*** *and* ***Shrink Font*** *buttons (⒜ and ⒜) on the* ***Home*** *tab. Publisher increases or decreases the font size with each click of the button.*

How do I apply formatting to my text?
Select the text you want to format, click the **Home** tab, and click the **Bold** (**B**), **Italic** (***I***), **Underline** (**U**), **Subscript** (**x₂**), or **Superscript** (**x²**) button.

What is the toolbar that appears when I select text?
When you select text, Publisher's mini toolbar appears, giving you quick access to common formatting commands. You can also right-click selected text to display the toolbar. If you want to use any of the tools on the toolbar, simply click the desired tool; otherwise, continue working, and the toolbar disappears.

continued

Change the Font, Size, and Color *(continued)*

Changing the text color can go a long way toward emphasizing it in your publication. For example, if you are creating an invitation, you might make the description of the event a different color to stand out from the other details. Likewise, if you are creating a newsletter, you might make the title of the newsletter a different color from the information contained in the newsletter or even color-code certain data in the newsletter. Obviously, when selecting text colors, you should avoid choosing colors that make your text difficult to read.

Change the Font, Size, and Color *(continued)*

Change the Color

1 Select the text that you want to format.

2 Click the **Home** tab on the Ribbon.

3 Click the ▾ next to the **Font Color** button (▣).

● You can click a color in the palette that appears to apply to the selected text.

4 Click **More Colors**.

The Colors dialog box opens.

5 Click the **Custom** tab.

6 Click a color in the **Colors** field.

7 Click a shade to refine your selection.

8 Click **OK**.

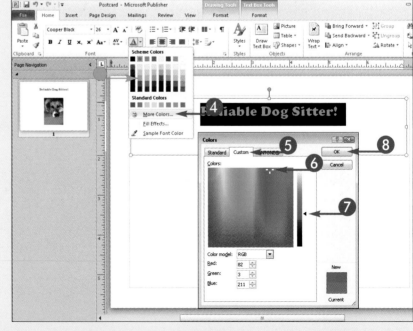

● Publisher applies the color to the text.

This example applies a blue color to the text.

Simplify It

Is there another way to change font characteristics?

Yes. You can also change font characteristics using the Font dialog box. Follow these steps:

1 Select the text that you want to format.

2 Click the **Home** tab on the Ribbon.

3 Click the corner group button (▣) in the Font group.

4 In the Font dialog box, click the font, style, size, color, underline style, or effect that you want to apply.

5 Click **OK**.

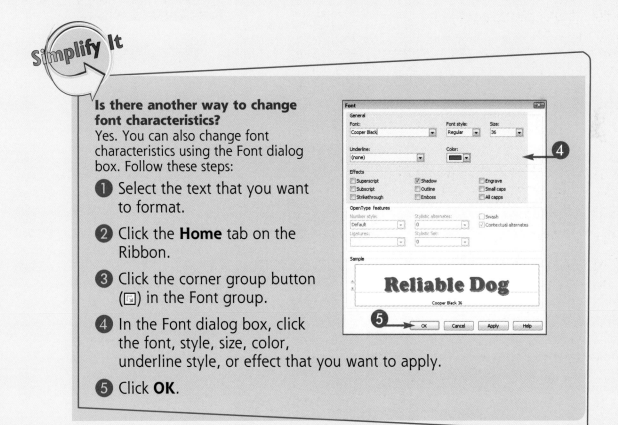

Apply a Text Effect

In addition to changing the font, size, and color of text in your publication, you can also apply text effects. These include a shadow effect, an outline effect, an emboss effect, and an engrave effect. Text effects can go a long way toward making your newsletter, brochure, postcard, or other type of publication appear more professional.

You apply text effects from the Format tab, under Text Box Tools. This tab appears on the Ribbon when you select text in your publication.

Be aware that applying too many different text effects can result in a publication that appears overdone or busy.

Apply a Text Effect

1. Select the text that you want to format.

2. Click the **Format** tab.

3. Click a button in the Effects group. (Here, the **Shadow** button is clicked.)

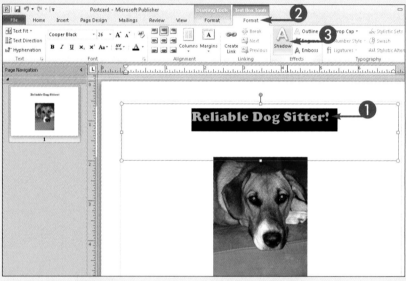

● Publisher applies the text effect.

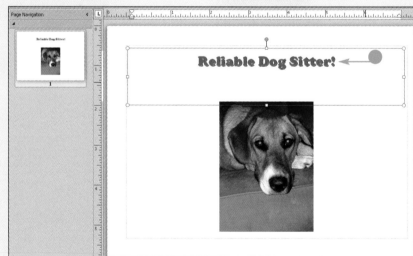

Change Text Alignment

Depending on the publication design that you select, alignment is preset to best suit the publication type. You can change the alignment to suit your own needs, however. You can use Publisher's alignment commands to change the way in which text is positioned both horizontally and vertically in a text object box.

For example, you might choose to align text in the bottom right corner of the text object box. There are nine alignment options in all: Align Top Left, Align Top Center, Align Top Right, Align Center Left, Align Center, Align Center Right, Align Bottom Left, Align Bottom Center, and **Align Bottom Right**.

Change Text Alignment

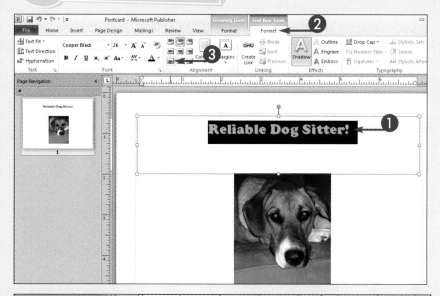

① Select the text that you want to format.

② Click the **Format** tab.

③ Click a button in the Alignment group. (Here, the **Align Bottom Left** button is clicked.)

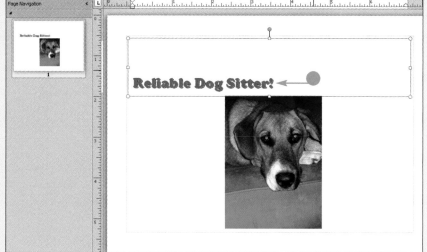

● Publisher applies the new alignment.

Add a Border

You can add a border to any object in a publication, including text boxes, clip art, and pictures, to add emphasis or make the publication more aesthetically appealing. Publisher comes with several predesigned borders, which you can apply to your publication. These include borders of various colors, shapes, and thicknesses, with or without background shading. Alternatively, you can create your own custom borders — for example, making each border line a different color or thickness. (Be aware that you should not add too many effects, such as borders, to your document because it will become difficult to read.)

Add a Border

1. Select the object to which you want to apply a border.

2. Click the **Format** tab.

3. Click a border in the Shape Styles list.

● You can click the **Shape Outline** button (⬚) to view available line styles and weights.

● You can click the **Change Shape** (⬚) button to view available shapes for the border.

● Publisher applies the border to the object.

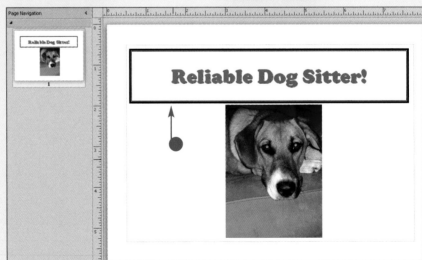

Control
Text Wrap

To add visual interest, many publications include text as well as objects, such as photographs, clip art images, tables, charts, or other visual elements. You can control the way in which text wraps around a picture, table, chart, or any other object in a publication. For example, you may want a column of text to wrap tightly around a clip art object, to appear above and below the object but not on the sides, and so on. Alternatively, you might prefer for the text to simply appear on top of the object.

Control Text Wrap

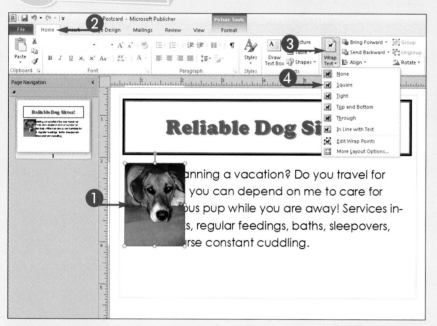

1 Click the picture object or other object that you want to wrap text around.

2 Click the **Home** tab.

3 Click the **Wrap Text** button.

4 Click a text-wrapping option.

Publisher applies the text wrapping.

● This example applies square text wrapping.

Link Text Boxes

When you add too much text to a text object, any text that does not fit in the text box is called *overflow*. In some cases, Publisher attempts to correct this problem with its AutoFit feature, which reduces the size of your text to make it fit. Alternatively, you can correct the problem of overflow text by creating a new text box adjacent to the existing one, linking the two text boxes, and flowing the extra text into the new text box. You use the Format tab's Linking tools to navigate and connect text boxes in a publication.

Link Text Boxes

Link Text Boxes

1. Click the text box that contains the overflowing text.
2. Click the **Format** tab.
3. Click the **Create Link** button.

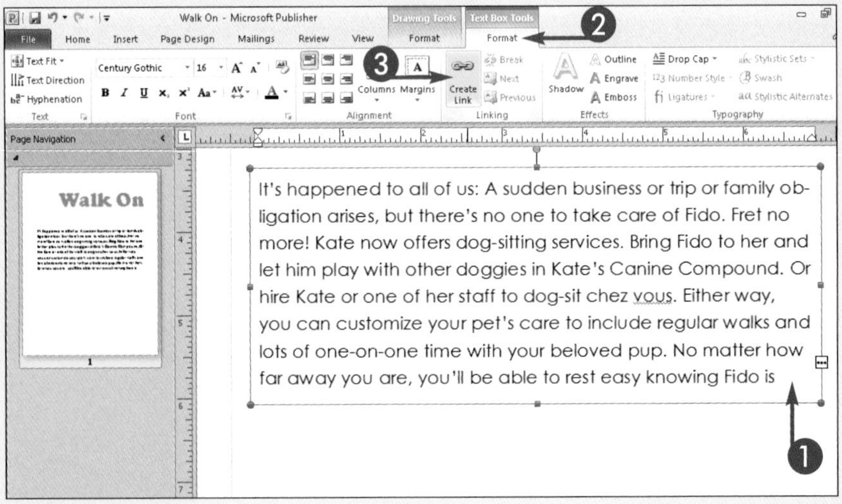

4. Click and drag to create a new text box for the text overflow (↖ changes to 🍺).

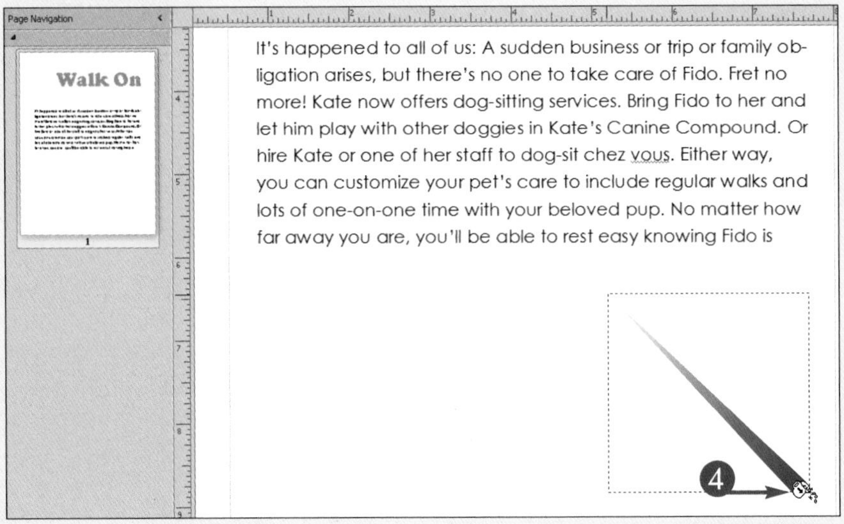

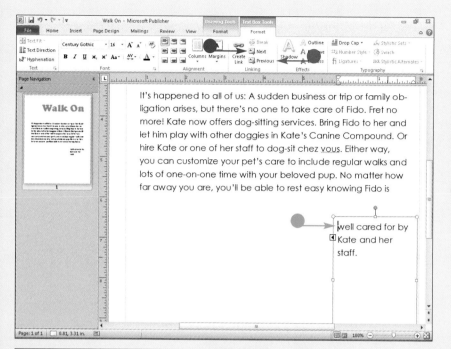

● Publisher links the two boxes, and moves any extra text from the first text box into the second text box.

● You can click the **Previous** button to return to the previous text box.

● You can click the **Next** button to go to the next text box.

Break a Link

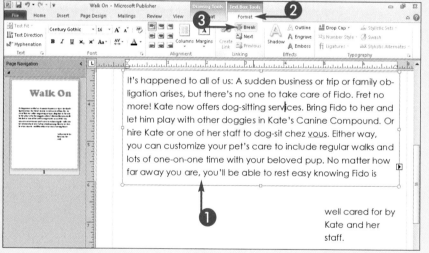

① Click the first text box that you want to disconnect.

② Click the **Format** tab.

③ Click the **Break** button.

Publisher breaks the link.

Are there other ways to handle overflow?
Yes. You can also use Publisher's Text Fit tools to auto-fit your text into the text box. To do so, click the text box to select it, and then click the **Format** tab. Next, click the **Text Fit** button in the Text group and choose **Best Fit**.

How do I turn off the AutoFit feature?
Select the text object to which AutoFit has been applied, click the **Format** tab, click the **Text Fit** button, and click **Do Not Autofit**.

Move and Resize Publication Objects

When you insert an object, such as a text box, photograph, clip art, table, and so on into a publication in Publisher, you may find that you need to make it larger or smaller in order to achieve the desired effect. For example, you may need to resize a text object to fit more text into the box. Fortunately, doing so is easy. When you select an object in a publication, handles appear around that object; you can use these handles to make the object larger or smaller. You can also move objects that you place in a publication.

Move and Resize Publication Objects

Move an Object

1. Click the object that you want to move.

- Publisher surrounds the selected object with handles.

2. Position the mouse pointer over the edge of the object until it changes from ↖ to ✥.
3. Drag the object to a new location.

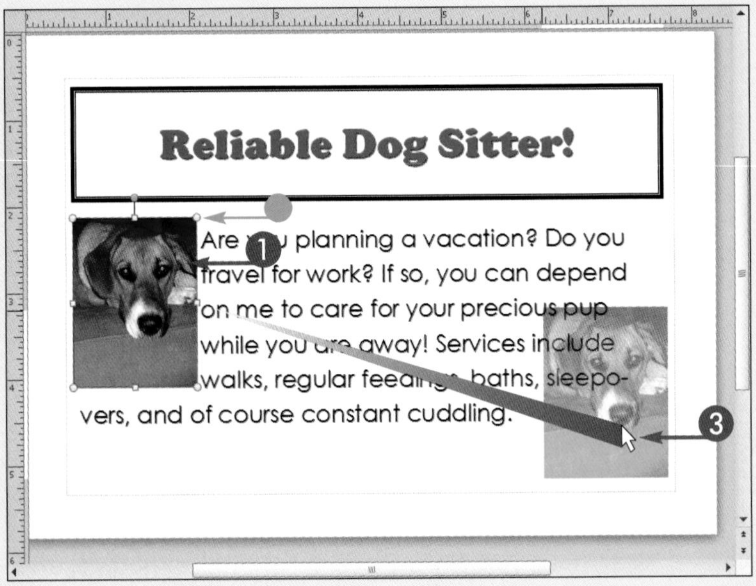

Publisher moves the object.

- This example moves a picture object.

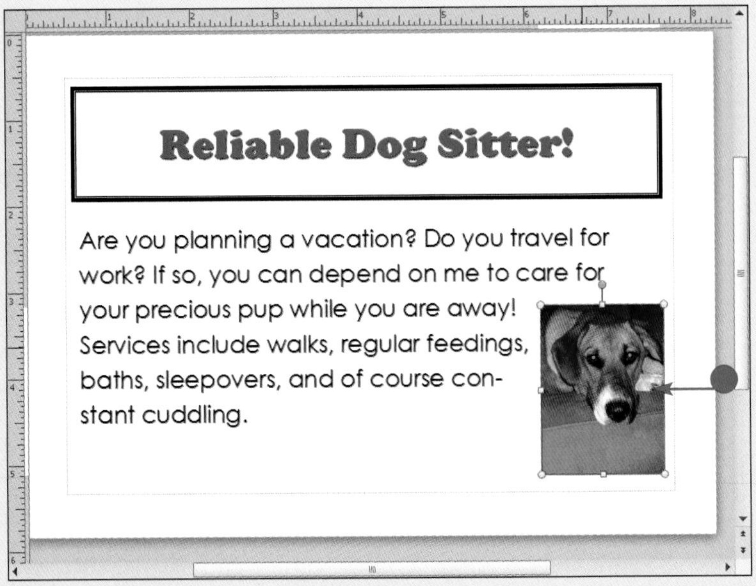

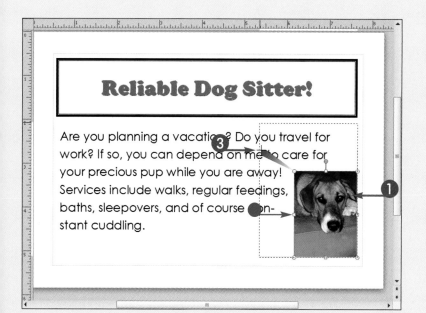

Resize an Object

1 Click the object that you want to resize.

● Publisher surrounds the selected object with handles.

2 Position the mouse pointer over the edge of the object until it changes from ↖ to ↗.

3 Click and drag a handle inward or outward to resize the object.

When you release the mouse button, Publisher resizes the object.

● This example resizes a picture object.

Can I rotate an object?
Yes. Click the object to select it, and then click the green rotation handle at the top of the selected object and drag it in the direction you want to rotate the object. When the object has been rotated to the desired degree, release the mouse button.

How do I delete an object?
To remove an object from a publication, click the object to select it and press **Delete**. Publisher removes the object from the page. You can select more than one object to delete by pressing and holding **Ctrl** while clicking each object.

Edit the Background

You can add visual interest to your publication by changing the background. Clicking the Background button in the Page Design tab enables you to quickly choose from among several solid backgrounds and gradient backgrounds; alternatively, you can choose from a variety of textures, patterns, and tints, or even apply one of your own photographs, from the Fill Effects dialog box. (For help using the Fill dialog box, see the tip at the end of this section.) If you decide you no longer want a background, you can quickly remove it.

Edit the Background

Apply a Background

1 Click the **Page Design** tab.

2 Click the **Background** button.

3 Click the background that you want to apply.

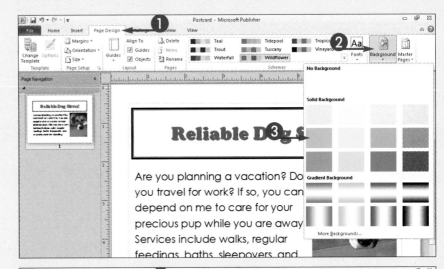

● Publisher applies the background.

Remove the Background

1 Click the **Page Design** tab.

2 Click the **Background** button.

3 Click the option under **No Background**.

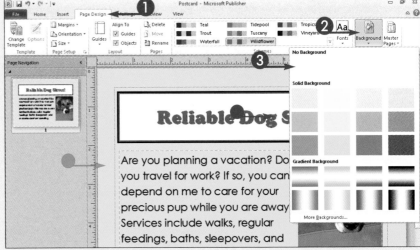

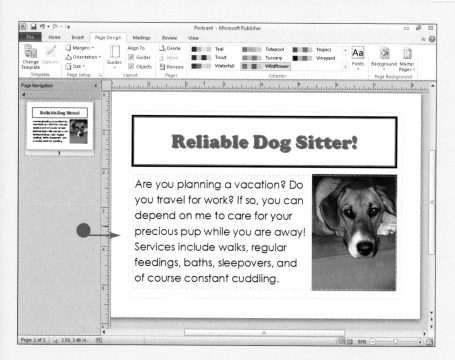

● Publisher removes the background.

Simplify It

Can I assign backgrounds from the Fill Effects dialog box?

Yes. You can assign a one-color or two-color gradient background using colors you choose; apply a texture background, such as Denim, Canvas, or Granite; apply a pattern, such as Plaid; choose your own photo for a background; or apply your own custom tint. You access these options from the Fill Effects dialog box. To open this dialog box, click the **Page Design** tab, click **Background**, and choose **More Backgrounds**.

Add a Building Block Object

You can use Publisher's Building Block objects to add all kinds of extra touches to your publication projects. For example, you can add a calendar to a newsletter or a graphical marquee to a letterhead. Publisher's Building Block objects encompass a wide variety of design objects, such as mastheads, borders, boxes, and even coupons and logos. You can customize the design of a Building Block object as needed — for example, you might change the border or fill color of an object. You can also change the text in a Building Block object by selecting it and typing over it.

Add a Building Block Object

① Click the **Insert** tab.

② Click a button in the Building Blocks group (here, **Advertisements**).

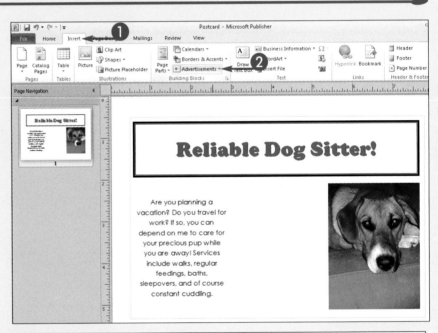

③ Click the Building Block object you want to insert.

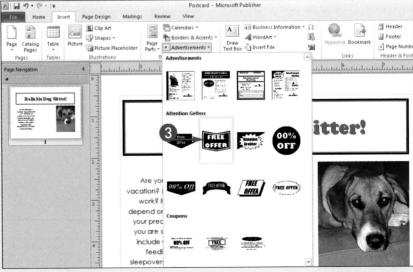

● Publisher adds the object to your publication.

● You can move and resize the object to suit your layout.

Note: *Refer to the section "Move and Resize Publication Objects" earlier in this chapter to learn more.*

How do I customize a Building Block object?
Many of the Building Block objects are composed of simple lines and shapes. You can customize the appearance of an object by selecting individual parts of it and making changes to the selection's formatting. Note that you may need to ungroup an object to edit individual elements of it. To do so, click the object, the **Home** tab, and then the **Ungroup** button (▣) as many times as necessary to free all the object's individual elements. When you finish making your edits, click the **Group** button (▣) to turn the elements back into a single object.

Create a Building Block Object

If you find yourself using an object you have created over and over, you can save that object as a Building Block object and reuse it as needed. For example, if you use the same headline in every publication you create, you can save it as a Building Block object; then, you can insert it into a publication anytime you need it (simply follow the steps in the preceding section, "Add a Building Block Object," to insert it). Anything you save as a Building Block object is accessible from any other Publisher files you open.

Create a Building Block Object

① Click the element that you want to save.

② Click the **Insert** tab.

③ Click a button in the Building Blocks group.

Click **Page Parts** if the Building Block object you want to create is a heading, sidebar, or something similar.

Click **Calendars** if the Building Block object you want to create is a calendar.

Click **Borders & Accents** if the Building Block object you want to create is a border or accent.

Click **Advertisements** if the Building Block object you want to create is a coupon or other advertisement.

④ Click **Add Selection to Building Block Gallery**.

Note: The precise name of this option varies depending on what button you click in Step **3**.

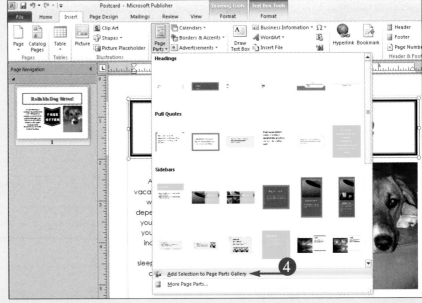

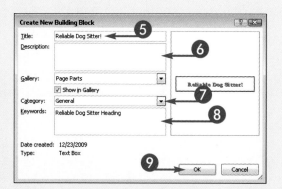

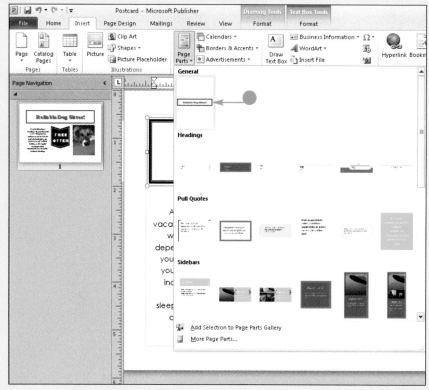

The Create New Building Block dialog box appears.

5 Type a name for the item.

6 Type a description for the item.

7 Choose a category for the item.

8 Enter keywords describing the item.

9 Click **OK**.

Publisher creates the Building Block object.

● You can view the item by clicking the button you clicked in Step **3**.

Simplify It

How do I remove a Building Block object?
Click the **Insert** tab and click the appropriate button in the Building Blocks group. Then right-click the Building Block object you want to delete, choose **Delete**, and click **OK** to confirm the deletion.

Are there more Building Block objects?
Yes. To access more Building Block objects, click the appropriate button in the Building Blocks group and choose **More *Building Blocks*** from the menu that appears. (The precise name of this option varies depending on what button you click.) The Building Block Library window opens, displaying all Building Block objects of the type you selected.

Part VIII

OneNote

OneNote acts like a digital notebook, enabling you to jot down ideas, sketch out plans, brainstorm business strategies, and compile scraps of information in one searchable, shareable, easy-to-access digital location. OneNote acts like a free-form canvas on which you can type, write, or draw, as well as paste in digital images such as a screenshot of a Web page or a digital photograph.

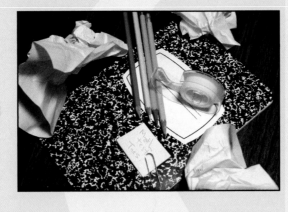

You might use OneNote to take notes during meetings and lectures, collect research materials from the Web, gather information about an upcoming trip, assemble ideas for a home improvement project, and more.

Navigate OneNote

OneNote acts like a digital binder, with notebooks that you can use to jot down ideas, sketch out plans, and compile scraps of information in one searchable, shareable, easy-to-access location. You can use OneNote to type, write, and draw your ideas, as well as paste in digital images such as a screenshot of a Web page or a digital photograph. By default, OneNote includes one notebook.

Navigate OneNote

1 In the OneNote Navigation bar, click the notebook you want to open.

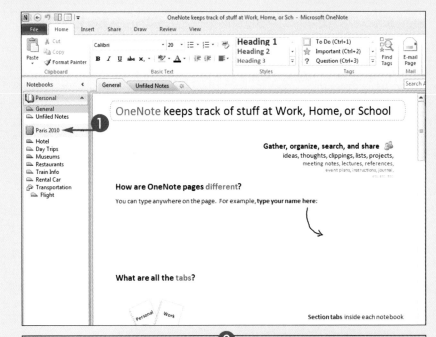

● OneNote opens the notebook you clicked.

2 Click a tab.

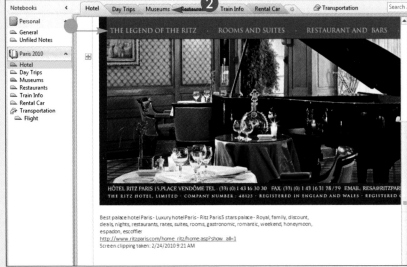

● OneNote displays the tab you clicked.

③ Click a page in the tab.

● OneNote displays the page you clicked.

How do I display the Navigation bar?
If the OneNote Navigation bar appears minimized on your screen, click the **Expand Navigation Bar** button (▷) to view it. To minimize the Navigation bar, thereby freeing up real estate in the OneNote window, click the **Collapse Navigation Bar** button (◁).

How do I view additional sections?
If OneNote does not display all the sections in a notebook, it displays a tab with a ▾. Click the ▾ to reveal links to additional sections in the notebook, and then click the link for the section you want to view.

Type and Draw Notes

As mentioned, OneNote acts like a binder, with notebooks that you can use to jot down ideas, sketch out plans, and compile scraps of information.

One way to enter these items into OneNote is by typing them with your keyboard. You can then format your text as desired, changing the font, size, and color; applying bold, italics, underline, subscript, or superscript formatting; and more.

Another approach is to use OneNote's drawing tools. When you create an item, also called a *note*, in OneNote, you can move it around the page as desired.

Type Notes

① With the page on which you want to type open in OneNote, click the **Draw** tab.

② Click the **Select & Type** button.

③ Click the spot on the page where you want to type.

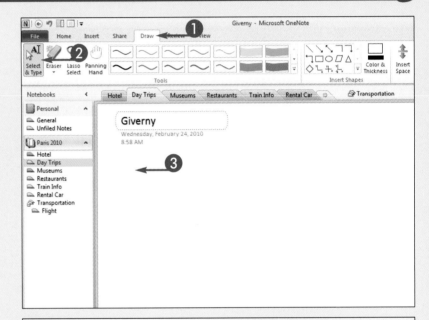

④ Type your note.

Note: *In the OneNote Home tab, you can change the text font, size, and color, and apply bold, italics, underline, subscript, or superscript formatting. You can also format text as a bulleted list or a numbered list and apply styles.*

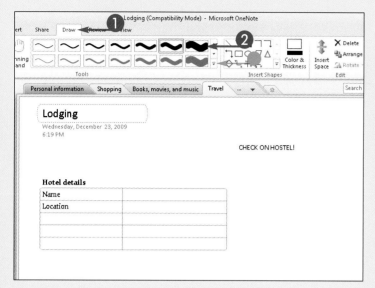

Draw Notes

1 With the page on which you want to draw open in OneNote, click the **Draw** tab.

2 In the Tools group, click a drawing tool.

● Click the **More** button (▫) to view all available drawing tools.

3 Draw your note.

How do I move a note?

If, after typing or drawing a note in OneNote, you decide you want it to appear elsewhere on the page, you can easily move it. To move a typed note, position your cursor over the text to reveal the note container; then move the cursor to the container's header. The cursor changes to ✥ ; click and drag the container to the desired location. To move a drawn note, press Shift while dragging over the drawing to select all its parts. Then position your cursor over the selection. When the cursor changes to ✥ , click and drag the selection to the desired location.

Paste a Picture into OneNote

You can paste digital photos you have saved on your hard drive into OneNote. For example, if you are using OneNote to plan a trip, you might paste in a photo of a hotel in which you would like to stay; alternatively, if you are using OneNote to help you run your business, you might paste in a photo of an office building in which you are considering renting space. You can move and resize pictures in OneNote much like you do graphics in other Office programs; for help, refer to Chapter 3.

Paste a Picture into OneNote

① With the page on which you want to paste a picture open in OneNote, click the **Insert** tab.

② Click the **Picture** button.

The Insert Picture dialog box opens.

③ Locate and select the picture you want to insert.

④ Click **Insert**.

● OneNote inserts the picture.

You can move and resize the picture as needed.

Attach Files to Notes

Sometimes it is helpful to attach a document or other file to a page in OneNote. For example, suppose you have created a spreadsheet for expense account transactions in Microsoft Excel; you can attach that spreadsheet to a OneNote page devoted to work. Likewise, you could attach a PowerPoint presentation to a OneNote

page devoted to a business meeting that you plan to attend.

When you attach a file to a note in a OneNote notebook, an icon for that file appears on the note; you can double-click the icon to open the file from within OneNote.

Attach Files to Notes

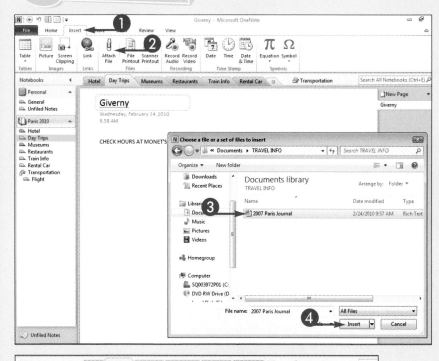

① With the page to which you want to attach a file open in OneNote, click the **Insert** tab.

② Click the **Attach File** button.

The Choose a File or a Set of Files to Insert dialog box opens.

③ Locate and select the file you want to insert.

④ Click **Insert**.

● OneNote inserts an icon for the file.

You can move the icon as needed.

Insert a Screen Clipping

You can use OneNote's Screen Clipping feature to "clip" portions of Web pages and paste them into OneNote. Screen clippings are especially helpful when you are researching on the Web, planning a trip, or comparing products. For example, you might clip an image of a Web page devoted to a car you are interested in buying or a price sheet for a service you are considering using. You can move a screen clipping the same way you move a note. For more information, refer to the tip "How do I move a note?" in the section "Type and Draw Notes," earlier in this chapter.

Insert a Screen Clipping

① In Internet Explorer, open the Web page containing the item you want to clip.

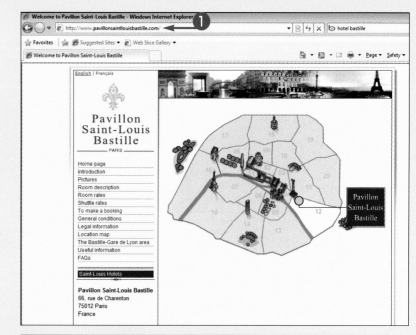

② In OneNote, click the spot on the page where you want to insert the clipping.

③ Click the **Insert** tab.

④ Click the **Screen Clipping** button.

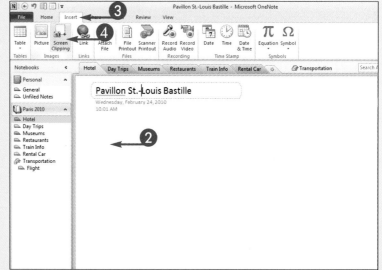

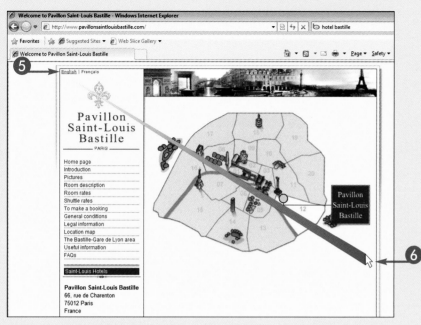

⑤ In Internet Explorer, click the top left corner of the area you want to clip.

⑥ Drag the cursor down and to the right until the area you want to clip is selected.

⑦ Release the mouse button.

● The clipping is pasted into OneNote.

Is there a faster way to paste clippings?
Yes. Open the Web site that contains the item you want to clip. Then perform the following steps. While holding down ⊞, press Ⓢ. Click the top left corner of the area you want to clip. Drag the cursor down and to the right to select the desired area. The Select Location in OneNote dialog box opens. Click the tab where you want the paste the clipping. Click **Send to Selected Location**. The clipping is pasted into OneNote.

Record an Audio Note

If you are attending a significant meeting or participating in an important conference call, you can use OneNote to record it and store the recording as part of your notes. As you record, you can type notes into OneNote; when you do, OneNote links the note to the recording, displaying a small icon alongside it. You can then click this icon to listen to the audio that was recorded at the time you typed the note.

Note that in order to record audio, you must have a microphone. Most laptop and tablet PCs come with microphones built-in. (Note: You should always ask permission before recording someone.)

Record an Audio Note

1 With the page to which you want to attach a file open in OneNote, click the **Insert** tab.

2 Click the **Record Audio** button.

OneNote begins recording.

● A shortcut icon for the audio file appears.

● The Audio & Video Recording tab appears, displaying playback controls.

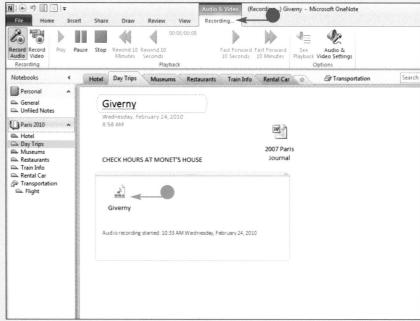

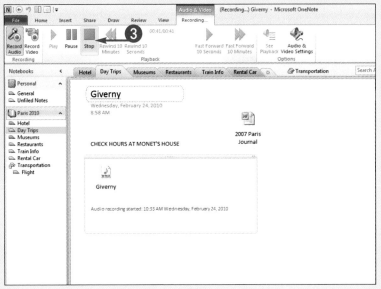

❸ To stop recording, click the
Stop button.

OneNote stops recording.

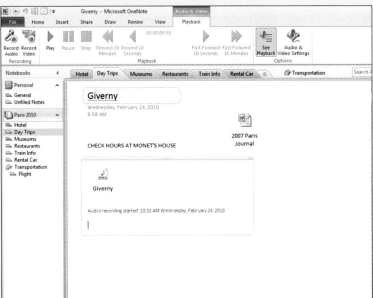

Can I record video notes?
Yes. If your computer features a webcam,
you can record video notes. To do so, click
the **Record Video** button in the Insert tab.
OneNote launches a video screen in which
you can view the footage as it is recorded
and displays the Audio & Video Recording
tab. To stop recording, click the **Stop** button
in the tab.

**How do I play back my
recording?**
When you create an audio or
video recording in OneNote,
a shortcut icon for that audio
file appears. To play back the
recording, double-click the
shortcut icon.

Create a New Notebook

By default, OneNote includes two notebooks: a Work notebook and a Personal notebook. If you want, you can create additional notebooks. For example, you might create a notebook to hold notes for a trip you are planning or a notebook to hold information relating to a home project.

New notebooks contain one section and one page by default; you can add more sections and pages as needed. (See the sections "Create a New Section" and "Create a New Page" in this chapter for details.)

When you create a new notebook, you specify where the notebooks should be stored — on the Web, on a network, or on your computer.

Create a New Notebook

① Click the **File** tab.

② Click **New**.

③ Choose where you want to store the notebook.

● Choose **Web** to store the notebook on the Web.

● Choose **Network** to store the notebook on a network.

● Choose **My Computer** to save the notebook on your computer's hard drive.

④ Type a name for the notebook.

● If you want to save the notebook somewhere other than the default, click the **Browse** button and select the folder in which the notebook should be saved.

⑤ Click **Create Notebook**.

● OneNote creates a new notebook.

● The new notebook contains one section.

● The section contains one page.

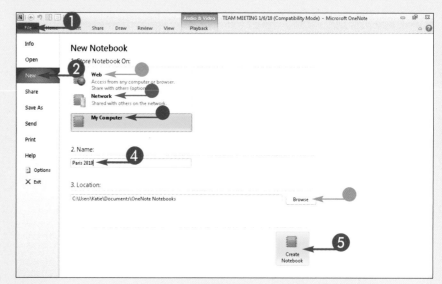

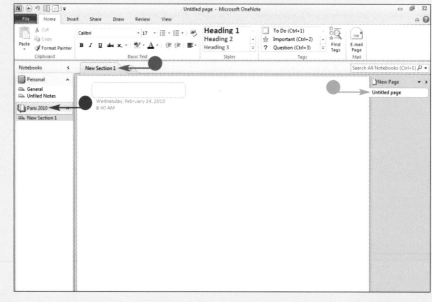

Create a New Section

The notebooks OneNote includes by default — the Work notebook and the Personal notebook — include several sections. These include Meeting Notes; Project A; Project B; Research; Travel; Planning; and Miscellaneous in the Work notebook. The Personal notebook contains sections labeled Personal Information; Shopping; Books, Movies, and Music; Travel; Recipes; To Do; and Miscellaneous.

You can easily add new sections to these notebooks or to any new notebooks you create. New sections are given names, such as New Section 1, New Section 2, and so on, by default; you can rename sections as needed. (For help renaming sections, see "Rename Sections and Pages," later in this chapter.)

Create a New Section

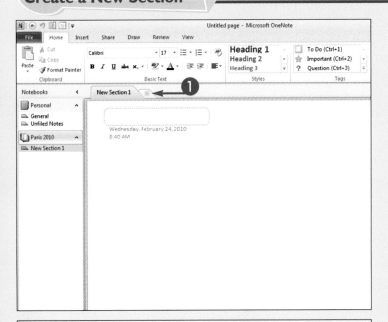

1 With the notebook for which you want to create a new section open in OneNote, click the **Create a New Section** tab (▦).

● OneNote creates a new section tab.

Create a New Page

You can easily add new pages to a notebook section. For example, if you are using OneNote to plan a vacation, you might create a notebook with one page for each phase of the trip. Or if you are using OneNote to plan a meeting, you might create a notebook with one page for each topic the meeting will cover.

When you create a new page, you can opt to create a subpage — that is, a page on a lower organizational level — in lieu of a regular page. You can also choose to use a page template — for example, to create a to-do list.

① Click the **New Page** ⊡.

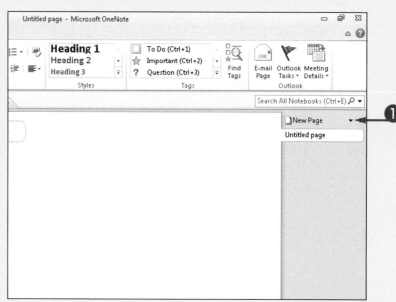

● Choose **New Page** to create a new page in the default style.

● Choose **New Subpage** to create a page on a lower organizational level.

② Click **Page Templates**.

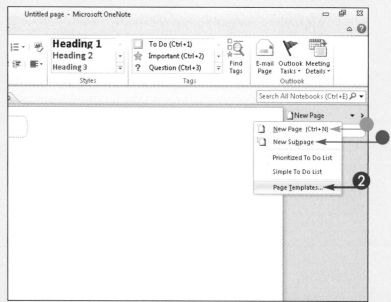

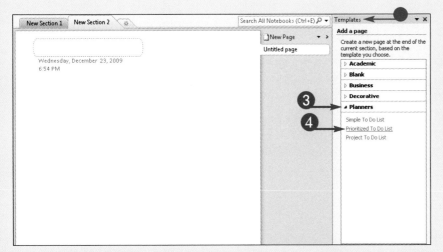

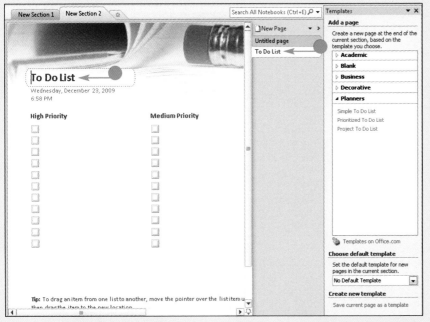

● The Templates pane opens.

③ Click a category's ▷ to reveal templates available in that category (▷ changes to ◢).

④ Click a template.

● OneNote creates a new page based on the template you selected.

What is the Unfiled Notes notebook?

If you want to create a note but are not sure in which notebook it should be filed, you can create it in the Unfiled Notes notebook. To do so, click **Unfiled Notes** in the Navigation pane; then create new pages and add notes as needed.

Can I move pages?

Yes. Right-click the page in the Page Tabs pane and choose **Move or Copy** from the menu that appears. In the Move or Copy Pages dialog box, click the ⊞ next to the notebook where you want to store the page, click the desired section, and click **Move** or **Copy**.

Rename Sections and Pages

New sections are given names, such as New Section 1, New Section 2, and so on, by default. Likewise, pages are given default names. You can assign your sections and pages more descriptive names to keep better track of where you have stored various pieces of information. For example, if your notebook relates to a project, you might create sections for each phase of the project and assign section names accordingly. Likewise, if a section of your notebook is devoted to attendees of a meeting, you might create a page for each person and assign page names accordingly.

Rename Sections and Pages

Rename a Section

① Right-click the tab for the section you want to rename.

② Choose **Rename**.

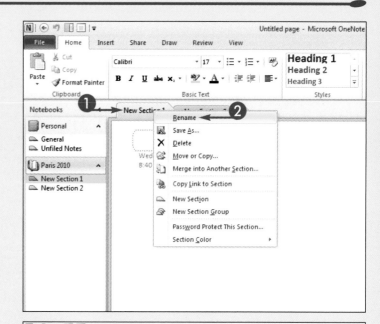

OneNote selects the current section name.

③ Type the new section name and press Enter.

OneNote applies the name you typed to the section tab.

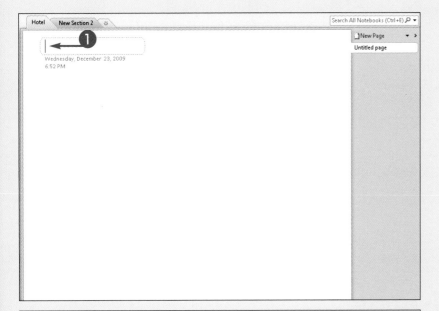

Rename a Page

1 Click in the page's **Title** field.

Note: *If the title field already contains text, select the text.*

2 Type a new title for the page.

● OneNote applies the title.

How do I delete pages and sections?
To delete a page, right-click it in the Page Tabs pane and choose **Delete**. To delete a section, right-click the section tab, choose **Delete**, and click **Yes** to confirm the deletion.

Can I delete a notebook?
Yes. Right-click the notebook in the Navigation pane and choose **Notebook Recycle Bin** from the menu that appears. OneNote places the contents of the notebook in the Notebook Recycle Bin. To remove the notebook completely, empty the Notebook Recycle Bin by clicking the **Share** tab, clicking the bottom half of the **Notebook Recycle Bin** button, and choosing **Empty Recycle Bin**.

Group
Sections

If your notebook contains several related sections, you can gather those sections into a group to make it easier to locate the section you need. For example, suppose you are planning a vacation and have created a OneNote notebook to keep track of your research. You might gather the notebook's

transportation-related sections — one with flight information, one for rental cars, one for train travel, and so on — into a group. Or if you are using OneNote to jot down ideas for your business, you might gather all the sections that pertain to a particular project in one group.

Group Sections

① Right-click the blank area to the right of the Create a New Section tab.

② Click **New Section Group**.

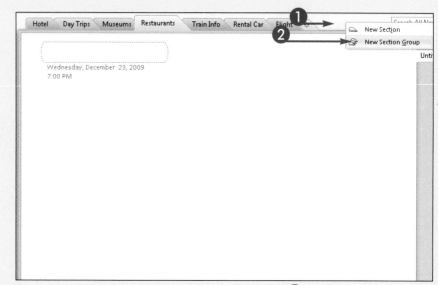

OneNote creates a new section group.

③ Type a name for the section group and press Enter.

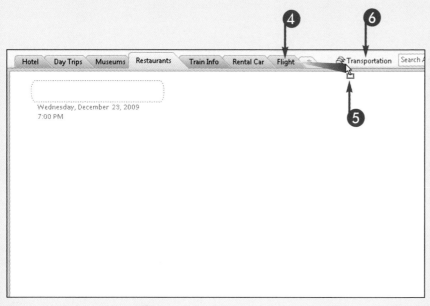

4 Click a tab.

5 Drag the tab to the section group.

The ⬚ changes to ⬚.

OneNote moves the tab to the section group.

6 Click the section group.

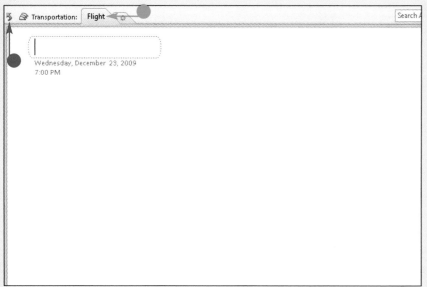

● The section tab appears in the section group.

● Click the **Navigate to Parent Section Group** button (⬚) to return to the regular view.

Can I remove a section tab from a group?	**Can I change the order in which sections appear?**
Yes. Open the section group, click the tab you want to move, and drag it to the Navigate to Parent Section Group button (⬚).	Yes. Click the tab for the section you want to move, drag the tab to the desired spot in the order, and release the mouse button. You can also change the order of pages in a section; to do so, click the page in the Page Tabs pane and drag it up or down to the desired spot in the order.

Search
Notes

As you enter more and more notes into OneNote, you may find it difficult to locate the information you need. Fortunately, OneNote offers a robust search function. Using it, you can locate any text in your OneNote notebooks — even text found in graphics. You can limit your search to a particular notebook or section or search all notebooks and sections. If you have enabled OneNote's Audio Search feature, you can also search audio and video for spoken words. (Note that in order to search audio and video, you must enable OneNote's Audio Search function. For help, see the tip at the end of this section.)

Search Notes

① Click in the OneNote **Search** field.

● OneNote displays a list of your notebooks and sections. To limit your search to a particular notebook or section, click it in the list.

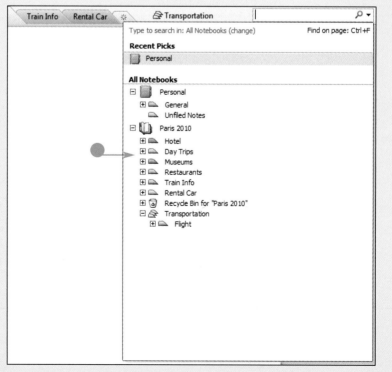

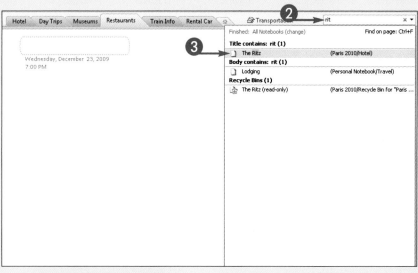

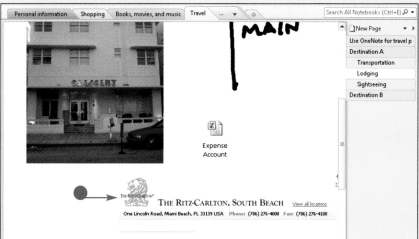

② Type your search text.

Note: As you type, the menu displays potential matches to your search criteria.

③ Click a match to view the page.

● OneNote displays pages containing the text you typed.

How do I enable Audio Search?

In order to search audio and video, you must enable OneNote's Audio Search function. To do so, click the **File** tab and choose **Options**. In the OneNote Options dialog box that appears, click **Audio & Video**, and select the **Enable searching audio and video recordings for words** check box. The Did You Know About Audio Search dialog box appears; click the **Enable Audio Search** button. Finally, click **OK** to close the OneNote Options dialog box.

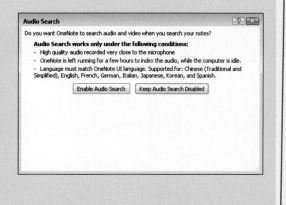

E-mail a Note Page

If you feel that a page in one of your OneNote notebooks could be beneficial to someone else, you can e-mail the page to that person. A page you send from OneNote is e-mailed in HTML format, meaning that the message recipient need not have OneNote installed to view the contents of the page.

You can launch the e-mail operation directly from OneNote. When you do, OneNote starts your e-mail program, creates a new message window containing the OneNote page, and applies the page's title to the message's Subject line. You simply enter the recipient's address and any additional text and send the message as normal.

E-mail a Note Page

① With the page you want to e-mail open in OneNote, click the **Home** tab.

② Click the **E-mail Page** button.

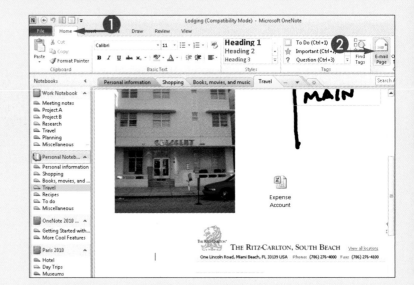

● OneNote launches your e-mail program, displaying a new message window containing the OneNote page.

● The message's Subject line contains the page's title.

③ Enter the recipient's e-mail address in the **To** field.

④ Click **Send**.

The message is sent.

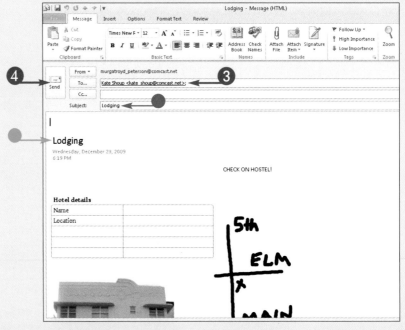

Convert Notes to PDF or XPS Format

One way to share your OneNote notes is to launch an e-mail operation from within OneNote. If, however, you want to share multiple pages, sections, or entire notebooks, a better route is to convert them into PDF or XPS format. You can then distribute the PDF or XPS file to others by e-mailing it as a file attachment or by publishing it on the Web. Assuming the intended recipient has a computer that has Adobe Acrobat Reader installed (for viewing PDF files) or that runs a version of Windows that includes an XPS viewer, the OneNote page, section, or notebook will be readable.

Convert Notes to PDF or XPS Format

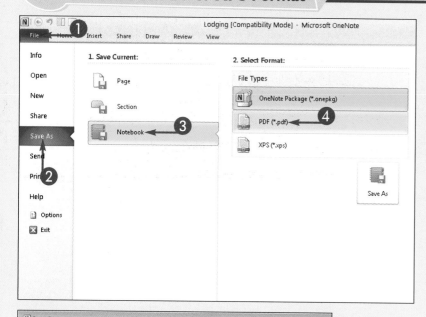

① With the page, section, or notebook you want to convert open in OneNote, click the **File** tab.

② Click **Save As**.

③ Click **Page**, **Section**, or **Notebook**.

④ Click **PDF (*.pdf)** or **XPS (*.xps)**.

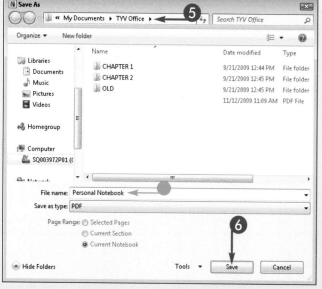

The Save As dialog box opens.

● The name of the page, section, or notebook appears in the File Name field.

⑤ Locate and select the folder in which you want to save the page, section, or notebook.

⑥ Click **Save**.

OneNote saves the page, section, or notebook in the format you specified.

Index

Index

Index

Index